FINALS

CRIMINAL PROCEDURE

CORE CONCEPTS AND KEY QUESTIONS

Second Edition

T. Leigh Hearn, Esquire
Series Editor

© 2009 by Kaplan, Inc.

Published by Kaplan Publishing, a division of Kaplan, Inc.
1 Liberty Plaza, 24th floor
New York, NY 10006

Printed in the United States of America

10   9   8   7   6   5   4   3   2   1

ISBN13: 978-1-60714-095-5

TABLE OF CONTENTS

KAPLAN) *pmbr*

I. THE FOURTH AMENDMENT

"The right of people to be secure in their persons, houses, papers, and effects against unreasonable searches and seizures, shall not be violated, and no Warrants shall issue, but upon probable cause, supported by Oath or affirmation, and particularly describing the place to be searched, and the persons or things to be seized."

A. ARREST

1. **General Principles**

    a. **Custody defined:** A person is in "custody" when the individual, in the presence of a law enforcement officer, is not free to leave, and is thus deprived of his freedom of action in a significant way [*Orozco v. Texas*, 394 U.S. 324 (1969)].

    b. **Arrest defined:** When a person is taken into custody for the purpose of commencing a criminal action, an arrest has occurred [*Dunaway v. New York*, 442 U.S. 200 (1979)]. More than a stop and frisk is required. Brief detentions by police are permissible for the purpose of questioning even without probable cause that the person has committed a crime, such a "stop" is not considered an arrest [*Terry v. Ohio*, 392 U.S. 1 (1968)].

    c. **Invalid arrest:** An unlawful arrest is no defense to a subsequent conviction of the crime charged, although a civil action for false arrest may lie.

    d. **Valid arrest:** A valid arrest may occur either with or without a warrant. Generally, no warrant is required for an arrest.

    (1) **In a public place:** Police need not obtain an arrest warrant before making an arrest in a public place even though there is time to get a warrant [*United States v. Watson*, 423 U.S. 411 (1976)].

    (2) **In one's home:** Absent exigent circumstances or consent an arrest warrant is required before police can arrest an individual in his own home [*Payton v. New York*, 445 U.S. 573 (1980)]. In cases of hot pursuit, when police have probable cause to arrest, they may follow a suspect into his home to effectuate a warrantless arrest and prevent escape [*United States v. Santana*, 427 U.S. 38 (1976)]. Also, police generally may not execute a warrant for a named individual in the home of another person [*Steagald v. United States*, 451 U.S. 204 (1981)]. In most states and according to federal law, an arresting officer must, absent exigent circumstances, announce his purpose before entry or the arrest is invalid.

2. **Common Law Rules for Warrantless Arrests**

    a. **Felonies:** Both police officers and private citizens may make arrests for *felonies committed in their presence.* A police officer may arrest a person for a felony **not** committed in his presence where he has reasonable grounds to believe the person committed the felony; however, such an arrest by a private citizen is valid only if the felony was **in fact committed**.

(1) **Use of deadly force against fleeing felons:** It is constitutionally unreasonable to use deadly force to prevent the escape of felony suspects. However, where an officer has probable cause to believe that either the suspect poses a threat of serious physical harm to the officer or to others, or that the suspect has committed a crime involving such infliction of harm deadly force may be used after feasible warning has been given and only if necessary to prevent escape [*Tennessee v. Garnor*, 471 U.S. 1 (1985)].

b. **Misdemeanors:** Both police officers and private citizens can make arrests for misdemeanors where 1) **the crime is committed in their presence,** and 2) **the misdemeanor amounts to a breach of the peace**.

(1) **Warrantless arrests for minor criminal offenses:** The Fourth Amendment does not forbid a warrantless arrest for a minor criminal offense, such as a misdemeanor seatbelt violation or other offense punishable only by a fine [*Atwater v. Lago Vista*, 121 S.Ct. 1536 (2001)].

3. **Other Detentions**

a. **Of third persons:** Persons present on the premises during the execution of a valid search warrant may be detained [*Michigan v. Summers*, 452 U.S. 692 (1981)].

b. **Vehicle stops:** Police officers may **not** randomly stop a vehicle to check license and registration without a reasonable suspicion of wrongdoing. Such a stop is unconstitutional because it leaves too much discretion with law enforcement [*Delaware v. Prouse*, 440 U.S. 468 (1979)]. At fixed checkpoints, a systematic stopping of vehicles **is permissible** for inspection purposes near a border; however, police must have probable cause to extend that stop to a search of the vehicle [*United States v. Martinez-Fuerte*, 428 U.S. 543 (1976)], and they may not order the driver out of the car absent a lawful detention for a traffic violation [*Pennsylvania v. Mimms*, 434 U.S. 106 (1978)].

(1) **Sobriety checkpoints:** Sobriety checkpoints are permissible [*Michigan v. Sitz*, 110 S.Ct. 2481 (1990)].

(2) **Illegal drugs:** When police set up a checkpoint program to search vehicles for evidence of illegal drugs, this program violates the Fourth Amendment because the checkpoint's primary purpose is indistinguishable from the general interest in crime control and because it is not based on individualized suspicion of wrongdoing [*Indianapolis v. Edmond*, 121 S.Ct. 447 (2000)]. However, a police highway checkpoint set up to obtain information from motorists about a recent crime does not violate the Fourth Amendment [*Illinois v. Lidster*, 124 S.Ct. 855 (2004)].

(3) **Probable cause not required in vehicle stops:** The Fourth Amendment is satisfied if a police officer's action is supported by reasonable suspicion to believe that criminal activity may be afoot. Probable cause is not required for a short investigatory stop. Courts must look to the totality of the circumstances of each case to see whether the police officer has a "particularized and objective basis" for suspecting legal wrongdoing [*United States v. Arvizu*, 122 S.Ct. 744 (2002)].

Example:

Tito was driving his van along a public road one night. Police officer Fuentes, who was driving behind Tito, decided to make a random stop of Tito's vehicle to check his license and registration. Officer Fuentes pulled Tito's van over to the side of the road and then walked up to the driver's side of the vehicle. When he came alongside the driver's window, Fuentes asked Tito for his identification. As Tito was thumbing through his wallet, the officer shined his flashlight into the van and spotted a plastic bag containing marijuana lying on the floor under the backseat. Officer Fuentes then arrested Tito and charged him with possession of marijuana.

At his trial for illegal possession of narcotics, Tito moved to suppress the use of the marijuana as evidence. His motion should be

(A) granted, because under the "poisonous tree" doctrine the marijuana was a fruit of an illegal search

(B) granted, because the police officer did not have probable cause or a reasonable suspicion to believe that Tito's van contained narcotics

(C) denied, because the marijuana was in plain view when the police officer shined his flashlight inside the van

(D) denied, because the seizure of the marijuana was made pursuant to a lawful investigatory stop

Answer:

(A) A random stopping of a vehicle on the highway where the officer has no suspicion of wrongdoing is unconstitutional because it leaves too much discretion in the police officer [*Delaware v. Prouse*, 440 U.S. 648 (1979)]. Applying the "fruits of the poisonous tree" doctrine, no evidence seized as a result of a Fourth Amendment violation may be admitted at trial [*Wong Sun v. United States*, 371 U.S. 471 (1963)]. **Caveat:** Be cognizant that the rule suppressing fruits of an illegal search applies not only to objects found, but also to verbal statements obtained because of the original tainted search, or as a result of an illegal arrest [*see Brown v. Illinois*, 422 U.S. 590 (1975)].

4. **Probable Cause Requirement:** Whether an arrest is made with or without a warrant, the Constitution requires probable cause to exist at the time of the arrest. The facts and circumstances within the police officer's knowledge must be such that a

reasonably prudent man would believe that the defendant had committed or was committing an offense [*Draper v. United States*, 358 U.S. 307 (1959); *Beck v. Ohio*, 379 U.S. 89 (1964)]. The same Fourth Amendment standards of probable cause apply to searches. [*See*, e.g., *Maryland v. Pringle*, 124 S.Ct. 795 (2003)—where large amounts of cash and drugs are found in a car during a routine traffic stop, probable cause exists to arrest all occupants of the vehicle, including passengers, when none claims ownership of suspect items.]

B. SEARCH AND SEIZURE

1. **The Exclusionary Rule**

   a. **In general:** The so-called exclusionary rule is a procedural rule of federal constitutional law used to deter unlawful police conduct. Under the exclusionary rule, evidence of all materials seized in violation of the Fourth Amendment is inadmissible in a criminal proceeding. This rule was made applicable to the states under *Mapp v. Ohio*, 367 U.S. 643 (1961).

   b. **Governmental conduct requirements:** The Fourth Amendment generally protects only against governmental conduct, and not against searches by private persons. It does not prevent the introduction of evidence obtained by illegal searches done by private citizens [*Burdeau v. McDowell*, 256 U.S. 465 (1921)]. Governmental agents include only publicly paid police and citizens acting under their direction, but not private security guards (unless deputized by police). **Note:** This same requirement of governmental conduct in Fourth Amendment cases applies to confessions as well. *Miranda* warnings only apply to interrogation by publicly paid police.

   c. **Fruits of the Poisonous Tree Doctrine:** In addition to excluding all evidence which has been illegally obtained, any additional evidence (including verbal statements as well as physical objects) acquired either directly or indirectly from the illegal arrest, search, or seizure must also be excluded as tainted fruit of the poisonous tree [*Wong Sun v. United States*, 371 U.S. 471 (1963)].

      (1) **Purging the taint:** Otherwise inadmissible "fruits" of an unlawful search or seizure may be admitted into evidence provided the taint is dissipated or purged by either:

         (a) **independent evidence**—evidence obtained from a source independent of the original illegality [*United States v. Crews*, 445 U.S. 463 (1980)];

         (b) **inevitable discovery**—evidence which would have been discovered regardless of the illegality [*People v. Fitzpatrick*, 32 U.S. 499 (1973)]; despite a violation of right to counsel in eliciting defendant's confession, the Court held that discovery of the victim's body was not a suppressible fruit of the confession, since the police already knew of the defendant's direction of flight and had found articles of the victim's clothing in the area [*Brewer v. Williams,* 430 U.S. 387 (1977)]; or

(c) **an intervening act of free will by the defendant** (i.e., a subsequent confession after release).

d. **Limitations on the exclusionary rule:**

(1) **In-court identification:** A witness's in-court identification of the defendant may not be excluded as a fruit of an unlawful detention where the victim's knowledge of the defendant's identity was acquired prior to the illegal arrest [*United States v. Crews,* supra].

(2) **Grand juries:** *The exclusionary rule has not been extended to grand jury proceedings.* Therefore, an indictment may be based on illegally obtained evidence [*United States v. Colandra,* 414 U.S. 338 (1974)]. Additionally, a grand jury may base its indictment on evidence which would be inadmissible hearsay at trial [*Costello v. United States,* 350 U.S. 359 (1956)].

Example:

Frankie Flame was arrested and indicted for arson. The evidence which the prosecutor presented to the grand jury consisted of two items. First, Patrolman Duffy testified to what eyewitnesses had told him about the crime. In addition, the prosecutor presented an empty gasoline can which the police had unlawfully seized without a warrant from the basement of Flame's home. The seizure of the gasoline can was in violation of the defendant's Fourth Amendment rights.

Flame moved to dismiss the indictment on grounds of violation of his constitutional rights. The motion should be

(A) granted, because there was no admissible evidence before the grand jury when it indicted Flame

(B) granted, because the indictment rests in part on evidence seized in violation of the Fourth Amendment

(C) denied, because no constitutional principle requires that indictments rest on evidence that would be admissible at trial

(D) denied, because since there is no constitutional right to indictment for noncapital offenses, Flame cannot challenge the validity of the indictment

Answer:

(C) Remember that the exclusionary rule has not been extended to grand jury proceedings. According to the decision in *Costello v. United States* (1956), a grand jury may base its indictment on evidence that would not be admissible at trial.

(3) **Civil proceedings:** Evidence illegally seized by one sovereign may be used in the civil proceedings of another sovereign [*United States v. Janis*, 428 U.S. 433 (1976)].

(4) **Impeachment exception:** Evidence obtained in violation of the Fourth, Fifth, or Sixth Amendments may be used to impeach the testimony given either on direct or cross-examination [*United States v. Havens*, 446 U.S. 620 (1980)]. A confession obtained without affording *Miranda* warnings may be used to impeach a defendant's testimony [*Harris v. New York*, 401 U.S. 222 (1971)], unless it is coerced [*Mincey v. Arizona*, 437 U.S. 385 (1978)] or immunized [*New Jersey v. Portash*, 440 U.S. 450 (1979)].

Statements taken in violation of the *Jackson* rule can be used to impeach [*Michigan v. Harvey*, 110 S.Ct. 1176 (1990)], but excluded evidence cannot be used to impeach defense *witnesses* [*Jaines v. Illinois*, 110 S.Ct. 648 (1990)].

(5) **Internal agency rules:** Where a search by electronic surveillance violated Internal Revenue Service rules, rather than federal law, such evidence was not subject to the exclusionary rule [*United States v. Caceres*, 440 U.S. 741 (1979)].

(6) **Search with a device not in general public use:** Where the government uses a device that is not in general public use to explore details of a private home that would previously have been unknowable without physical intrusion, the surveillance is a search under the Fourth Amendment and is presumptively unreasonable without a warrant [*Kyllo v. United States*, 121 S.Ct. 2038 (2001)].

(7) **Habeas Corpus:** Fourth Amendment claims will not be relitigated in federal habeas corpus proceedings [*Stone v. Powell*, 428 U.S. 465 (1976)].

e. **Procedural considerations:**

(1) **Suppression hearing:** A defendant has a right to a suppression hearing at which time the judge, as a matter of law, determines the admissibility of the evidence out of the jury's presence [*Jackson v. Denno*, 378 U.S. 368 (1964)]. The defendant has the burden to prove by a preponderance that the evidence should be suppressed in cases where the evidence was seized pursuant to a warrant [*United States v. Vigo*, 413 F.2d 691 (1969)]. The defendant's testimony at the suppression hearing may not be used against him at trial on the substantive issue of guilt [*Simmons v. United States*, 390 U.S. 377 (1968)]. The government's burden is to establish admissibility of the evidence by a preponderance where the evidence is seized as a result of a warrantless search [*Lego v. Twomey*, 404 U.S. 477 (1972)].

(2) **Harmless Error Standard:** Admission of illegally obtained evidence constitutes reversible error, unless the error is "harmless." To be found

"harmless," the evidence must **not** have contributed to the defendant's conviction [*Chapman v. California*, 386 U.S. 18 (1967)]. In this case, the prosecution's burden of proof must meet the "beyond a reasonable doubt" standard. **Note:** Denial of right to counsel is never harmless error, nor is a coerced confession.

2. **Reasonable Expectation of Privacy:** A person's Fourth Amendment rights may be raised where a reasonable expectation of privacy exists. This requirement is satisfied *only when the defendant has shown standing and when the objects to be seized are not "held out to the public."*

   a. **Standing:** A defendant may establish standing to assert a Fourth Amendment claim only where *his own* rights are violated. He may not assert the Fourth Amendment rights of another. An *ownership or possessory interest* in the premises is sufficient to establish standing.

   A defendant has standing when he is an overnight guest in another's home [*Minnesota v. Olson*, 110 S.Ct. 1684 (1990); *but see Minnesota v. Carter*, 119 S.Ct. 795 (1998)—short-term commercial guests have no reasonable expectation of privacy in a host's home].

CRIMINAL PROCEDURE MULTISTATE CHART #1

STANDING REQUIREMENTS

	Constitutional Law	Criminal Procedure
Party Asserting Right	plaintiff	defendant
Prima Facie **Showing**	personal stake in the outcome	defendant's own Fourth Amendment rights must be violated
Elements To Be Established	direct, immediate injury and causation (subject to prudential limitations of court)	possessory interest in premises
Assertion of Third-Party Rights	denied, unless close relation and special need demonstrated	denied, unless third party had joint access and control of the property

   (1) **Examples:**

      (a) A passenger in an automobile *lacks standing* to challenge the validity of a search of the vehicle [*Rakas v. Illinois*, 439 U.S. 128 (1978)]. Mere lawful presence in the car is only a factor the courts consider in determining existence of a legitimate expectation of privacy. This is not consistently the rule under state law; some states still confer automatic standing for state prosecutions.

      Exception: When police *unlawfully make a random stop of an automobile*, the passenger has standing to challenge the search and seizure of items inside the vehicle. [LaFave on **Criminal Law**, p. 492.]

(b) Standing was denied a defendant who placed drugs in a friend's purse just before the contents were searched [*Rawlings v. Kentucky*, 448 U.S. 98 (1980)]. The Court held that standing based on a legitimate expectation of privacy is not necessarily determined by mere ownership.

(c) Similarly, in crimes where a defendant is charged with possession, Fourth Amendment standing is no longer "automatic." The defendant must show a ***legitimate expectation of privacy*** in the items seized or in the premises searched [*United States v. Salvucci*, 448 U.S. 83 (1980)].

(2) **Standing improper to establish guilt:** In crimes where a defendant is charged with possession, a showing of possession to establish standing may not be admitted against him at trial as substantive evidence of guilt [*Simmons v. United States*, 390 U.S. 377 (1968)].

b. **Items "held out to the public":** Such items afford a defendant with no reasonable expectation of privacy and therefore no Fourth Amendment protections can be raised.

(1) **Examples:**

(a) **Handwritten samples:** [*United States v. Mara*, 410 U.S. 19 (1973)]

(b) **Voice exemplars:** *United States v. Dionisio*, 410 U.S. 1 (1973)]

(c) **Bank records:** [*United States v. Miller*, 425 U.S. 435 (1976)]

(d) **Pen registers:** that is, police may record numbers dialed on a telephone [*Smith v. Maryland*, 442 U.S. 735 (1979)]

(e) **"Private conversations":** defendant assumes the risk that an eavesdropping "friend" will report or tape-record a conversation [*Hoffa v. United States*, 385 U.S. 293 (1966)]; **Caveat:** A person in a closed telephone booth *does* have an actual (subjective) and reasonable expectation of privacy such that attachment of electronic eavesdropping devices on the exterior of the phone booth constitutes an impermissible search [*Katz v. United States*, 389 U.S. 347 (1967)].

(f) **Public school students:** School officials may search students' personal items where there is a reasonable belief that contraband will be found [*New Jersey v. T.L.O.*, 469 U.S. 325 (1985)]; it is yet unresolved whether a student has a legitimate expectation of privacy in lockers, desks, and other school property. However, drug testing of students who participate in competitive extracurricular activities does not violate the Fourth Amendment [*Board of Education of Independent School District No. 92 of Pottawatomie County, Okla. v. Earls*, 122 S.Ct. 2559 (2002)].

(g) **"Open fields" doctrine:** Any unoccupied or undeveloped area outside of the curtilage is not extended Fourth Amendment protection. Specifically, it was held to be no search to engage in aerial photography of the outdoor areas of a large fenced-in industrial complex [*Dow Chemical Co. v. United States,* 90 L.Ed.2d 226 (1986)].

Also, use of police aircraft flying over a defendant's home and observing marijuana plants growing within the fenced curtilage was held to be no search since the plants were readily discernible to the naked eye within a public navigable airspace [*California v. Ciraolo,* 90 L.Ed.2d 210 (1986)]. In contrast, the use of high technology devices which use infrared or other parts of the spectrum not visible to the naked eye has been determined to require a warrant.

(h) **Discarded property:** i.e., commingled garbage and abandoned rental premises

(i) **Sniffing dogs:** Exposure of luggage (not persons) in a public place to a trained canine sniff is constitutionally permissible, regardless of reasonable suspicion [*United States v. Place,* 462 U.S. 696 (1983)].

(j) **Sobriety checkpoints:** A DUI roadblock is constitutional if conducted properly as to such factors as time, location, manner and regularity of stopping, and otherwise neutral criteria.

(2) **Caveat:** The MBE (Multistate Bar Examination) often asks students to determine on what grounds a defendant may raise a valid defense against admission of specific evidence. The above examples deal with the Fourth Amendment exclusionary rule. However, students must also be aware of the Fifth and Sixth Amendment grounds which bar examiners combine in these situations. First of all, the Sixth Amendment right to counsel is only applicable to *"critical stages"* of criminal procedure (see chapter IV, section C, 8), and would be inapplicable here. Also, note that the Fifth Amendment privilege against self-incrimination ***only protects against evidence that is testimonial in nature*** and would likewise not be helpful as a defense in regard to the preceding examples.

(3) **Impermissible searches:** Pumping a defendant's stomach to obtain evidence of heroin was held to "shock the conscience" and thus violate due process [*Rochin v. California,* 342 U.S. 165 (1952)].

3. **Searches Pursuant to a Warrant**

    a. **General rule:** The Fourth Amendment requires that a warrant be issued for a search to be lawful, unless the search falls within one of the seven recognized exceptions to the warrant requirement.

b. **Warrant requirements:**

(1) **Neutral magistrate:** The warrant must be issued by a *neutral and detached magistrate* who reviews evidence submitted by police officers and determines if there is probable cause to issue the warrant [*Giordenello v. United States*, 357 U.S. 480 (1958)].

  (a) A justice of the peace who also happens to be the state attorney general is not neutral and detached [*Coolidge v. New Hampshire*, 403 U.S. 443 (1971)]; however, a court clerk is a neutral judicial officer regarding warrants for city ordinance violations [*Shadwick v. City of Tampa*, 407 U.S. 345 (1972)].

  (b) A warrant is invalid if the magistrate takes a monetary reward in return for issuing the warrant [*Connelly v. Georgia*, 429 U.S. 245 (1977)].

  (c) A neutral magistrate may not "supervise" the scope of the search [*Lo-Ji Sales, Inc. v. New York*, 442 U.S. 319 (1979)].

(2) **Supported by oath or affirmation:** Either oral testimony or an affidavit must set forth the facts or circumstances which constitute the probable cause relied upon by the magistrate. The magistrate must then make an independent finding that probable cause exists based on those facts and circumstances [*Shadwick v. City of Tampa, supra*].

(3) **Specificity of the warrant:** The warrant must describe with particularity the place to be searched and the items or persons to be seized. Absent independent justification, a search warrant confers upon police only the authority to search named places or persons.

  (a) Where only the search of one apartment is required, a warrant authorizing the search of the entire apartment building is imprecise and thus invalid [*United States v. Minton*, 219 F.2d 326 (1955)].

  (b) Note, however, that contraband not named in the warrant may be lawfully seized—under the *"plain view" doctrine*—where the police are acting under a valid warrant [*Harris v. New York*, 331 U.S. 145 (1947)]. Nevertheless, the scope of the search is limited by the *premise described* in the warrant [*Marron v. United States*, 275 U.S. 192 (1927)].

  (c) **Search of third-party premises:** Where probable cause of criminal activity exists, a place owned by nonsuspects may be searched upon obtaining a warrant [*Zurcher v. Stanford Daily*, 436 U.S. 547 (1978)]. No First Amendment privilege for a newspaper office was found to override the Fourth Amendment justification for the search.

  (d) **Detention of occupants:** A warrant properly issued for the search of contraband carries with it the implicit authority to detain occupants on the premises [*Michigan v. Summers*, 452 U.S. 692 (1981)].

c. **Probable cause:** In order to be valid a warrant must be based upon probable cause.

(1) **Definition:** Probable cause is satisfied when the testimony or affidavit presented to the magistrate contains facts or circumstances sufficient that a reasonable person would conclude it to be more probable than not that such evidence of named items or persons will be found [*Carroll v. United States,* 267 U.S. 132 (1925)]. Probable cause may be invalidated if the information is too remote in time.

(2) **Administrative warrants:** Where reasonable standards exist for inspecting buildings involving municipal, health, or safety functions, strict probable cause is not required for issuance of a warrant. "Area search warrants" based on a lower standard of reasonableness will suffice [*Camera v. Municipal Court,* 387 U.S. 523 (1968)]. Warrantless searches, however, have been held valid regarding emergency health situations [*See v. Seattle,* 387 U.S. 541 (1967)].

An administrative warrant is not necessary when the search/seizure is of a closely regulated business. Furthermore, because of the public need, drug testing of railroad employees associated with an accident or customs agents seeking promotion is permissible [*Skinner v. Railway Labor Executives' Assoc.* 108 S.Ct. 1402 (1989); *Nat'l Treasury Employee's Union v. Von Raab,* 104 S.Ct. 1384 (1989)].

d. **Use of informants:** To determine probable cause when the police officer's affidavit contains hearsay information based on an informant's tip, the courts *formerly applied* the so-called *Aguilar-Spinelli* Test.

(1) **Elements of Aguilar-Spinelli Test:** Under the two-pronged test, the magistrate must receive 1) *credible information* (i.e., facts sufficient to show a fair probability that contraband or evidence of a crime will be found) from a 2) *reliable informant* (i.e., an informant with fresh, personal observation of the evidence who has been previously used as an informant, or who gives information subjecting himself to criminal penalty) [*Aguilar v. Texas,* 378 U.S. 108 (1964) and *Spinelli v. United States,* 393 U.S. 410 (1969)]. In some cases, corroboration is also required to verify an informant's tip.

(2) **Modern approach:** Under *Illinois v. Gates,* 462 U.S. 213 (1983), a warrant based on an informant's tip should be issued when probable cause is established under the "totality of the circumstances." The relevant factors to be taken into account are:

(a) *credible information;*

(b) *reliable informant;*

(c) *police corroboration; and*

(d) *declaration against interest.*

Exam Tip: The *Gates approach* should be followed for exam purposes.

(3) **Identity not required:** An informant's identity usually does not need to be revealed, even to the magistrate issuing the warrant [*McCray v. Illinois,* 386 U.S. 300 (1983)].

e. **Attacking the validity of a warrant:** A defendant may challenge the affidavit upon which a warrant was issued by proving by a preponderance of the evidence the following conditions [*Franks v. Delaware,* 438 U.S. 154 (1978)]:

(1) a substantial showing that the affidavit contained false statements;

(2) the statements were made intentionally, knowingly, or in reckless disregard for the truth; and

(3) the magistrate's finding of probable cause could not have been made without the false statements.

Absent any of the above, a warrant will be upheld if there was a "substantial basis" to issue it in the first instance [*Massachusetts v. Upton,* 466 U.S. 727 (1984)].

f. **Execution of a warrant:** A search warrant need not specify the precise manner for its execution, yet specific limitations do apply:

(1) Only the police may execute a warrant, not private citizens;

(2) A search warrant must be executed promptly while probable cause still exists;

(3) Absent exigent circumstances, a police officer must knock and announce his presence before attempting a forcible entry [*Ker v. California,* 374 U.S. 23 (1964); *but see U.S. v. Banks,* 124 S.Ct. 521 (2003)—where police waited 15–20 seconds after knocking with no response, there was reasonable suspicion that occupants would destroy evidence if officers waited longer, and forcible entry was constitutional under the Fourth Amendment]; however, the Supreme Court recently held that violation of the knock-and-announce rule did not require the suppression of all evidence found in the search [*Hudson v. Michigan,* 126 S.Ct. 2159 (2006)].

(4) Persons unnamed in a warrant may not be searched merely because of their presence [*Ybarra v. Illinois,* 444 U.S. 85 (1979)—patrons of a bar, where only search of the bartender and the premises was authorized in the warrant, cannot be searched for weapons, absent reasonable suspicion].

g. **General requirement of reasonableness:** It is improper to issue a warrant—even when there is probable cause—if the intrusion is unreasonable, for example, requiring the removal of a bullet from an individual suspected of robbery when the bullet is deeply embedded in the body, removal would damage the body, and the removal would require general anesthesia [*Winston v. Lee,* 105 S.Ct. 1611 (1985)].

h. **When warrant is obtained after police enter defendant's home:** When police do not have a search warrant or an arrest warrant until after they enter the defendant's home and conduct a search, such a search is not permissible under the Fourth Amendment absent exigent circumstances, even where the police believe that they have probable cause to search [*Kirk v. Louisiana*, 122 S.Ct. 2458 (2002)].

4. **Exceptions to the Warrant Requirement:** Since the warrant requirement is central to the Fourth Amendment protection against unreasonable searches and seizures, all warrantless searches are unconstitutional unless they fall within one of the seven exceptions discussed below:

a. **Search incident to a lawful arrest:** To protect the arresting police officers and to prevent the destruction of evidence, the person of the defendant and the area within his immediate control (i.e., his wingspan) may be searched without a warrant [*Chimel v. California,* 395 U.S. 752 (1969)—warrantless search of *defendant's house* following his lawful arrest held unconstitutional].

A search incident to arrest includes a cursory scan or "protective sweep" of adjoining rooms. Additionally, provided there is reasonable suspicion of an armed accomplice, the entire domicile may be scanned [*Maryland v. Buie,* 110 S.Ct. 1093 (1990)].

Furthermore, where police officers had probable cause to believe that a defendant had hidden drugs in his home and good reason to fear that he would destroy drugs if given opportunity to do so, they did not violate the Fourth Amendment's proscription of unreasonable seizures by temporarily barring defendant, who had exited his home during discussion with police, from re-entering his home alone while officers sought search warrant [*Illinois v. McArthur,* 121 S.Ct. 946 (2001)].

(1) **Time requirements:** A search incident to a lawful arrest must be contemporaneous to the arrest [*United States v. Chadwick,* 433 U.S. 1 (1977)—search of a footlocker one-and-a-half hours after arrest held invalid], it may even precede the arrest [*Rawlings v. Kentucky,* 448 U.S. 98 (1980)—where probable cause to arrest exists, the search may immediately precede the actual arrest; *but see Knowles v. Iowa,* 119 S.Ct. 484 (1998)— exception does not apply where officer only issues citation and does not arrest defendant].

(2) **Where full search permissible:** When an offense authorizes a full custodial arrest, a search incident to that arrest may follow, even where the police do not fear for their safety or believe contraband will be found [*United States v. Robinson,* 414 U.S. 218 (1973)—search of defendant's pack of cigarettes which contained heroin held lawful as incident to his arrest for a traffic violation].

Examples:

(1) A driver was ordered out of his vehicle and a full search was held lawful, even though the arrest was only for a traffic violation [*Pennsylvania v. Mimms,* 434 U.S. 106 (1977)].

(2) Following a lawful custodial arrest during which the defendant was hand-cuffed, police were permitted to search the entire passenger compartment of his car and its contents, as being within the defendant's control (i.e., "lunge doctrine") [*New York v. Belton,* 453 U.S. 454 (1981)].

b. **Stop and frisk:** Where a police officer has a reasonable and articulable suspicion that a suspect is armed and dangerous he may, without probable cause, perform a pat-down search for concealed weapons (i.e., frisk) [*Terry v. Ohio,* 392 U.S. 1 (1968)].

(1) **Limitations:**

(a) **Weapons only:** Under the *Terry* standard a frisk is generally limited to a pat-down of the outer clothing for the purpose of finding concealed weapons. The evidence must reasonably be believed by the officer to be a possible weapon before the frisk is made [*Sibron v. New York,* 392 U.S. 40 (1968)—a pat-down yielding a soft plastic bag of heroin was held unconstitutional].

(b) **Identification alone insufficient:** An officer cannot, without probable cause to arrest, stop and frisk an individual on the street for mere failure to show identification [*Brown v. Texas,* 443 U.S. 47 (1979)].

(c) **Suspicion based on hearsay sufficient:** A hearsay tip from an unnamed informant may justify a weapons search by police prior to an arrest [*Adams v. Williams,* 407 U.S. 143 (1972)—search of defendant's belt permitted to locate weapon without initial pat-down].

(d) **Investigating past criminal activity:** A *Terry* stop based on less than full probable cause is permitted where the detainee is suspected of involvement in a past crime constituting a felony or a threat to public safety [*United States v. Hensle,* 469 U.S. 221 (1985)—upon reasonable suspicion that the driver was armed and dangerous and wanted for investigation of robbery, a police officer properly stopped a vehicle, ordered the driver and passenger out of the car, and then observed a gun through the passenger door].

c. **Plain view:** Two requirements must be met in order for the plain view doctrine to justify a warrantless seizure of property [*Coolidge v. New Hampshire,* 403 U.S. 443 (1971)].

(1) **Requirements:**

   (a) The police must be lawfully positioned; and

   (b) it must be ***immediately apparent*** that the evidence is incriminating [*Horton v. California,* 110 S.Ct. 2301 (1990)].

(2) **Specific case:**

   (a) A police officer may follow an arrestee into his house and then lawfully seize any contraband evidence which is in plain view [*Washington v. Chrisman,* 455 U.S. 1 (1982)].

   (b) Once a vehicle is lawfully impounded, items found during an ***inventory search*** may be seized 1) to safeguard the defendant's property and 2) to protect the police against false claims of theft [*South Dakota v. Opperman,* 428 U.S. 364 (1967)].

Example:

Mason Perry was sitting at home one evening working on his new book, soon to be published by the Lucre Press. As he was typing away, he heard a knock at the door. He opened the door, and two local police officers were standing at the entrance, displaying a valid arrest warrant for Perry. The officers announced that Perry was under arrest for possession of illegally grown grapes, a violation of the state's criminal code. Arresting Officer Chablis then ordered Perry to accompany him downstairs to the basement, where Perry had a refrigerator. Chablis opened the refrigerator and saw a shipping box. Perry's attempt to grab the box from Chablis was not fruitful, and Chablis saw that grapes were hidden in the box. These grapes, which were illegally grown, were the subject of a suppression hearing.

The seizure of the grapes was

(A) unlawful

(B) lawful, since the grapes were in "plain view"

(C) lawful, because Perry gave his implied consent to the search

(D) lawful, since the search was incident to an arrest

Answer:

(A) The seizure of the grapes by Officer Chablis was unlawful as violative of Mason Perry's Fourth Amendment rights. If a valid arrest has been made, a police officer may make a search without a warrant incident to the arrest. The scope of the search incident to an arrest is limited to the area within the control or grasp of the arrested person. See *Chimel v. California,* 395 U.S. 752 (1969). In the present case, Mason Perry was placed under arrest as he opened the door to his home. Consequently, Officer Chablis had no right to order Perry downstairs to the basement of his house, since the basement was not within the "area of reach" of the defendant. Thus, the seizure was the illegal fruit of an unlawful search. Choice (B) is incorrect as the grapes were not in "plain view" since Officer Chablis was not properly in a place where he had a right to be. Choice (C) is also wrong because there was no implied consent to search.

d. **Automobile exception:** Warrantless search and seizure of items from an automobile may be justified under several theories—search incident to a lawful arrest, plain view, an inventory search following a lawful impounding, or a border search. However, the main authority for a warrantless automobile search is based on the holding of *United States v. Ross,* 456 U.S. 798 (1982). If probable cause justifies the search of a lawfully stopped vehicle, it justifies the search of every part of the vehicle and its contents that may conceal the object of the search.

(1) **Requirements:**

(a) **Caveat:** A mere lawful stop based on reasonable suspicion or criminal violation can ripen into probable cause necessary for a warrantless search [*Colorado v. Bannister,* 449 U.S. 1 (1980)—a lawful vehicle stop for speeding developed into probable cause to search when officers observed fruits of crime they had learned of through a police broadcast].

(2) **Contemporaneity *not* required**: Where a warrantless search is lawful, the police may bring the vehicle to the station and search it at a later time [*Chambers v. Maroney,* 399 U.S. 42 (1970)].

(3) **Scope of automobile search:** Where probable cause to conduct a warrantless search exists, the police may search the entire vehicle, including closed containers and luggage, to find the objects for which the probable cause existed [*United States v. Ross,* 456 U.S. 798 (1982); *see also Wyoming v. Houghton,* 119 S.Ct. 1297 (1999)—rule is true whether containers belong to driver or passenger]. However, the Court held it to be an improper invasion of privacy to open a footlocker without a warrant, even though the item was obtained from an automobile over which the police had

custody [*United States v. Chadwick*, 433 U.S. 1 (1977)—a lesser expectation of privacy exists in an automobile, boat, or airplane than in one's home or personal property].

e. **Search of bus passengers:** The Fourth Amendment does not require police officers to advise bus passengers of their right not to cooperate and to refuse consent to searches, provided that a reasonable person would feel free to decline the requests to search or otherwise terminate the encounter. Factors worth noting in this analysis are (1) whether a police officer makes intimidating movements; (2) whether he brandishes his weapon; (3) his conduct and politeness to passengers; and (4) his leaving a departure route open and available [*United States v. Drayton*, 122 S.Ct. 2105 (2002); *see also Florida v. Bostick*, 501 U.S. 429 111 S.Ct. 2382 (1991); *but see Bond v. U.S.*, 120 S.Ct. 1462 (2000)—where law enforcement officer felt and examined soft-sided luggage stored by bus passenger in an overhead luggage compartment it was considered a Fourth Amendment search].

f. **Consent:** A search is proper without a warrant or probable cause where effective consent is given. To be effective, the defendant's consent must be a voluntary and intelligent decision made without coercion [*Schneckloth v. Bustamonte*, 412 U.S. 218 (1973)]. Voluntariness is determined by the ***"totality of the circumstances."*** The police need not inform the defendant that she has a right to withhold consent [*Schneckloth v. Bustamonte, supra*]. Consent given pursuant to an invalid warrant is deemed involuntary [*Bumper v. North Carolina*, 391 U.S. 543 (1968)].

(1) **Scope of consent:** The consenting party controls the scope of the search and any conduct exceeding the scope of the consent is unlawful. Consent may be revoked, in which case the search must cease.

(2) **Implied consent:** In certain industries regulated by statute (i.e., sale of drugs, firearms, and toxic chemicals), implied consent to inspection searches is valid, where reasonable. Likewise, baggage searches at airports and U.S. borders are generally valid.

(3) **Third-party consent:** The general rule is that any person who has joint control or use of the premises may consent to a valid search, and any evidence obtained may be used against the other occupants [*Frazier v. Cupp*, 394 U.S. 731 (1969)—a duffel bag having co-owners may be searched upon consent of one of the owners]. Such consent applies to common areas, but not to private, reserved areas where the defendant has exclusive control [*United States v. Matlock*, 415 U.S. 164 (1974)].

The police need only have a reasonable belief that the third party has actual authority [*Illinois v. Rodriguez*, 110 S.Ct. 2793 (1990)].

(a) **Examples of specific situations:**

(1) A landlord may ***not*** consent to the search of a tenant's apartment [*Chapman v. United States,* 365 U.S. 610 (1961)].

(2) A motel owner may ***not*** consent to the search of a guest's room [*Stoner v. California,* 376 U.S. 483 (1964)].

(3) An employer may ***not*** consent to the search of an employee's private storage area.

(4) School officials ***may search a student under their authority upon a showing of reasonableness*** under the circumstances [*New Jersey v. T.L.O.,* 83 L.Ed.2d 720 (1984)—search of 14-year-old girl's purse which yielded drug paraphernalia and marijuana held proper without a warrant or probable cause].

Example:

Dagwood and Daisy were second-year law students at Pepperdine Law School in Malibu. They shared a small three-room apartment and lived together as roommates and lovers. One morning they had a bitter argument after Dagwood found out that Daisy was having an affair with Dean McGoldfinger, her Islamic law instructor.

During their squabble, Dagwood lost his temper and punched Daisy in the mouth. He then stormed out of the apartment to attend classes. While he was gone, Daisy called the police and told them that she had just been assaulted by her boyfriend. Thereafter, two police officers arrived at the apartment and Daisy gave them permission to enter.

As she was being questioned about the incident, Daisy said that Dagwood was "high" on cocaine when he struck her. She then told the officers that Dagwood kept cocaine in the bedroom closet. Thereupon, she led them into the bedroom. While searching Dagwood's closet, the officers found a vial which contained a small amount of cocaine. When Dagwood returned to the apartment, he was arrested for possession of illegal narcotics.

At his hearing, Dagwood moves to suppress the narcotics found by the police. His request should be

(A) granted, because Dagwood had a reasonable expectation of privacy in the confines of his bedroom closet

(B) granted, because the police should have obtained a search warrant before searching the closet

(C) denied, because Daisy consented to the search of a shared area

(D) denied, because the police had probable cause to suspect that there was cocaine in the closet

Answer:

(C) As a general rule, in the absence of the defendant, a third party who has joint control with the defendant over the premises to be searched can consent to a search over those areas where he has joint control. In *State v. Thibodeau,* 317 A.2d 172 (1974), it was held that "where two or more persons occupy a dwelling place jointly, the general rule is that a joint tenant can consent to police entry and search the entire house or apartment, even though they occupy separate bedrooms." Therefore, Daisy's consent is apparently valid because (as Dagwood's lover) she shared the bedroom with him.

g. **Hot pursuit:** A warrantless search is lawful when police are pursuing a dangerous suspect to apprehend him, and they may seize "mere" evidence as well as any contraband they find [*Warden v. Haden,* 387 U.S. 294 (1967)]. Police may enter and search a private dwelling while in reasonable pursuit [*United States v. Santana,* 427 U.S. 38 (1976)].

   (1) **Caveat:** There is no exception to the warrant requirement for searches at the scene of a crime [*Mincey v. Arizona,* 437 U.S. 385 (1978); *Thompson v. Louisiana,* 83 L.Ed.2d 246 (1984)—a warrantless search of the defendant's home soon after she killed her husband held unconstitutional, since there is no "murder scene" exception; however, police may search without a warrant to seek other victims or a remaining killer].

h. **Exigent circumstances:** In certain emergency situations where evidence may be lost or destroyed before a warrant can be obtained, a warrantless search and seizure is permitted [*Schmerber v. California,* 384 U.S. 757 (1966)—blood sample allowed to determine driver's alcohol level; *Cupp v. Murphy,* 412 U.S. 291 (1973)— fingernail scrapings permitted].

   (1) **Scope:** No general emergency exception exists, so courts are cautious not to overexpand the areas permissible for warrantless searches [*Michigan v. Tyler,* 436 U.S. 499 (1978)—a warrantless search of a fire was permitted at the scene and a few hours later to determine the cause of the fire, although a search several days later to investigate for arson was held illegal without a warrant].

i. **Private Party:** The police are permitted to repeat and incidentally expand a private citizen's search [*United States v. Jacobsen,* 466 U.S. 109 (1984)].

j. **Inventory:** Provided there are standard police procedures so allowing, an officer is permitted to inventory all effects lawfully in police possession [*Florida v. Wells,* 110 S.Ct. 1632 (1990)].

5. **Other Searches**

a. **Administrative searches:** Administrative warrants are generally issued upon a lesser showing of probable cause. Periodic inspections regarding building codes and health regulations are permitted where reasonable, so as not to foster selective enforcement [*Camara v. Municipal Court*, 387 U.S. 523 (1967)].

CRIMINAL PROCEDURE MULTISTATE CHART #2
EXCEPTIONS TO THE WARRANT REQUIREMENT

Exception	Main Case
(1) Search incident to a lawful arrest	*Chimel v. California*
(2) Stop and Frisk	*Terry v. Ohio*
(3) Plain view	*Coolidge v. New Hampshire*
(4) Automobile exception	*Carroll v. United States*
(5) Consent	*Schneckloth v. Bustamonte*
(6) Hot pursuit	*Warden v. Hayden*
(7) Exigent circumstances	*Schmerber v. California*

(1) **Examples allowing warrantless searches:**

(a) Search of a locked storeroom of a firearms warehouse is permitted during reasonable hours because of public interest involved [*United States v. Biswell*, 406 U.S. 311 (1972)].

(b) Search for highly contaminated food is justified without warrant [*North American Cold Storage v. City of Chicago*, 211 U.S. 306 (1908)].

(2) **Airport searches and detentions:** To protect passengers from weapons and explosives, under federal law warrantless administrative searches are permitted at airports. A passenger may avoid being searched by declining to board the plane.

(a) **Specific cases of airport detentions:**

(1) Although narcotics-sniffing dogs may smell a passenger's luggage, any resulting detention must be brief and a seizure of the luggage is subject to Fourth Amendment limitations [*United States v. Place*, 77 L.Ed.2d 110 (1983)].

(2) Seizure of a debarking passenger by narcotics agents, who took the suspect's ticket and identification and escorted him in custody to a detention room, violated the *Terry* standard for reasonable suspicion and was held unconstitutional [*Florida v. Royer*, 460 U.S. 491 (1983)].

(3) At an airport, a consensual encounter where police ask to talk to a suspect involves no Fourth Amendment interest. A temporary detention for questioning requires no showing of probable cause, but only an *"articulable suspicion"* by police [*Florida v. Rodriguez*, 83 L.Ed.2d 165 (1984)—detention justified where suspects spoke furtively, were overheard to say "(let's) get out of here," and made evasive movements when sighted by officers].

b. **Border searches:** As an incident of national sovereignty, routine warrantless searches of individuals and their personal effects may be conducted by governmental agents without probable cause upon crossing an international border or its "functional equivalents" (i.e., international airports, post offices where foreign mail enters) [*Alameida-Sanchez v. United States*, 413 U.S. 266 (1973)]. Because of increasing drug traffic at U.S. borders, the Court may soon reconsider the standard of suspicion required for body cavity searches, but at present such intrusive searches are only permitted where agents have a clear indication that there is contraband [*Henderson v. United States*, 390 F.2nd 805 (9th Cir. 1967)].

(1) **Fixed checkpoints:** Vehicles may be stopped without cause for questioning, but *probable cause* is required to fully search [*United States v. Martinez-Fuerte*, 428 U.S. 543 (1976)].

(2) **Roving patrols:** Vehicles may be stopped where police have *a reasonable suspicion* (i.e., more than the appearance of Mexican ancestry alone) [*United States v. Brignoni-Ponce*, 422 U.S. 872 (1975)], but searched only where probable cause exists [*Alameida-Sanchez v. United States, supra*].

(3) **Search of alimentary canal:** Where a suspect declines to submit to an X-ray by customs agents at the border, and reasonable justification for detention initially exists, the detention may continue until a bowel movement occurs [*United States v. de Hernandez*, 87 L.Ed.2d 381 (1985)].

c. **Seizure of a person's conversations:** Only where an invasion of a person's reasonable expectation of privacy exists will the Fourth Amendment protect against unlawful searches and seizures.

(1) **Eavesdropping:** Each party to a conversation assumes the risk that the other party will reveal, transmit, or tape-record the substance of the conversation [*Hoffa v. United States*, (1966)]. There is no constitutional right to protect misplaced confidences. A defendant has no Fourth Amendment basis to object to such eavesdropping—even if the person turns out to be a police informer—as an unlawful warrantless search [*United States v. White*, 401 U.S. 745 (1971)].

(2) **Wiretapping:** A different situation exists in this case since any form of wiretapping or use of electronic surveillance devices violates a defendant's right

to a reasonable expectation of privacy [*Katz v. United States*, 389 U.S. 347 (1967)]. Such a search is permitted only after a warrant is issued. *Berger v. New York*, 388 U.S. 41 (1967) set forth the requirements for such a warrant:

(a) Probable cause must be shown that a crime has been or is being committed;

(b) The warrant must name the suspects as well as describe the particular conversation to be overheard; and

(c) The wiretap must be valid only for a brief period after which time it will be terminated and the recorded conversations returned before the court.

(3) **National security:** In foreign matters of national security, warrantless wiretaps are allowed; however, in domestic matters, even the president cannot request such surveillance without a warrant being issued upon approval by a neutral magistrate [*United States v. U.S. District Court (Eastern District of Michigan)*, 407 U.S. 297 (1972)].

d. **Diagnostic tests:** A state hospital's performance of a diagnostic test to obtain evidence of a patient's criminal conduct for law enforcement purposes is an unreasonable search if the patient has not consented to the procedure. The interest in using the threat of criminal sanctions to deter pregnant women from using cocaine is not adequate to justify a departure from the general rule that an official nonconsensual search is unconstitutional if not authorized by a valid warrant [*Ferguson v. Charleston*, 121 S.Ct. 1281 (2001)].

e. **Warrantless searches as a probation condition:** Where a person on probation agrees as a condition of that probation to submit to random, unannounced warrantless searches that are not based on probable cause, such a search may be valid under the Fourth Amendment, especially where it is actually based on reasonable suspicion [*United States v. Knights*, 122 S.Ct. 587 (2001)].

II. STATEMENTS, CONFESSIONS, AND IDENTIFICATIONS

A. INTRODUCTION

The Court uses several approaches to determine the admissibility of statements and confessions made by a defendant and the propriety of both pre-indictment and post-indictment identification procedures. A defendant's rights in these areas derive from the Fourth, Fifth, and Sixth Amendments.

B. STATEMENTS AND CONFESSIONS

1. In General

A statement *may be found inadmissible* if it is either (a) involuntary under the Due Process Clauses of the Fifth and Fourteenth Amendments; (b) in violation of the Fifth Amendment privilege against self-incrimination as applied by the *Miranda* standard; (c) in violation of the Sixth Amendment right to counsel under the *Massiah* rule; or (d) a fruit of an illegal arrest or search under the Fourth Amendment exclusionary rule.

a. **When the right to counsel begins:** Although the *Massiah* right to counsel had generally been interpreted as arising only upon indictment, in *Brewer v. Williams* the Court declared that "the right to counsel granted by the Sixth and Fourteenth Amendments means at least that a person is entitled to the help of a lawyer at or after the time that judicial proceedings have been initiated against him—'whether by way of formal charge, preliminary hearing, indictment, information, or arraignment.'" Noting that a warrant had been issued for Williams's arrest, that he had been arraigned on that warrant before a judge, and that he had been committed by the court to confinement in jail, the Court concluded there "can be no doubt in the present case that judicial proceedings had been initiated."

Clearly this test is not met merely because the defendant had been arrested without a warrant, nor is it met merely because the investigation has focused upon the defendant. Though "focus" was one of the several elements in *Escobedo*, that case has been limited to its own facts, and the Supreme Court later held in *Hoffa v. United States* that focus alone did not ripen the Sixth Amendment right to counsel. Even against the contention that indictment was delayed for the specific purpose of allowing the government to "beef up" its case with admissions to be obtained by stealth and trickery, it has been held that the government is under no obligation to cease an ongoing investigation when probable cause to obtain an indictment comes into existence.

CRIMINAL PROCEDURE MULTISTATE CHART #3

FOUR BASES TO EXCLUDE STATEMENTS AND CONFESSIONS

Approach	Constitutional Basis
(1) **Voluntariness Approach**—To be admissible, a statement must be voluntarily made based on the totality of the circumstances.	Due Process Clause of Fifth and Fourteenth Amendments
(2) *Miranda* **Standard**—statements made during custodial interrogation are inadmissible in the absence of *Miranda* warnings.	Fifth Amendment Privilege Against Self-Incrimination
(3) **Right to Counsel Approach**—statements made during any "critical stage" of a criminal proceeding are inadmissible unless the defendant is afforded the right to counsel.	Sixth Amendment Right to Counsel
(4) **Fruits of Illegal Conduct**—otherwise admissible voluntary statements obtained as fruits of prior illegal searches and seizures are inadmissible.	Fourth Amendment Exclusionary Rule

2. **Voluntariness Approach:** Historically, the voluntariness standard, based on trustworthiness and reliability of the proffered evidence, was used to determine the admissibility of a confession based on the totality of the circumstances [*Brown v. Mississippi*, 297 U.S. 278 (1936)—physical abuse by police rendered confession involuntary]. Such factors as the defendant's age, sex, education, and mental and physical health are considered as factors of coercion. Police have broad reign to trick and deceive the defendant during interrogation, but may not offer false promises of dropping charges to elicit a confession [*Spano v. New York,* 360 U.S. 315 (1959)].

   a. **"Harmless Error" Standard:** Admission of a coerced confession no longer results in automatic reversal. Rather, the harmless error rule is now applicable to the admission of involuntary confessions [*Arizona v. Fuhninante,* U.S. S.Ct. Docket No. 89-839 (1991)]. Note: Confessions elicited in violation of both the Sixth and Fourteenth Amendments are thus subject to the harmless error standard.

3. **The *Miranda* Standard:** In *Miranda v. Arizona,* 384 U.S. 436 (1966) the Fifth Amendment privilege against self-incrimination was determined to be a basis to evaluate the admissibility of a confession. The objective standard imposed by the *Miranda* warnings is now the main source of excluding a confession, but it does not replace the case-by-case analysis used in the "voluntariness approach."

   a. **Background: The Fifth Amendment Privilege Against Self-Incrimination:** The Fifth Amendment states that "no person shall be compelled in a criminal case to be a witness against himself." The privilege, which applies **only to natural persons, must be asserted to be effective.** It may be so asserted in any criminal, civil, or administrative proceeding where incriminating testimony can be used in a subsequent prosecution (i.e., a defendant may assert privilege before a grand jury, but may not do so where immunity has been granted).

      (1) **Applicability of the privilege:** The privilege against self-incrimination protects only against admission of evidence that is **testimonial** in nature (i.e., lie detector test), but not against the admission of real or physical evidence (i.e., blood, hair, and handwriting samples). The privilege applies only to *"compelled" self-incriminating testimony* [*California v. Byers*, 402 U.S. 424 (1971)—a California law requiring motorists to give their names at the scene of an accident was upheld since the identification requirement presented no substantial risk of self-incrimination].

      Examples:

      > Wayne Wilson was arrested at Kansas City Municipal Airport when the small satchel he was carrying was found to contain cocaine. Wilson, who did not challenge the legality of the airport search, was subsequently prosecuted for possession of cocaine.

      > At trial, Wilson testified in his own behalf and said that the satchel belonged to his girlfriend, Jerri Martin, who was accompanying Wilson when he was

arrested. (Martin died in a skydiving accident two weeks before Wilson's trial.) Moreover, Wilson testified that although he was a former cocaine addict, he had not used any drugs in the past three years. On cross-examination, the prosecuting attorney asked Wilson to roll up the sleeves of his shirt and exhibit his arms to see if there were any needle marks.

This request is

(A) objectionable, because Wilson has a privilege against self-incrimination

(B) objectionable, because the probative value is substantially outweighed by the danger of unfair prejudice

(C) permissible, because such evidence is relevant to Wilson's credibility

(D) permissible, because Wilson waived his privilege against self-incrimination by taking the stand

Answer:

(C) Students must be aware that choice (D) is wrong because the privilege against self-incrimination only applies to evidence that is ***testimonial in nature.*** Here, choice (C) is correct because the prosecuting attorney is attempting to attack Wilson's credibility. According to **F.R.E.** 806, "When a hearsay statement, or a statement defined in Rule 801(d)(2), (C), (D), or (E), has been admitted in evidence, the credibility of the declarant may be attacked, and if attacked may be supported, by any evidence which would be admissible for those purposes if declarant had testified as a witness." In our case, Wilson testified that he "had not used any drugs for the past three years." Consequently, it is proper for the prosecution to attack his credibility by seeing if there are any needle marks on his arms.

The state of Newton has the following hit-and-run statute in effect:

> "Any driver of a motor vehicle (including but not limited to automobiles, trucks, buses, or motorcycles) involved in an accident or collision resulting in injury or death to a human being shall immediately stop his or her vehicle at the scene of such accident or collision, render necessary aid to the injured victim and furnish the police or other person(s) at the scene with his or her name, address, and driver's license. Any violation or noncompliance with said statute shall be punished by imprisonment of not less than three years nor more than seven years."

At 3:30 P.M. on the afternoon of January 13, 1997, nine-year-old Goldie Hand was riding her bicycle along Pacific Coast Highway. As Goldie swerved into the southbound lane, her bicycle was struck by a car driven by Ellen Brennan. Goldie was knocked off her bike and thrown onto the sidewalk adjacent to the highway. Although Goldie received some minor scrapes and bruises, she was not seriously injured. Following the accident, the car driven by Brennan sped away.

Moments later, however, a tractor-trailer crashed into the rear of a Ford Pinto about thirty feet from where Goldie was lying. The Pinto almost instantly caught fire as its gas tank exploded. Goldie, who was engulfed in the flaming wreckage, burned to death.

Assume for the purposes of this question only that Brennan is charged with violating the aforementioned statute. She files a motion to dismiss on the grounds that the disclosure requirement of the statute violates her privilege against self-incrimination. Her motion should be

(A) granted, because the statute makes no provision for *Miranda* warnings concerning her right to remain silent

(B) granted, because the statute requires her to provide incriminating information that can be used against her in a criminal prosecution

(C) denied, because the legislative intent in enacting the statute was designed to require disclosure of information to be used primarily in civil litigation

(D) denied, because in accordance with public policy considerations the required disclosures are insufficiently testimonial

Answer:

(D) The facts in this hypothetical are taken from *California v. Byers*, 402 U.S. 424, 91 S.Ct. 1535 (1971), in which the U.S. Supreme Court held that a statute requiring a motorist involved in an accident to stop and give his name and address did not involve self-incrimination in a constitutional sense. Students should be aware that choice (C) is wrong because violation of the statute results in a (criminal) sentence of imprisonment. Therefore, clearly, the legislative intent was not directed for the disclosure requirement to be used primarily in civil litigation.

(2) **Availability of privilege when witness denies all culpability:** Where a witness has reason to fear that answers to possible questions might tend to incriminate her, she has a valid Fifth Amendment privilege against self-incrimination [*Ohio v. Reiner*, 121 S.Ct. 1252 (2001)].

(3) **Procedural considerations:**

(a) **Prosecutorial comment:** No comment on the ***defendant's failure to testify*** may be made by the prosecution [*Griffin v.*

California, 380 U.S. 609 (1965)]. Furthermore, the defendant may request the judge to instruct that no adverse inference may be drawn from the defendant's failure to testify [*Carter v. Kentucky,* 450 U.S. 288 (1981)]. However, where a prosecutor argued during summation that the testifying defendant's *presence* at trial afforded opportunity to tailor testimony to that of other witnesses, there was no Fifth Amendment violation [*Portuondo v. Agard,* 120 S.Ct. 1119 (2000)]. **Note:** Even in civil cases, the prevailing view is that if a witness is "equally available" to both parties, ***no adverse inference may spring from a failure of the witness to be called*** [McCormick, **Law of Evidence,** p. 657]. Furthermore, even where a defendant has pled guilty, he does not waive his Fifth Amendment rights in the sentencing hearing, and the sentencing judge may not draw adverse inferences from the defendant's silence at sentencing [*Mitchell v. United States,* 119 S.Ct. 1307 (1999)].

Example:

During the murder trial of Slick Savage, the prosecution presented four witnesses to the brutal slaying of Melody Mercy. The evidence pointed to the fact that Slick beat her about the head and neck with a thirty-two inch baseball bat, causing severe injuries to her brain and her ultimate death.

The prosecution rested, and Slick presented two witnesses—his brother and his girlfriend—who testified that Slick was dining at an elegant French restaurant on the other side of town at the time of the alleged murder. Slick presented no other witnesses.

During his closing argument to the jury, the assistant district attorney, Don Dandee, called attention to the fact that the prosecution witnesses had no apparent reason to have any bias toward the prosecution or against the defendant. He then noted that Slick's witnesses had clear motives to falsify their testimony and favor Slick. Dandee added, "If Slick was on the other side of town, why didn't he tell us himself? Why didn't he get on the stand? What was he hiding? Those are questions for you, the jury to answer."

Slick was convicted of first-degree murder and sentenced to life imprisonment.

On appeal his conviction should be

(A) reversed, because the prosecutor improperly referred to the possible motives or interests of the defense witness

(B) reversed, because Slick's constitutional rights were violated in Dandee's closing argument

(C) reversed, because Dandee referred to Slick's failure to testify

(D) reversed, because Dandee's argument violated Slick's rights under the Fifth and Fourteenth Amendments

Answer:

(D) In *Griffin v. California,* 380 U.S. 609, 85 S.Ct 1229 (1965), the U.S. Supreme Court held that the self-incrimination guarantee of the Fifth Amendment, as applicable to the states under the Fourteenth Amendment, forbids either comment by the prosecution of an accused's silence or instructions by the court that such silence is evidence of guilt. The comments by the prosecutor during his closing argument that Slick failed to take the stand would be violative of the defendant's right against self-incrimination.

Example:

Marshall sued Gelson's Market for injuries allegedly sustained from a collision with the store's automatic doors. Marshall contended that the doors (which were programmed to swing inward) swung outward and injured him as he attempted to enter the store one afternoon. Brock, Marshall's brother-in-law, who was an eyewitness to the accident was not called to testify at trial. Moreover, Marshall's attorney failed to depose Brock, who redomiciled out of state shortly after the accident.

With respect to Marshall's failure to offer Brock's testimony at trial, on request by Gelson's attorney the court should

(A) instruct the jury that it raises the presumption that Brock's testimony would have been unfavorable to Marshall

(B) instruct the jury that it constitutes an adoptive admission that Brock's testimony would have been unfavorable to Marshall

(C) permit Gelson's attorney to argue that it raises a presumption that Brock's testimony would have been unfavorable to Marshall

(D) neither instruct the jury on the matter nor permit Gelson's attorney to argue the matter

Answer:

(D) A very popular Multistate testing area deals with whether the ***failure of a party to call a particular witness*** (or the failure to take the stand himself as a witness) allows his adversary to use this failure as a basis for invoking an adverse inference. Although there are a large number of cases supporting the inference, under the prevailing view if the witness is "equally available" to both parties no inference springs from the failure of either to call him. [McCormick, **Law of Evidence,** p 657]. McCormick points out that "the possibility that the inference may be drawn invites waste of time in calling unnecessary witnesses or in presenting evidence to explain why they were not called." Most importantly, McCormick notes that "the availability of modern discovery procedures serves to diminish both the justification and the need for the inference." [McCormick, **Law of Evidence,** p 657].

(b) **Failure to testify:** Invocation of the privilege during an investigation may not be used as a valid basis to fire a police officer [*Garrity v. New Jersey*, 385 U.S. 493 (1967)].

(c) **Immunity:** Where either use or transactional immunity has been granted a defendant, the privilege against self-incrimination is eliminated [*Kastigar v. United States*, 406 U.S. 441 (1972)]. Immunized testimony cannot be used to impeach *(New Jersey v. Potash*, 440 U.S. 450 (1979)], but it can be used to prove perjury [*United States v. Apfelbaum*, 445 U.S. 115 (1980)].

(d) **Waiver:** A defendant may choose not to take the stand, but once he does permit questioning on direct examination, he may be cross-examined regarding the substance of his testimony [*Brown v. United States*, 356 U.S. 148 (1958)]. Generally, the defendant is thought not to waive the privilege "in toto" (i.e., a blanket waiver), but only to the extent necessary for reasonable scrutiny by the prosecution.

(e) **Requirement to participate in sexual abuse treatment program:** Where inmates are offered minimal incentives (such as visitation rights, work opportunities, ability to send money to family, canteen expenditures, access to a personal television, and incarceration in a lower-level security facility) to participate in a sexual abuse treatment program in which they "accept responsibility" for and admit to their crimes and any uncharged sexual criminal offenses, such a policy is not compelled self-incrimination prohibited by the Fifth Amendment [*McKune v. Lile*, 122 S.Ct. 2017 (2002)].

(f) Notably, a witness may not assert the Fifth Amendment privilege against self-incrimination based on his fear that his testimony will subject him to prosecution in a foreign country [*U.S. v. Balsys*, 118 S.Ct. 2218 (1998)].

b. **The *Miranda* Rule:**

(1) **Applicability of the rule:** The *Miranda* rule applies only to statements made during ***custodial interrogation.*** However, because *Miranda* derives from the Fifth Amendment, a federal statute that attempted to make the voluntariness of a suspect's custodial statements the touchstone of their admissibility and allowed admission of such statements in the absence of

Miranda warnings was unconstitutional [*Dickerson v. United States*, 120 S.Ct. 2326 (2000)].

(a) **Custody:** A person is in custody *when a significant deprivation of freedom of movement occurs and the person is not free to leave* [*Orozco v. Texas*, 394 U.S. 324 (1969)].

For *Miranda* purposes *a Terry "stop" is not considered to be custodial*. Therefore, *Miranda* warnings are not required [*Berkemer v. McCarty*, 468 U.S. 420 (1984)].

(b) **Subjective vs. objective approach:** A fundamental question concerning the *Miranda* "custody" issue is whether it is determined by some subjective factor (either that the suspect in fact believed he was in custody or that the police officer intended to take custody), or whether instead an objective test of the "reasonable man" type governs. Under the subjective approach, *which focuses upon the state of mind of the suspect*, a defendant would be in custody for *Miranda* purposes if he believed he was in custody. In defense of this approach, it may be said that it relates directly to the "potentiality for compulsion" with which the Court was concerned in *Miranda:* if the combination of custody and questioning is sufficiently coercive to call for warnings, then certainly the situation is no less coercive as to the defendant who actually but erroneously believes he is in custody. The trouble with this approach, however, is that it would place upon the police the burden of anticipating the frailties or idiosyncracies of every person they question.

On the other hand, the objective approach requires a careful examination of all the circumstances of the particular case. Account must be taken of those facts intrinsic to the interrogation: *when and where it occurred, how long it lasted, how many police were present, what the officers and the defendant said and did, the presence of physical restraint* or the equivalent (e.g., drawn weapons, guard stationed at the door), *and whether the defendant was being questioned as a suspect or as a witness*. Events before the interrogation are also relevant, especially how the defendant got to the place of questioning—whether he came completely on his own, in response to a police request, or escorted by police officers. The Supreme Court and the lower courts have also looked to what happened after the interrogation, relying upon the fact *that the suspect was allowed to leave following the interrogation as strong evidence that the interrogation was not custodial*.

MBE Exam Tip: For MBE Exam purposes, *the objective approach is the majority view* and should be followed whenever possible.

Example:

Smelson was employed by the B&O Railroad Company as a watchman at its crossing, to give warning to the public of approaching trains. Late one evening he fell asleep in his shanty and failed to warn of the approach of an oncoming train. Fishbone, who was driving his car, knew of the usual presence of the watchman. As he approached the crossing, he received no warning. Driving onto the track, Fishbone's car was struck and crushed by the train. Fishbone died instantly.

A few minutes after the accident, Police Officer Rose arrived at the crossing and walked into the shanty. As he entered, Smelson then awoke. Rose asked him, "What happened here?" Smelson made incriminating statements.

Smelson is subsequently charged with involuntary manslaughter. His motion to prevent the introduction of his incriminating statement into evidence will most likely be

(A) granted, because Police Officer Rose failed to give Smelson his *Miranda* warnings

(B) granted, because Police Officer Rose's conduct in questioning Smelson immediately after he awoke was unfairly prejudicial to the defendant

(C) denied, because the exchange took place in a noncustodial setting and the question was investigatory in nature

(D) denied, because Smelson's incriminating statements were volunteered

Answer:

(C) With *Miranda,* the Fifth Amendment privilege against compelled self-incrimination became the basis for ruling upon the admissibility of a confession. It should be noted that *Miranda* warnings (and a valid waiver) are prerequisites to the admissibility of any statement made by the accused **during a custodial interrogation.** Generally speaking, an interrogation will be considered custodial if the individual is *not* free to leave. According to *Orozco v. Texas,* 394 U.S. 324, 89 S.Ct. 1095 (1969), the U.S. Supreme Court held that a person is in "custody" if he (or she) is not free to leave, even if the questioning occurs in the individual's bedroom. In the present example, the facts do not indicate that Smelson was in police "custody" for *Miranda* purposes. Therefore, choice (C) is the best answer because Smelson's statements were not made during a custodial interrogation. Note that choice (C) is a better answer than (D) because the issue here is whether the police questioning was "on the scene" or "custodial."

CRIMINAL PROCEDURE MULTISTATE CHART #4
CRIMINAL PROCEDURE

MIRANDA	*MASSIAH*	*HOFFA*
1. *custodial* interrogation 2. Once a defendant is in police custody, he must be advised of his *Miranda* warnings: (a) right to remain silent; (b) any statement he does make may be used against him; (c) he has the right to have an attorney present; and (d) if he cannot afford an attorney, one will be appointed for him. 3. Only the defendant in custody must be warned. 4. *Miranda* does not apply to spontaneous, unsolicited confessions (as when a defendant blurts out incriminating statements or voluntarily confesses without prodding.	1. *post-indictment* interrogation 2. Defendant has the right to counsel when the police seek to interrogate him. 3. interrogation by police informant 4. Interrogation results when the police (or its informants) seek to elicit incriminating statements from the defendant.	1. defendant *not* in police custody 2. Government did *not* "plant" or encourage informant to interrogate (or elicit incriminating information from the defendant). 3. Eavesdropping was committed by defendant's "friend" who later volunteered to become an informer. 4. Eavesdropping is permissible because there is no constitutional right to protect misplaced confidences. 5. Each party to a conversation must assume the risk that the other will reveal the substance of the conversation.

(c) **Interrogation:** Interrogation occurs where *police know or should reasonably know that their actions or inquiries are reasonably likely to elicit an incriminating response* from the suspect [*Rhode Island v. Innis,* 446 U.S. 21 (1980)]. Volunteered statements are not the product of interrogation and are thus admissible, since *Miranda* warnings do not apply.

This test focuses on the susceptibility of the suspect. Thus, if there are no objective indications of particular susceptibility, such as youth, then it is likely to be permissible for the police to converse in the presence of the suspect provided there is no direct questioning. It should also be noted that *Miranda* bars only "official" interrogation. Thus, informant questioning in jail does not require the giving of *Miranda* warnings [*Illinois v. Perkins,* 110 S.Ct. 2394 (1990)].

(d) **Situations where the *Miranda* rule is inapplicable:**

(1) **questioning by private security guards** [*People v. Baugh,* 311 N.E.2d 607 (Ill. 1974)];

(2) **on-the-scene questioning;**

(3) **statements made before a grand jury investigation** [*United States v. Mandujano*, 425 U.S. 564 (1976)];

(4) **spontaneous, unsolicited statements;**

(5) **interrogation of a taxpayer during a criminal investigation by the I.R.S.** [*Beckwith v. United States*, 425 U.S. 341 (1976)]; and

(6) **questioning by a parole officer where the defendant was free to leave the police station** [*Oregon v. Mathiason*, 429 U.S. 492 (1977)].

(7) **"Public safety" exception:** The right to receive *Miranda* warnings was held to be outweighed by the immediate threat posed to the public safety in *New York v. Quarles*, 81 L.Ed.2d 550 (1984)—after chasing an armed rape suspect into a supermarket, police asked him "Where is the gun?" Thereupon, the police found the weapon, and the court held no violation of *Miranda* occurred.

(8) **Routine booking:** Police questions regarding age, date of birth, height, weight, and the like are permissible and do not require *Miranda* protections. Thus a slurred response (relevant to drunken driving) is admissible when answering such a question [*Pennsylvania v. Muniz*, 110 S.Ct. 2638 (1990)].

(2) **The *Miranda* warnings:** No statement made by a defendant will be admitted into evidence unless, prior to custodial interrogation, she is warned of the following:

(a) *She has a right to remain silent;*

(b) *Anything she says can be used against her in court;*

(c) *She has the right to the presence of an attorney; and*

(d) *If she cannot afford an attorney, one will be provided for her.*

c. **Limitations on the *Miranda* standard:**

(1) **Specificity of reciting the warnings:** The *Miranda* warnings need not be given verbatim, provided the defendant is sufficiently informed of his rights [*California v. Prysock*, 453 U.S. 355 (1981)].

(2) **Harmless error rule:** Failure to recite the *Miranda* warnings at all is a proper basis to render a statement inadmissible. Admission of evidence in violation of a person's *Miranda* rights **does not result in automatic reversal**, but is analyzed under the harmless error standard [*Milton v. Wainwright*, 407 U.S. 371 (1972)]. **Note:** Failure to advise a defendant of the right to appointed counsel is also analyzed under the harmless error standards [*Michigan v. Tucker*, 417 U.S. 433 (1974)].

(3) **When interrogation must cease:** If a defendant either requests an attorney or states that she wishes to remain silent, ***all interrogation must stop***. These requests can be made at any point during the course of interrogation and must be "scrupulously honored" by law enforcement.

(4) **When questioning can resume:**

  (a) A defendant who has exercised his right to remain silent may properly be questioned about ***an unrelated crime*** following a significant lapse of time and ***provided a new set of warnings are given*** [*Michigan v. Mosely*, 423 U.S. 96 (1975)].

  (b) A defendant who has requested an attorney may not be further questioned until either counsel is furnished or the defendant voluntarily initiates a discussion [*Edwards v. Arizona*, 451 U.S. 477 (1981)].

  Provided there is no Fourth Amendment violation, admissions obtained after the giving of *Miranda* warnings are admissible—even if prior admissions on the same matter were obtained in violation of *Miranda* [*Oregon v. Elstad*, 105 S.Ct. 1285 (1985)].

  (c) Warnings need not be repeated because of ***a short (as opposed to "significant") break in interrogation*** or because a new police agency begins questioning [*Westover v. United States*, (1966)].

(5) **Impeachment:** Statements taken in violation of *Miranda* may not be used substantively, but may be used to impeach [*Harris v. New York*, 401 U.S. 222 (1971)].

(6) **Effect of right to remain silent on adoptive admissions:**

  (a) **Following custody:** To afford due process, once a defendant ***is in custody, his silence may not be used for impeachment*** [*Doyle v. Ohio*, 426 U.S. 610 (1976)], because at this time he is viewed as relying on the warnings. Only if no *Miranda* warnings are given may a defendant be cross-examined about his post-arrest silence [*Fletcher v. Weir*, 455 U.S. 603 (1982)].

  (b) **Before custody:** On the other hand, the defendant's silence may be used as an adoptive admission ***in a precustodial situation*** [*Jenkins v. Anderson*, 447 U.S. 231 (1980)].

(7) **Corroboration:** Proof of a defendant's guilt requires more than just a confession alone. The ***corpus delicti*** or some independent corroborating evidence must be shown.

(8) **Waiver:** ***A knowing and intelligent waiver of one's* Miranda *rights is permitted***, but the prosecution has a "heavy burden" to prove that there was compliance with the warnings and that the waiver was effec-

tive. A written waiver is not required [*North Carolina v. Butler*, 441 U.S. 369 (1979)]. **Waiver must be specific:** It cannot be presumed from a defendant's silence, nor can a request to consult with a probation officer be construed as a request for the assistance of counsel [*Fare v. Michael C.*, 442 U.S. 707 (1979)]. However, the general inquiry is whether there was police overreaching. Thus, admissions from a mentally disabled person can be used [*Colorado v. Connelly*, 479 U.S. 157 (1986)].

(a) **Use of trickery by police:** *Miranda* waivers have been *upheld* even when obtained after police had misrepresented the strength of the case or the seriousness of the crime being investigated. For example, a defendant can effectively waive his rights and talk to the police about a robbery without knowing specific facts, such as that the victim is now dead (i.e., felony murder)—no new *Miranda* warnings regarding the nature of the charges are required. Although trickery cannot per se invalidate a waiver under *Miranda,* the use of police deception may, in some circumstances, rise to the level of a due process violation under the voluntariness approach.

(b) **Police withholding information:** In *Moran v. Burbine,* 89 L.Ed.2d 410 (1986), the court ruled that the defendant's waiver of counsel was sufficiently "knowing and intelligent" where police withheld from the defendant information that an attorney had sought to consult with him—events occurring outside a suspect's presence and entirely unknown to him do not bear on his own capacity to knowingly relinquish a constitutional right. A different result would arise where the defendant knows an attorney has been barred access.

4. **Exclusion of Statements Under the Right to Counsel Basis of *Massiah***

a. **Rule:** Absent an effective waiver, once formal charges have been filed the deliberate eliciting of any incriminating statements from a defendant without the assistance of an attorney violates the Sixth Amendment right to counsel [*Massiah v. United States,* 377 U.S. 201 (1964)—secret police agents recording defendant's conversations while out on bail violated his right to counsel]. The rule of *Massiah* applies to any adversarial proceeding as well as to noncustodial settings. Once the Sixth Amendment right to counsel has attached, subsequent waiver of this right as to any police-initiated interrogation is invalid [*Michigan v. Jackson,* 89 L.Ed.2d 631 (1986)].

b. **Application:** Where a paid government informant deliberately elicited statements from a defendant in his jail cell, a violation of the right to counsel occurred, and such statements were held inadmissible [*United States v. Henry,* 447 U.S. 264 (1980)]. In *Brewer v. Williams,* 430 U.S. 387 (1977), the defendant's Sixth Amendment right to counsel was violated when police used a "Christian burial speech" to deliberately elicit information, since this tactic was tantamount to formal interrogation. **Caveat**: In *Maine v. Moulton,* 88 L.Ed.2d 481 (1985), the Court rejected the claim that a decisive fact in *Massiah* was that the police set up the confrontation between the accused and a police agent—a violation of the right to counsel occurred even where the defendant himself initiated the conversation with his codefendant, who by the time of the meeting had become a police agent. The police cannot knowingly exploit or intentionally create an opportunity to confront the accused without counsel, absent waiver. However, passive listening by a cell mate informant does not violate the right to counsel [*Kuhlmann v. Wilson,* 106 S.Ct. 2616 (1986)].

5. **Exclusion of Statements as Fruits of Illegal Conduct:** The fruits doctrine was developed in the context of the Fourth Amendment exclusionary rule to deter unreasonable searches no matter how probative their fruits. Even a voluntary statement or confession made after a waiver of *Miranda* rights may be inadmissible if it is obtained as a fruit of an illegal arrest, search, or seizure [*Wong Sun v. United States,* 371 U.S. 471 (1963)—defendant's voluntary confession following an illegal arrest was admitted because his intervening act of free will dissipated the taint]. The time frame between the illegal arrest and the confession, and the intervening circumstances are factors the courts use to determine whether the taint has been purged [*Brown v. Illinois,* 442 U.S. 590 (1975)—giving of *Miranda* warnings between the time of an illegal arrest and the obtaining of a confession does not by itself render the "fruit" admissible].

6. **The McNabb-Mallory Rule:** Formerly, when federal courts failed to arraign a defendant promptly after arrest—in hopes of obtaining a confession—no statement obtained during the undue delay could be held admissible [*McNabb v. United States,* 318 U.S. 332 (1943); *Mallory v. United States,* 354 U.S. 449 (1957)]. Presently, Congress has declared that delay in bringing a defendant before a judicial officer cannot be the sole basis for inadmissibility of a confession.

C. IDENTIFICATION PROCEDURES

Two specific bases exist to attack identifications of a defendant. Pre-indictment identifications are judged under the due process standard, while post-indictment identifications are examined under the right to counsel approach. Remember, the Fifth Amendment privilege against self-incrimination only applies to testimonial evidence used for identification. **Note:** A defendant nevertheless may be properly asked to recite certain words for identification purposes.

1. **Pre-Indictment Identifications: The Due Process Standard**

   Any lineup, showup, or photo identification will be inadmissible as violative of due process where the identification is "unnecessarily suggestive and conducive to irreparable mistaken identification" [*Stovall v. Denno,* 388 U.S. 293 (1967)—a one-on-one showup in a hospital room was justified on the basis of expediency, namely a victim close to death and the impracticability of using a lineup].

   a. **Reliability:** Since one-on-one identifications require very close judicial scrutiny because of the high likelihood of misidentification, courts have

adopted a specific approach for both out-of-court and in-court identifications: where an identification is both suggestive and unnecessary, it can
still be admissible if it is reliable based on a "totality of the circumstances"
approach [*Manson v. Brathwaite*, 432 U.S. 98 (1977)]. The following factors are
considered:

(1) the opportunity to view the criminal at the scene;

(2) the witness's degree of attention;

(3) the accuracy of the witness's descriptions;

(4) the degree of certainty of the witness; and

(5) the time interval between the crime and the identification.

These factors are then balanced against the degree of suggestiveness.

b. **Effect of due process violation:** Where an out-of-court identification is
excluded for *suggestiveness or unreliability*, a subsequent in-court identification will not be allowed.

Examples:

(1) An unnecessarily suggestive showup seven months after the crime was
held proper, since it satisfied the criteria for reliability [*Neil v. Biggers*, 409
U.S. 188 (1972)].

(2) Showing of a single photograph to a police officer two days after a crime was
permitted [*Manson v. Brathwaite, supra,*—no misidentification or reliability
problems were present]. **Note:** Some factors which may taint a photo identification include repetitive display of a photo, or making distinctive marks upon
the photo.

(3) In a lineup where the defendant was six inches taller than the other
suspects and the only suspect from the first lineup to wear similar
clothes to the actual thief and to reappear in the second lineup, a due
process violation was found [*Foster v. California*, 394 U.S. 440 (1969)].

2. **Post-Indictment Lineups: The Right to Counsel Basis**

a. **Rule: After formal charges have been filed (i.e., post-indictment):** The
defendant *has the right to the presence of an attorney at a lineup* [*United States
v. Wade*, 388 U.S. 218 (1967)]. The right to counsel attaches once adversary
criminal proceedings have begun [*Moore v. Illinois*, 434 U.S. 220 (1977)—a
rape victim's identification of defendant at a preliminary hearing was held
inadmissible at trial because defendant was arraigned at the hearing without
counsel].

b. **Pre-indictment lineups:** *No right to counsel exists at police lineups conducted before the accused is indicted* [*Kirby v. Illinois,* 1406 U.S. 682 (1972)]. **Note:** Still unresolved is the issue regarding at what point counsel may be present at a lineup—after a defendant is in custody under warrant (i.e., a formal charge), or only upon indictment.

c. **Compare: photo identifications:** There is no right to counsel at pretrial photographic (or scientific) displays because it is not an adversarial procedure [*United States v. Ash,* 413 U.S. 300 (1973)].

d. **In-court identifications:** The inadmissibility of a previous out-of-court identification made at a lineup does not bar the witness from making an in-court identification of the accused at trial where the prosecution can clearly and convincingly show that the subsequent identification stemmed from an independent, "purging" source [*Gilbert v. California,* 388 U.S. 263 (1967)].

e. **Appellate review:** improper admission of an identification will result in overturning a conviction, unless the prosecution can show harmless error (i.e., that the illegal identification in no way contributed to the conviction [*Chapman v. California,* 386 U.S. 18 (1967)].

III. PRETRIAL PROCEDURES

A. CHRONOLOGY OF PROCEDURES FROM ARREST TO TRIAL

CRIMINAL PROCEDURE MULTISTATE CHART #5

1. **Timeline of Criminal Proceedings from Arrest to Trial**

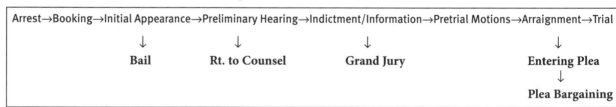

2. **Booking:** The booking stage is an administrative procedure recording the arrest. At this time certain identifications and evidenciary tests are performed (i.e., blood samples, fingerprints, photographs). Neither the right to counsel nor the privilege against self-incrimination apply to protect the defendant during these preliminary tests. In some instances bail is available after booking.

3. **Initial Appearance:** The defendant is given formal notice of the charges against her and advised of her rights, including appointment of counsel. Bail is generally set at this time.

a. *"Gerstein"* **hearing:** In situations where a defendant is arrested without a warrant or a prior indictment (i.e., grand jury indictment prior to arrest), there exists a Fourth Amendment right to a hearing to determine probable cause to detain. This right arises, however, only where "significant restraints" on the defendant's liberty are present (such as being held in jail or being released only upon posting of bail) [*Gerstein v. Pugh*, 420 U.S. 103 (1975)].

    (1) **Type of hearing:** An informal, nonadversarial procedure is conducted in which no right to counsel exists. Hearsay evidence is allowed.

  b. **Bail:** The Eighth Amendment *prohibits "excessive bail."* **Note:** There is no explicit constitutional right to bail, yet most states grant a right to bail in their constitutions. The purpose of bail is to assure the presence of the defendant at trial [*Stack v. Boyle*, 342 U.S. 1 (1951)]. *No right to bail exists for capital offenses.* A denial of bail may be raised at any time during criminal proceedings.

    There is no right to bail—even federally. The Constitution only requires that if bail is given, it not be excessive [*United States v. Salerno*, 479 U.S. 1026 (1987)].

4. **Preliminary Hearing:** The preliminary hearing is an adversarial procedure used to determine probable cause to prosecute. Presentation of evidence is allowed by both sides and the defendant may assert any of her defenses. The preliminary hearing is essentially a minitrial with witnesses testifying and being cross-examined. Most importantly, the defendant *has a right to counsel at this stage* [*Coleman v. Alabama*, 399 U.S. 1 (1970)]. A defendant may waive her right to a preliminary hearing.

5. **Indictment by a Grand Jury:** An indictment is a written accusation of charges against the defendant which a grand jury reviews to determine if the prosecution's evidence justifies a trial. Upon indictment, the prosecutor then decides whether to prosecute. A Fifth Amendment right to a grand jury exists in all federal felony cases. **Note:** The right to indictment by a grand jury for capital and infamous crimes has not been held binding on the states [*Hurtado v. California*, 110 U.S. 516 (1884)]; however, grand jury indictment is required in felony cases in several states. Special grand juries which investigate unlawful activity (such as political corruption) on their own can bring an indictment to commence a criminal proceeding. A federal grand jury is composed of between 16 and 23 persons, 12 of whom must agree to issue an indictment.

  a. **Characteristics of grand jury proceedings:**

    (1) Proceedings are conducted in secret and the defendant has no right to be present.

    (2) The defendant may not present or confront witnesses, or introduce evidence.

    (3) A grand jury witness has no right to counsel (except for consultation outside the grand jury room).

    (4) *Miranda* warnings are not required [*United States v. Mandujano*, 425 U.S. 564 (1976)], yet a witness is still subject to penalty of perjury [*United States v. Wong*, 431 U.S. 174 (1977)].

(5) A grand jury indictment *may be based on illegally obtained evidence* [*United States v. Calandra*, 414 U.S. 338 (1974)] or even on hearsay evidence [*Costello v. United States*, 350 U.S. 359 (1956)].

(6) In federal court the accused can waive a grand jury hearing except in capital offenses.

(7) An accused may not challenge a grand jury subpoena for lack of probable cause.

(8) However, if the jury pool was chosen in a racially discriminatory manner, reversal of a subsequent conviction is the proper course [*Vasquez v. Hillery*, 474 U.S. 254 (1986)].

6. **Information:** An information is a written accusation of charges filed in the name of the state by a prosecutor on the basis of information submitted by police or private citizens. As an alternative to an indictment, it is used either where a grand jury indictment is not required or has been waived. An information is more common than an indictment in felony cases and is almost always used in misdemeanors. A preliminary judicial hearing on probable cause prior to filing an information is afforded in most states, but it is not an explicit constitutional right [*Gerstein v. Pugh, supra*].

7. **Pretrial Motions:** At some point following indictment, a defendant may raise motions to dismiss, motions to suppress, or motions to compel discovery.

8. **Arraignment and Pleading:** At the arraignment, the defendant is called upon to answer the indictment, elect a trial by judge or jury (if available), and enter her plea. In felony cases, counsel for indigent defendants is usually appointed at this time. When the accused pleads not guilty (or remains silent), a trial date is set. Upon a guilty plea which constitutes a waiver of a jury trial, the judge then determines if the plea was voluntarily and intelligently made [*McCarthy v. United States*, 394 U.S. 459 (1969)].

   a. **Plea of nolo contendere:** By pleading "no contest," a defendant can forego a trial without admitting guilt. A plea of *nolo contendere* is admissible to prove guilt both in subsequent criminal and civil cases.

   b. **Guilty pleas:**

      (1) **Requirements:** To be *voluntary and intelligent,* the plea must be taken on the record and the judge must personally be certain that the defendant understands the following [*Boykin v. Alabama*, 395 U.S. 238 (1969)]:

         (a) the nature of the charge against him [*Henderson v. Morgan*, 426 U.S. 637 (1976)];

(b) the maximum possible sentence and any mandatory minimum penalty;

(c) the fact that he has a right not to plead guilty; and

(d) that by pleading guilty, the right to a jury trial is waived.

(2) **No admission of guilt required:** A guilty plea is valid to impose criminal punishment, even where the defendant never makes a formal admission of his guilt [*North Carolina v. Alford*, 400 U.S. 25 (1970)].

(3) **Withdrawal of a guilty plea:** A defendant may withdraw her guilty plea and plead again where any form of error occurs during the taking of the plea [*McCarthy v. United States, supra*]. A withdrawn guilty plea is inadmissible in a subsequent civil trial.

c. **Collateral attacks on guilty pleas after sentencing:**

(1) **General rule:** On the theory that the defendant knew the risks involved before choosing to waive a jury trial, the Court affords a defendant no right to collaterally attack a guilty plea for prior constitutional violations [*Brady v. United States*, 397 U.S. 742 (1970); *Tollet v. Henderson*, 411 U.S. 258 (1973)—even a claim of grand jury racial discrimination will not provide relief at this point].

(2) **Exceptions (i.e., where collateral attack is permitted):**

(a) in a plea bargain situation where the prosecutor fails to keep his promise [*Santobello v. New York*, 404 U.S. 257 (1976)].

(b) where the court lacks jurisdiction [*Blackledge v. Perry*, 417 U.S. 21 (1974)—jurisdiction barred due to double jeopardy].

(c) where ineffective assistance of counsel occurs.

d. **Plea bargaining:**

(1) **In general:** A defendant may agree to plead guilty to an offense in return for the prosecutor's recommendation for a lesser sentence or a dismissal of charge.

(2) **Enforcement of the bargain:** A defendant has a right to have a plea bargain kept once the guilty plea has been accepted by the court. Failure to enforce the bargain can result in either specific performance of the plea or withdrawal of the guilty plea by the defendant [*Santobello v. New York, supra*]. The plea bargain is ***enforceable against the prosecutor***, not the judge. Since the plea bargain is viewed as a contract negotiation, it is permissible for the prosecution to drive a hard bargain and even to

threaten the defendant with a more serious charge if he does not plead guilty [*Bordenkircher v. Hayes*, 434 U.S. 357 (1978)].

B. PRETRIAL RIGHTS

1. **Rights During Discovery Stage**

   a. **Equal access:** Although state courts are not required to permit liberal pretrial discovery, they must grant the defense such reciprocal rights as are given the prosecution [*Wardius v. Oregon*, 412 U.S. 470 (1973)].

2. **Notice of Alibi:** The defendant may be compelled to give the prosecution ***advance notice of an intent to present an alibi defense*** in some states [*Williams v. Florida*, 399 U.S. 78 (1970)].

   a. **Disclosure of names:** Some states also require the defendant to disclose the names and addresses of the alibi witnesses. The state must then do likewise for witnesses refuting the alibi [*Williams v. Florida*, supra]. The defendant's Fifth Amendment privilege against self-incrimination is not violated by this procedure.

   b. **Prosecutorial comment:** The prosecutor may not comment on either the defendant's failure to present the alibi or failure to produce a named alibi witness; however, a defendant may be impeached where she has given notice of one alibi, but then testifies as to a different alibi.

   Example:

   > Ken Klinger was arrested and charged with burglarizing Young's Pharmacy. The break-in allegedly occurred late one evening after the store had closed for business. Klinger was identified as the perpetrator of the crime by a film that was recorded during the burglary from a hidden camera. When Klinger was apprehended, he denied involvement in the crime and told the arresting officers that he had been out of town when the burglary occurred.
   >
   > Prior to trial, Klinger's court-appointed attorney filed a motion requesting discovery of the videotape film that was recorded during the perpetration of the crime. The trial judge granted the defense request and ordered a duplicate copy of the videotape be sent to Klinger's attorney. Following the judge's ruling, the prosecuting attorney, pursuant to state law, then filed a discovery motion specifically asking Klinger whether he planned to raise an alibi defense. The prosecuting attorney also sought discovery of the identity of such an alibi witness.
   >
   > > Assume that the judge requires Klinger to respond as to whether the defendant intends to raise an alibi defense. Should the judge also require Klinger to disclose the identity of the alibi witness?

(A) yes, because if the defendant is constitutionally required to give notice of an alibi, then the disclosure order only affects the time of disclosure of the witness's identity

(B) yes, because the defendant waived any claim of privilege ab initio when he sought discovery of the film from the prosecution

(C) no, because requiring the defendant to reveal information before he is tactically ready to do so substantially impairs his ability to successfully defend himself

(D) no, because such disclosure constitutes an implied representation that is testimonial in character, and thus violates the defendant's privilege against self-incrimination

Answer:

(A) As noted earlier, the MBE is testing students on very subtle distinctions or nuances in the hornbook law. Here is a truly classic Multistate example where the correct answer is derived from a footnote in McCormick's hornbook on **Evidence**. McCormick points out that a "1963 study indicated that 14 states required a defendant to give advance notice of intent to assert an alibi and to furnish specific information as to the place where he claims to have been at the time of the crime [McCormick, **Law of Evidence,** p 284, footnote 63]. Seven states require a list of witnesses who will be called to support the defense." In a similar case, the Florida requirement was upheld against constitutional attack in *Williams v. Florida*, 399 U.S. 916 (1970). In this PMBR example, since the prosecuting attorney's discovery motion was pursuant to state law, choice (A) is correct.

3. **Duty of Disclosure of Prosecution:** To satisfy due process requirements, the defendant must be informed of the charges against him in sufficient detail that an adequate defense is possible [*Russell v. United States,* 369 U.S. 749 (1962)].

   a. **Exculpatory information:**

      (1) **Duty to disclose:** Upon request by the defense, the prosecution must disclose evidence which is favorable to the accused [*Brady v. Maryland,* 373 U.S. 83 (1963)]. However, a prosecutor need not disclose to the defendant information about the impeachment of witnesses or affirmative defenses before the defendant enters into a binding plea agreement which includes information that may tend to impeach the credibility of a prosecution witness such as a plea agreement or conflicting statements [*United States v. Ruiz,* 122 S.Ct. 2450 (2002)].

      Upon request by the defense, the prosecution must disclose evidence when there is a reasonable probability it is favorable to the defense [*United States v. Bagley,* 105 S.Ct. 3375 (1985)].

      (2) **Unrequested information:** Unrequested exculpatory evidence is required to be disclosed only in situations where it "creates a reasonable

doubt that did not otherwise exist" [*United States v. Agurs*, 427 U.S. 97 (1976)].

b. **Automatic reversal:** Failure to disclose any evidence affecting the outcome of a conviction results in automatic reversal [*United States v. Agurs, supra*]. A conviction must also be reversed whenever knowingly false evidence leads to the conviction [*Napue v. Illinois*, 360 U.S. 264 (1959)].

c. **Duty to preserve evidence:** The defendant, in order to obtain a reversal, must show that nonpreserved evidence was 1) actually exculpatory and 2) that he was unable to obtain such evidence on his own [*California v. Troinbetta*, 467 U.S. 479 (1984)]. The focus is on police bad faith [*Arizona v. Youngblood*, 109 S.Ct. 337 (1988)].

4. **The Right to a Public Trial**

a. **In general:** The Sixth Amendment provides the defendant a right to a public trial in all criminal prosecutions. However, in some situations, limitations may be placed on the public and on the media, subject to the discretion of the judge.

b. **Right of the public and the press:** Members of the press and general public have a Sixth Amendment right to be present at all criminal proceedings except the grand jury. In states that use preliminary hearings instead of grand juries, there is no general right to be present at those proceedings even if they take place in a courtroom.

(1) **Compare:** There is a First Amendment right of the public ***to attend the trial itself*** [*Richmond Newspapers, Inc. v. Virginia*, 448 U. S. 555 (1980)], unless the judge specifically finds some overriding interest to necessitate a closed trial [*Globe Newspaper Co. v. Superior Court*, 102 S.Ct. 2613 (1982)]. Whereas evidence which would be inadmissible at trial could tend to influence potential jurors at pretrial proceedings, at the trial stage there is no danger of such a problem, since the judge can prevent the jury from considering prejudicial evidence.

c. **Pretrial publicity:** A defendant has a right to an impartial jury which is unaffected by media coverage. Adverse pretrial publicity can amount to a ***denial of due process*** [(*Irwin v. Dowd*, 366 U.S. 717 (1961); *Groppi v. Wisconsin*, 400 U.S. 505 (1971)—state law denying change of venue for misdemeanors found unconstitutional where adverse pretrial publicity prevented a fair trial].

d. **Effect of exposure to media:** Prejudicial error occurs and the right to a fair trial has been denied where jurors are exposed to out-of-court media information concerning the trial [*Sheppard v. Maxwell*, 384 U.S. 333 (1966)].

e. **Caveat:** Television coverage of a trial may be permitted where the defendant and the jurors are not unfairly or prejudicially affected by the coverage [*Chandler v. Florida*, 449 U.S. 560 (1981)].

Example:

Defendant was arrested and prosecuted for the crime of confidence game (which in several states is a form of aggravated false pretenses). At trial, Defendant testified that she dressed as a gypsy and prophesized Victim's imminent death. Defendant admitted that she told Victim she could save him if he brought a large sum of money wrapped in a handkerchief to a ritual. After the ritual, Defendant returned the handkerchief to Victim filled with waste paper rather than the money. After Defendant was convicted of confidence game, she moved for a new trial and offered the affidavits of several jurors who sat on the case.

An affidavit containing which of the following facts will most likely furnish Defendant's best basis for securing a new trial?

(A) A juror misunderstood the judge's instruction regarding the burden of proof.

(B) A juror in violation of the court's instruction read a newspaper article implicating Defendant in several other confidence game schemes.

(C) A juror fell asleep during defense counsel's closing argument.

(D) A juror admittedly stated during deliberations that he had a personal animosity toward Defendant.

Answer:

(B) The Sixth Amendment provides that in all criminal prosecutions the accused shall enjoy the right to a speedy and public trial, **by an impartial jury** of the state wherein the crime shall have been committed. In this respect, a defendant is entitled to be tried by a jury which is unaffected by media coverage of the events which are the subject of the trial. If publicity (pretrial or otherwise) surrounding a particular trial has been so extensive that the minds of potential jurors are no longer impartial, the trial will be violative of the Due Process Clause [*Irwin v. Dowd*, 366 U.S. 717 (1961)]. Choice (B) is therefore correct because a fair trial may be impossible when potential jurors are exposed to prejudicial inadmissible evidence or to prejudicial evidence which is never even offered at trial.

5. **Right to a Speedy Trial**

   a. **Constitutional requirements:** The Sixth Amendment guarantees a criminal defendant the right to a speedy trial. This guarantee has been made applicable to the states [*Klopfer v. North Carolina*, 387 U.S. 213 (1967)]. Violation of this right results in a complete dismissal of the charges against the defendant [*Strunk v. United States*, 412 U.S. 434 (1973)].

   b. **When the right attaches:** The right to a speedy trial attaches once a defendant has become an "accused," such as upon arrest or filing of charges. Pre-arrest delays may violate due process, however, if sufficient prejudice is found [*United States* v. Lovasco, 431 U.S. 783 (1977); *United States v. Marion*, 404 U.S. 307

(1971)—*pre-arrest investigation and discovery are not subject to time limits* based on the right to a speedy trial]. Where a defendant, subject to being arrested and released, is not indicted until a long time interval has passed, the right to a speedy trial does apply [*Dillingham v. United States*, 423 U.S. 64 (1975)]. The Speedy Trial Act of 1974 requires federal indictment within 30 days of arrest and trial within 70 days of indictment. But, refiling is permitted.

  c. **Determining unreasonable delay:** The Court judges violations of the right to a speedy trial by balancing the factors set forth in *Barker v. Wingo*, 407 U.S. 514 (1972):

    (1) **Length of the delay**

    (2) **Reason for the delay**

      (a) **Delay by the defendant:** The right to a speedy trial is waived where the defendant willfully delays the proceedings. This most commonly occurs when the defendant files a pretrial motion or seeks a suppression hearing. The time from the filing of such motion or request until resolution is excluded because it was caused by the defendant.

      (b) **Delay by the prosecution:** Courts evaluate the good faith and the justifiability of the delay. In *Barker*, repeated continuances by the prosecution delayed the trial for five years, but the Court found no prejudice or any violation of the right to a speedy trial, since the defendant only asserted the right after three-and-one-half years.

    (3) **Defendant's assertion of her right to a speedy trial;** and

    (4) **Prejudice to the defendant** (i.e., oppressive incarceration, memory loss by witnesses, loss of evidence, anxiety to the defendant).

IV. GUARANTEES OF A FAIR TRIAL

A. CONSTITUTIONAL BASIS

The Sixth Amendment and the Due Process Clauses of the Fifth and Fourteenth Amendments establish the basic rights of a defendant at a criminal trial. The Sixth Amendment guarantees include the right to a fair, public, and speedy trial by an impartial judge or jury; the right to counsel; and the rights of confrontation and compulsory process.

1. **Due Process Basis:** A defendant must be able to understand the nature of the charges against him or have the capacity to consult with his lawyer in preparing his defense; otherwise, due process is violated.

2. **Competency Hearing:** The defendant has a right to a hearing to determine competency. The finding is usually made by a judge, but it is often allowed by

a jury. Competency to stand trial is an issue which cannot be waived. **Note:** Competency, *which is determined by a defendant's mental condition at the time of trial* (not at the time of the crime, as in insanity) can even be raised after the completion of the trial [*Pate v. Robinson,* 383 U.S. 375 (1966)]. The test: oriented as to time and place and the defendant also must have a fair recollection of the events surrounding the charge [*Dusky v. United* States, 362 U.S. 402 (1960)].

3. **Procedure for Incompetent Defendant:** A defendant found to be incompetent is generally committed for treatment, but cannot remain indefinitely in a mental hospital. The criminal proceedings are suspended until the defendant regains competence. The government may administer antipsychotic drugs to a mentally ill defendant against the defendant's will for the purpose of rendering the defendant competent to stand trial on serious criminal charges [*Sell v. United States,* 123 S.Ct. 2174 (2003)].

B. IMPARTIALITY: DUE PROCESS AND SIXTH AMENDMENT BASES

1. **Unbiased Judge:** The due process right to an unbiased judge requires that the defendant be tried before a magistrate who is neither prejudiced against the defendant nor financially interested in the outcome of the trial [*Ward v. City of Monroeville,* 409 U.S. 57 (1972)—a village mayor, who collects the town's revenues including traffic fines, may not serve as a judge because of his financial interest]. **Compare:** In a minor misdemeanor case the defendant's trial by a nonlawyer judge was allowed, provided an appeal *de novo* was made available before a legally-trained judge [*North v. Russell,* 427 U.S. 328 (1976)].

C. THE RIGHT TO COUNSEL

The Sixth Amendment provides that "the accused shall enjoy the right to have the assistance of counsel for his defense." This right has been applied to the states [*Gideon v. Wainwright,* 372 U.S. 335 (1963)].

1. **General Rule:** Absent waiver, a defendant may not be *"imprisoned for any offense, whether classified as petty, misdemeanor, or felony unless he was represented by counsel"* [*Argersinger v. Hamlin,* 407 U.S. (1972)]. Thus, where *imprisonment is actually imposed, the right to counsel exists.* An uncounselled conviction cannot be used in recidivist sentencing [*Baldasur v. Illinois,* 446 U.S. 222 (1980)].

   a. **Caveat:** On the Multistate Bar Examination, note that where punishment consists of a fine or imprisonment and the defendant is only fined, no denial of the right to counsel has occurred. On the other hand, if *actual imprisonment* is imposed, then the appointment of counsel requirement attaches.

   Example:

   Defendant is arrested and charged with shoplifting. He claims he intended to pay for the item he took and requests an attorney and a jury trial. Both requests are denied by the judge and Defendant is found guilty. The maximum penalty for shoplifting is a $500 fine and six months in jail. Defendant is sentenced to three months in jail which he is allowed to serve on weekends in the county detention center.

> Defendant claims his constitutional rights have been violated. Is he correct?
>
> (A) no, because his actual sentence was only three months
>
> (B) yes, because Defendant was denied the right to counsel
>
> (C) yes, because Defendant was denied the right to a jury trial
>
> (D) yes, because Defendant was denied both the right to counsel and the right to a jury trial

Answer:

(B) The Sixth Amendment provides that the accused shall have "the assistance of counsel for his defense." This right not only encompasses the right to hire private counsel, but also the right to be provided with counsel without charge if the accused is unable to afford counsel. Choice (B) is correct because in *Argersinger v. Hamlin,* 92 S.Ct. 2006 (1972), the U.S. Supreme Court held that "absent a knowing and intelligent waiver, no person may be imprisoned for any offense, whether classified as petty, misdemeanor, or felony unless he was represented by counsel." Note that choice (D) is not correct because the right to jury exists **whenever the accused faces a sentence of possibly more than six months** [*Baldwin v. New York,* 399 U.S. 66 (1970)]. In this example, since Defendant's maximum sentence was six months in jail (**not more than six months imprisonment**), he would not have the right to a jury trial.

2. **Rights of Indigents:** The right to counsel includes the right to be provided with free counsel when the accused cannot afford an attorney. With respect to appointment of counsel, courts are quite liberal. There is no constitutional standard for indigency, although some states do require a defendant to pay back the amount of attorney's fees at a later time, if possible [*Fuller v. Oregon,* 417 U.S. 40 (1974)].

3. **Waiver:** A defendant may waive the right to counsel where the court finds that she does so knowingly and intelligently [*Faretta v. California,* 422 U.S. 806 (1975)]. Although some courts appoint attorneys to advise a defendant who is representing herself, the accused may not divide the actual representation between herself and the attorney [*United States v. Condor,* 423 F.2d 904 (1970)]. An indigent must be informed of her right to free counsel before a valid waiver can arise [*Kitchens v. Smith,* 401 U.S. 847 (1971)]. Although a defendant has the right to go *pro se,* the court is permitted to appoint a standby counsel—even over defendant's objection—provided the defendant maintains actual control of his case *and* appears in control of his case [*McKaskle v. Wiggins,* 465 U.S. 168 (1984)].

4. **Joint Representation:** It is a violation of the Sixth Amendment to represent more than one defendant in a criminal action. Whenever a conflict of interest is shown to exist which jeopardizes the rights of any defendant or adversely affects the

attorney's performance the attorney will not be permitted to represent multiple parties [*Cuyler v. Sullivan*, 446 U.S. 335 (1980)]. Either the defendant or the court may raise this issue. Otherwise, defendants may choose to share an attorney, or have their own separate counsel appointed.

5. **Denial of the Right to Counsel:** Failure to provide counsel at trial results in an automatic reversal [*Gideon v. Wainwright, supra*]. The harmless error rule applies, however, to denial of counsel at criminal proceedings other than the trial [*United States v. Wade*, 388 U.S. 218 (1967)].

6. **Right to Counsel Is Offense Specific:** Because the right to counsel is offense specific, it does not necessarily extend to offenses that are "factually related" to those that have actually been charged (such as when a suspect, under arrest only for burglary, confesses without counsel to the murder of the home's inhabitants) [*Texas v. Cobb*, 121 S.Ct. 1335 (2001)].

7. **Suspended Sentences:** A suspended sentence that may end up in the "actual deprivation of a person's liberty" (i.e., jail time) may not be imposed under the Sixth Amendment unless the defendant was provided assistance of counsel in the prosecution for the crime charged [*Alabama v. Shelton*, 122 S.Ct. 1764 (2002)].

8. **Stages at Which the Right to Counsel Attaches:** The right to counsel attaches to all *critical stages* of the proceedings which affect the defendant's right to a fair trial [*Gilbert v. California*, 388 U.S. 263 (1967)].

   a. **The following stages are deemed "critical stages" because they constitute adversary proceedings:**

CRIMINAL PROCEDURE MULTISTATE CHART #6
Critical Stages

	(1) **Custodial interrogation** [*Miranda v. Arizona, supra*]; But note: The *Miranda* counsel right is based on the Fifth not the Sixth Amendment. Therefore, exceptions are permissible, *supra*;	
Pre-trial	(2) **Post-indictment lineups** [*Kirby v. Illinois, supra*];	
	(3) **Preliminary hearing** [*Coleman v. Alabama, supra*];	**RIGHT**
	(4) **Arraignment** [*Hamilton v. Alabama*, 368 U.S. 52 (1961)];	**TO**
	(5) **Felony trials** [*Gideon v. Wainwright, supra*];	
Trial	(6) **Misdemeanors where imprisonment is actually imposed** [*Scott v. Illinois*, 440 U.S. 367 (1979)]; (a) **Probation revocation hearing** [*Mempa v. Rhay* 389 U.S. 128 (1967)];	**COUNSEL** **EXISTS**
Post-trial	(7) **Sentencing** [*Mempa v. Rhay*, 389 U.S. 128 (1967)]; and	
	(8) **Appeals as a matter of right** [*Douglas v. California*, 372 U.S. 353 (1963)—right to counsel attaches on equal protection grounds and an indigent may also obtain a free transcript].	

b. **The following stages are not deemed "critical" and no right to counsel exists:**

CRIMINAL PROCEDURE MULTISTATE CHART #7

Noncritical Stages

Pre-trial	(1) **Preliminary identification procedures** [*Schmerber v. California, supra*—blood samples; *Gilbert v. California, supra*—handwriting samples; *United States v. Ash, supra*—photo identifications];	NO
	(2) **Police lineups prior to indictment** [*Kirby v. Illinois, supra*];	RIGHT
	(3) **Nonadversarial detention hearings** [*Gerstein v. Pugh, supra*];	
	(4) **Grand jury proceedings** [*United States v. Mandujano, supra*];	TO
	(5) **Discretionary appeals** [*Ross v. Moffitt*, 417 U.S. 600 (1974)];	
Post-trial	(6) **Probation and parole revocation** [*Gagnon v. Scarpelli*, 411 U.S. 778 (1973)]; and	COUNSEL
	(7) **Habeas corpus proceedings.**	EXISTS

9. **Right to Self-Representation:** Although an intelligent waiver of the right to counsel will generally be recognized and approved, there is no absolute Sixth Amendment right to waive counsel at the appellate level [*Martinez v. Court of Appeal of California, Fourth Appellate Dist.*, 120 S.Ct. 684 (2000)].

10. **Ineffective Counsel:** The Sixth Amendment right to counsel is the right to effective counsel. This claim is often raised on collateral appeal, but may be raised in any appeal. Under *Strickland v. Washington*, 466 U.S. 668 (1984) a defendant making this claim must prove both 1) counsel was ineffective, that is, counsel deviated from reasonably prevailing norms, and 2) there is a reasonable probability the verdict would have been not guilty.

   a. **Examples:**

      (1) **Inexperience of counsel:** Where counsel is inexperienced and has significantly less time to prepare, reversal is not proper unless both prongs of *Strickland* are satisfied. There must be a specific allegation of specific attorney errors [*United States v. Cronic*, 466 U.S. 648 (1984)].

      (2) **Strategy:** As a general rule, since there is a presumption of effective counsel, strategic decisions of the attorney are not open to attack [*Strickland v. Washington, supra*].

      (3) **Perjury:** Threatening the defendant with withdrawal, with telling the judge why, and with impeaching the defendant's testimony so as to prevent his perjury are not ineffective, per se [*Nix v. Whiteside*, 475 U.S. 157 (1986)].

(4) **Choosing appellate issues:** Ignoring the defendant's requested appellate issues and arguing issues of the attorney's choice is not ineffective [*Jones v. Barnes,* 103 S.Ct. 3308 (1988)].

(5) **Public defender assigned:** A defendant does not have the right to have a specific public defender—only the right to have a competent one [*Morris v. Slappy,* 103 S.Ct. 1610 (1983)].

(6) **Misinformation regarding length of sentence:** Misinforming the defendant of the length of prison term does not invalidate a plea of guilty, because no claim was made that with knowledge of this longer sentence the defendant would have altered his plea (prong 2 of *Strickland* not satisfied) [*Hill v. Lockhart,* 477 U.S. 52 (1985); *see also Glover v. United States,* 121 S.Ct. 696 (2001)—where prison sentence under sentencing guidelines increased because of counsel's performance, no minimum length required for prejudice under Sixth Amendment].

(7) **Government wiretap:** Effective assistance of counsel was denied where the government tapped into conversations between the defendant and his attorney [*Beach v. United States,* 386 U.S. 26 (1966)].

(8) **Informants:** If a government informant were to reveal accounts of the defendant's conversation with his attorney to the prosecution, the accused would be denied effective assistance of counsel [*Weatherford v. Bursey,* 429 U.S. 545 (1977)].

(9) **Interference by the court:** Counsel may determine at what point to put the defendant on the stand [*Brooks v. Tennessee,* 406 U.S. 605 (1972)], and counsel may confer with the defendant during an overnight recess [*Geders v. United States,* 425 U.S. 80 (1976)] without interference from the court, but barring conference during a 15-minute recess is acceptable [*Perry v. Leeke,* 109 S.Ct. 595 (1989)].

(10) **Failure to present mitigating evidence:** Assistance of counsel is effective under *Strickland* even where the lawyer fails to present mitigating evidence, fails to mount a case for life imprisonment, and waives final argument during the sentencing phase of a death penalty proceeding. Assistance of counsel is only ineffective under *Strickland* where the attorney's failure to test the prosecutor's case is complete, not merely at specific points [*Bell v. Cone,* 122 S.Ct. 1843 (2002); *see also Wiggins v. Smith,* 123 S.Ct. 2527 (2003)—failure to argue without investigation into mitigating circumstances may be ineffective assistance of counsel].

(11) **Conflicts of interest:** To demonstrate that violation of Sixth Amendment right to counsel resulted from counsel's conflict of interest, the defendant must show that the conflict adversely affected counsel's representation,

even if the trial court knew or should have known about the conflict but failed to inquire about it [*Mickens v. Taylor*, 122 S.Ct. 1237 (2002)].

(12) **Note:** In two analogous situations the Strickland test is not to be used.

(a) **Multiple representation:** If there is an actual conflict which adversely effected the attorney's performance, reversal is proper [*Cuyler v. Sullivan*, 446 U.S. 335 (1980)]. Furthermore, if the defense attorney indicates to the court that such a conflict exists, the defense *must be severed* [*Holloway v. Arkansas*, 435 U.S. 475 (1978)].

(b) **Withdrawal:** An attorney is permitted to withdraw if she feels there are no valid issues [*Anders v. California*, 386 U.S. 738 (1967)] and in such instance, additional counsel need not be appointed. But, if there are colorable issues, an attorney must be appointed—the *Strickland* test is not proper [*Penson v. Ohio*, 488 U.S. 75 (1988)].

D. JURY TRIAL

The Sixth Amendment right to a jury trial in criminal prosecutions was held applicable to the states as being "fundamental to the American scheme of justice" [*Duncan v. Louisiana*, 391 U.S. 145 (1968)].

1. **When the Right Attaches:** The right to a jury trial attaches in any criminal proceeding where the defendant faces the possibility of receiving a sentence of *more than six months* [*Baldwin v. New York*, 399 U.S. 66 (1970)]. Such a crime is classified as a *serious* (i.e., not petty) offense.

   a. **Criminal contempt:** The right to a jury trial was extended to criminal contempt cases [*Bloom v. Illinois*, 391 U.S. 194 (1968)] in which the punishment imposed exceeded six months in jail [*Frank v. United States*, 395 U.S. 147 (1969)]. Reduction of a contempt sentence to six months or less by an appeals court eliminates the right to a jury trial [*Taylor v. Hayes*, 418 U.S. 488 (1974)].

   b. *Compare*—**civil contempt**: No right to jury trial exists. Since the purpose of civil contempt is to compel testimony, the defendant can be released upon compliance, whereas in criminal contempt, the purpose is to punish for failure to testify.

   c. **Waiver:** The defendant can expressly and intelligently waive his right to a jury trial [*Singer v. United States*, 380 U.S. 24 (1965)].

2. **Size of Jury**

   a. **State courts:** A six-member jury was upheld in noncapital cases in state courts as long as the group functioned as a representative cross-section of the community [*Williams v. Florida*, 399 U.S. 78 (1970)]; however, *a unanimous* *verdict is required with a six-person jury* [*Burch v. Louisiana*, 441 U.S. 130 (1979)]. Five-person juries were held unconstitutional as a denial of due process [*Ballen v. Georgia*, 435 U.S 223 (1978)].

b. **12-member juries:**

(1) **Federal courts:** Federal criminal trials require unanimous verdicts from 12-member juries.

(2) **State courts:** State criminal trials having 12-member juries need not be unanimous [*Johnson v. Louisiana*, 406 U.S. 356 (1972)—9–3 verdict not violative of due process; *Apodaca v. Oregon*, 406 U.S. 404 (1972)—10–2 verdict held not to violate the Sixth Amendment in non-first-degree murder cases].

Criminal Procedure Multistate Chart #8

JURY SIZE AND UNANIMITY REQUIREMENTS

Criminal Proceedings	No. of Jurors Required	Jury Verdict Requirement
State Court	no 12-person requirement	—
	6-person jury allowed, except in capital cases	unanimity required
	12-person jury	9–3 verdict permitted 10–2 verdict permitted
Federal Court	12-person jury	unanimity required

3. **Jury Selection:** Discrimination in the selection of a jury is prohibited by the Equal Protection Clause. The defendant has a right to a jury selected from a cross-section of the community [*Carter v. Green City Jury Commissioner*, 396 U.S. 320 (1970)—a state may apply neutral, nondiscriminatory guidelines to select a jury, even though the eventual jurors comprise only a small percentage of minorities]. This cross-section need not include members of all minority groups.

a. **Showing of discrimination:** To rebut a charge of racial discrimination, the state must show it followed racially neutral selection procedures [*Alexander v. Louisiana*, 405 U.S. 625 (1972)]. The underrepresentation of a distinct and significant racial group from the number of individuals sequestered for jury selection (i.e., the *venire*) provides adequate grounds for a *prima facie* showing of discriminatory jury selection [*Taylor v. Louisiana*, 419 U.S. 522 (1975)].

(1) **Standing:** Standing to challenge jury selection can be conferred even where the defendant is not a member of the excluded group [*Peters v. Kiff*, 407 U.S. 493 (1972)—a white person can challenge the exclusion of blacks from a grand jury].

      (2) **Discrimination based on sex:** Statutes giving women, but not men, the right to exempt themselves from jury selection are invalid [*Taylor v. Louisiana, supra; Duren v. Missouri*, 439 U.S. 357 (1979)—jury composed of only 15 percent women (since women could refuse jury duty) held unconstitutional].

   b. **Exclusion of prospective jurors:** In contrast to striking potential jurors for cause, a prosecutor generally may exercise peremptory challenges for any rational or irrational reason. However, ***exclusion of prospective jurors based on race and gender is forbidden under the Equal Protection Clause*** [*J.E.B. v. Alabama*, 511 U.S. 127 (1994)]. In *Batson v. Kentucky*, 476 U.S. 79 (1989), based on principles of equal protection, the court held that a *prima facie* showing of purposeful racial discrimination in jury selection can be established solely on the prosecutor's exercise of peremptory challenges at the defendant's trial, thus shifting the burden to the state to provide a neutral explanation for such exclusion.

      (1) It is reversible error to exclude jurors who simply have misgivings about ordering capital punishment [*Witherspoon v. Illinois*, 391 U.S. 510 (1968)].

  4. **Revelation of impeachment evidence:** The Constitution does not require the government to disclose material impeachment evidence prior to entering a plea agreement with a criminal defendant. Although the Fifth and Sixth Amendments provide, as a part of the Constitution's "fair trial" guarantee, that defendants have the right to receive exculpatory impeachment material from prosecutors, a defendant who pleads guilty forgoes a fair trial as well as various other accompanying constitutional guarantees [*United States v. Ruiz*, 122 S.Ct. 2450 (2002)].

E. RIGHT OF CONFRONTATION

  1. **In General:** The Sixth Amendment right of a defendant "to be confronted with witnesses against him" in all criminal prosecutions is a fundamental right and has been made applicable to the states through the Fourteenth Amendment Due Process Clause [*Pointer v. Texas*, 380 U.S. 400 (1965)]. The primary purpose of the right of confrontation is to give the defendant an opportunity to cross-examine witnesses.

  2. **Nonapplicability of the Right of Confrontation:** Although the defendant has the right to be present at the trial, this right is not absolute and may be waived.

   a. **Exclusion of disruptive defendant:** The court may first warn and then physically remove a disorderly defendant from the courtroom, thereby waiving the right to confrontation [*Illinois v. Allen*, 397 U.S. 337 (1970)]. **Note:** The trial judge may either bind and gag the defendant, cite him for contempt, or remove him from the courtroom.

b. **Absence of defendant:** A waiver of the right to confrontation also exists where a defendant voluntarily leaves the trial after its inception [*Taylor v. United States*, 414 U.S. 17 (1973)—the trial may continue in defendant's absence].

c. **Grand jury hearings:** No right to confront witnesses arises before a grand jury [*Jenkins v. McKeithen*, 395 U.S. 411 (1969)].

d. **Child abuse:** Placing a screen between a child abuse victim and the defendant violates the confrontation clause [*Coy v. Iowa*, 108 S.Ct. 2798 (1988)], but excluding the defendant and electronically transmitting the child's testimony to him while allowing him the immediate opportunity to electronically communicate with his attorney does not violate the clause [*Maryland v. Craig*, 110 S.Ct. 3157 (1990)].

3. **Cross-Examination of Witnesses:** Impeachment of both prosecution and defense witnesses is allowed to determine the credibility of the witness as well as to discover possible bias.

4. **Relationship of Confrontation Clause and Use of Hearsay Evidence:** The introduction of an out-of-court statement must not deny the defendant the right of confrontation. The Sixth Amendment issue predominates over the hearsay question. However, all hearsay evidence is not automatically excluded because of the Confrontation Clause.

a. **Factors required for admission of hearsay statements:** The prosecution must demonstrate that the witness *is unavailable after good-faith efforts have been made and that the hearsay statement is trustworthy.* Trustworthiness is shown where the hearsay statement either (1) falls within one of the recognized hearsay exceptions or (2) is made under oath and the defendant had the opportunity to cross-examine [*Mancuri v. Stubbs*, 408 U.S. 204 (1972)].

b. **Examples:**

(1) The incriminating hearsay statement of a defendant's co-conspirator was held properly admitted at trial, despite the defendant's absence, since a Georgia statute allowing post-indictment coconspirator admissions did not violate the Sixth Amendment, even though it did conflict with the Federal Rules of Evidence [*Dutton v. Evans*, 400 U.S. 74 (1970)].

(2) The right to confrontation is satisfied where the defendant had the right to cross-examine at an earlier hearing and the prosecution made a good-faith effort to produce the unavailable witness's testimony at the trial [*Barber v. Page*, 390 U.S. 719 (1968)—unavailable because witness was out of the state; *California v. Green*, 399 U.S. 149 (1970)—unavailable due to drug-related memory loss].

(3) The hearsay rule cannot be "mechanistically applied to defeat the ends of justice" where constitutional rights directly affecting ascertainment of a defendant's guilt are involved [*Chambers v. Mississippi,* 410 U.S. 284 (1973)—application of state hearsay rule held improper where exclusion of testimony of defendant's hearsay witnesses would have denied him the right to confront and cross-examine a material witness].

(4) A codefendant's confession cannot be used against the defendant at a joint trial unless the codefendant takes the stand, the defendant makes similar confession, or references to the defendant are omitted [*Richardson v. Marsh,* 481 U.S. 200 (1988)].

(5) **Testimonial statements.** Out-of-court statements that are "testimonial" in nature, such as statements made to the police or 911 after an emergency has ceased, are inadmissible under the Confrontation Clause, even if such statements would be considered to be excited utterances [*Crawford v. Washington,* 541 U.S. 36 (2004); *Davis v. Washington & Hammon V. Indiana,* 126 S.Ct. 2266 (2006)].

5. **Right of Severance**

   a. **When right exists:** If either codefendant is unfairly prejudiced at any stage of a joint trial (i.e., when differences in proof arise or confessions by one codefendant incriminate the other defendant), a right of severance may be properly granted.

   b. **Confessions of codefendants:** In a joint trial where a codefendant's confession implicates the other defendant, the Court held that the right to confrontation prohibits the use of such a confession and that ***the defendants are entitled to separate trials*** [*Bruton v. United States,* 391 U.S. 123 (1968)]. The *Bruton* case found that the traditional approach of giving jury instructions to consider the confession only against the confessing defendant was constitutionally inadequate.

      (1) **Exceptions to the *Bruton* rule:**

         (a) Severance of joint trials is not necessary where the incriminating portions of the confession can be deleted;

         (b) Where the codefendant takes the witness stand after making a confession and is subject to cross-examination, the *Bruton* rule does not apply [*Nelson v. O'Neil,* 402 U.S. 622 (1971)—this result follows even where the codefendant testifies at trial that he never made the confession];

         (c) Separate trials are not necessary where the codefendant's statement is subject to the harmless error rule [*Schneble v. Florida,* 405 U.S. 427 (1972)—overwhelming evidence of defendant's guilt, including his own confession, allowed the Court to proceed without requiring a severance]; and

(d) In situations where the confessions of both codefendants overlap, the Court has not definitively ruled, although the harmless error rule would appear to be applicable [*Parker v. Randolph*, 442 U.S. 62 (1979)].

F. RIGHT TO COMPULSORY PROCESS

The Sixth Amendment right to compulsory process for obtaining witnesses has been incorporated to apply to state criminal proceedings [*Washington v. Texas*, 388 U.S. 14 (1967)]. The right of compulsory process provides a defendant not only with the power to present his own witnesses, but with a fair opportunity to present a defense free from intimidation or prejudicial exclusion of material evidence [*Washington v. Texas, supra*—the Court held unconstitutional a state statute prohibiting defendant's accomplice from testifying as a defense witness, since, in effect, the statute excluded relevant evidence and thereby violated defendant's right to present a defense].

G. PROCEDURAL RIGHTS FOR CONVICTION

1. **Burden of Proof:** The prosecution must prove beyond a reasonable doubt that the defendant is guilty of each element of the crime charged to satisfy the due process requirement of a fair trial [*Speiser v. Randall*, 358 U.S. 860 (1958); *Taylor v. Kentucky*, 436 U.S. 478 (1978)].

   a. **Examples:** To reduce a charge of murder to voluntary manslaughter, the defendant may be required to prove an affirmative defense (i.e., extreme emotional disturbance) by a preponderance of the evidence [*Patterson v. New York*, 432 U.S. 197 (1977)], yet it is a violation of due process to require the defendant to prove reasonable provocation to mitigate a killing from murder to manslaughter because provocation is an element of voluntary manslaughter [*Mullaney v. Wilbur*, 421 U.S. 684 (1975)].

   b. **Affirmative defenses:** The defendant may be required to prove an affirmative defense (such as insanity or self-defense) by a preponderance [*Leland v. Oregon*, 343 U.S. 790 (1952)]; however, in insanity defenses, generally ***the prosecution must prove sanity beyond a reasonable doubt*** once the defendant raises some evidence of insanity.

2. **Presumption of Innocence:** Since there is no absolute right to a jury instruction on the presumption of innocence, failure to so instruct the jurors cannot by itself amount to a denial of a fair trial [*Kentucky v. Whorton*, 441 U.S. 786 (1979)—the need for a jury instruction is determined by weighing the evidence and considering the arguments of counsel and the other jury instructions].

3. **Presumptions:** A ***mandatory presumption*** (which the jury must accept) is unconstitutional in a criminal case because it violates the defendant's due process

[*Sandstrom v. Montana,* 442 U.S. 510 (1979)]. A ***permissive presumption*** (which the jury may accept) is allowed in criminal proceedings only where a "rational connection" exists between the prosecution's proof of the basic fact and the jury's inference of the ultimate fact or element of the crime [*Ulster County Court v. Allen,* 442 U.S. 140 (1979)].

V. POSTTRIAL STAGE

A. DEFENDANT'S RIGHTS DURING SENTENCING

1. **Right to Counsel:** The accused has a right to counsel during sentencing since it is a critical stage of the criminal proceeding [*Mempa v. Rhay,* 389 U.S. 128 (1967)].

2. **No Confrontation of Witnesses:** During sentencing, the court may use hearsay evidence and information not subject to cross-examination [*Williams v. New York,* 333 U.S. 241 (1949)—reports from probation officers admitted without cross-examination by defendant]. Where the death penalty is involved, however, the defendant is given greater confrontation rights since a death sentence may not be based on a presentence report which is off the record and undisclosed to the defendant [*Gardner v. Florida,* 430 U.S. 349 (1977)].

3. **Discretion of Judge:** The judge may not consider the defendant's conduct and evaluate factors apart from the actual record of the trial.

   a. **Sentencing by a judge:** Other than the fact of prior conviction, any fact that increases the penalty for a crime beyond the prescribed statutory maximum must be submitted to the jury and proved beyond a reasonable doubt [*Apprendi v. New Jersey,* 120 S.Ct. 2348 (2000)]. The Supreme Court recently held that a sentencing judge, sitting without a jury, could not find an aggravating circumstance necessary for imposition of the death penalty. Evidence of such an aggravating circumstance would have to be heard and decided by a jury. A defendant may not be exposed to a penalty exceeding the maximum he would receive if punished according to the facts reflected in the jury verdict alone [*Ring v. Arizona,* 122 S.Ct. 2428 (2002)].

   b. **Jury consideration of mitigating circumstances:** A jury must be able to consider and give effect to a defendant's mitigating evidence in imposing sentence [*Penry v. Johnson,* 121 S.Ct. 1910 (2001)].

4. **Due Process Rights During Resentencing:** Generally, if the defendant has appealed and is then reconvicted, a more severe penalty may not be imposed upon retrial [*North Carolina v. Pearce,* 395 U.S. 711 (1969)]. To prevent vindictive punishment, *Pearce* held that a harsher sentence may only be imposed where it is based on new, objective information of defendant's conduct occurring *after* the first sentence was decreed. **Note:** In a ***trial de novo*** (where no review of the original conviction or appeal is considered in reaching a new verdict) an increased

punishment can result since a different court is rendering the sentence [*Colten v. Kentucky*, 407 U.S. 104 (1972)].

B. PUNISHMENT

1. **"Cruel and Unusual" Punishment:** The Eighth Amendment guarantee against cruel and unusual punishment is applicable to the states [*Francis v. Resweber*, 329 U.S. 459 (1946)].

   a. **Example:**

      (1) Doubling of inmates in one jail cell in a state prison is not cruel and unusual [*Rhodes v. Chapman*, 450 U.S. 906 (1981)].

      (2) On the other hand, excessive jail terms which are grossly disproportionate to the crime committed are in violation of the Eighth Amendment [*Weems v. United States*, 217 U.S. 349 (1910)—unconstitutional to impose hard labor for falsifying public records], *but see Ewing v. California*, 123 S.Ct. 1179 (2003); *Lockyer v. Andrade*, 123 S.Ct. 1166 (2003)—California's "three strikes" rule, which mandated sentence of 25 years to life for third felony conviction, not grossly disportionate, even if crime relatively small (e.g., where third felony was stealing three golf clubs worth $399 apiece or $150 worth of videotapes)].

   b. **Recidivist statutes:** The concept of imposing harsher sentences for repeat offenders has been held constitutional [*Rummel v. Estelle*, 445 U.S. 263 (1980)–mandatory life sentence with possibility of parole upheld against a defendant who had three prior convictions of petty theft].

   c. **Status crimes:** It constitutes cruel and unusual punishment to convict an individual for the crime of being a narcotics addict [*Robinson v. California*, 370 U.S. 660 (1962)]. **Note:** Being a drug addict, or an alcoholic, cannot of itself be criminal; however, being drunk in public can be a punishable crime [*Powell v. Texas*, 392 U.S. 514 (1968)].

   d. **Equal Protection limitation:** A defendant cannot be imprisoned because of her inability to pay a fine [*Tate v. Short*, 401 U.S. 395 (1971)—imprisonment in lieu of payment of a fine discriminates against individuals without financial means].

2. **Capital Punishment:** The death penalty is not considered cruel and unusual punishment, nor grossly disproportionate to the crime, provided the court's review procedure affords procedural safeguards to prevent arbitrary or discriminatory sentencing [*Gregg v. Georgia*, 428 U.S. 153 (1976)]. As noted below, there are indications that the Supreme Court will, in the future, limit application of the death penalty to a limited range of crimes.

a. **Procedural safeguards:**

(1) **Bifurcated trial:** The likelihood of discriminatory sentencing is lessened where one jury determines guilt and a second jury recommends the sentence.

(2) **Aggravating factors:** Presentation of evidence concerning aggravating circumstances is crucial before imposing the death penalty. Nevertheless, a killing cannot be raised to a capital offense under a vague state statute where none of the express aggravating factors were proven [*Godfrey v. Georgia*, 446 U.S. 420 (1980)—disfiguration accompanying a homicide is not alone determinative of torture or aggravated battery].

(3) **Mitigating factors:** The court must review mitigating factors before imposing the death penalty. However, the jury need not receive instructions on the concept of mitigation or on particular mitigating factors allowed by a state [*Buchanan v. Angelone*, 118 S.Ct. 757 (1998)]. Mandatory capital punishment for specified crimes, such as shooting a police officer, is unconstitutional since it precludes consideration of mitigating factors [*Woodson v. North Carolina*, 428 U.S. 280 (1976); *Lockett v. Ohio*, 438 U.S. 586 (1978)—mitigating circumstances cannot be limited in number by statute, rather the court must consider defendant's overall conduct, age, and police record; *Eddings v. Oklahoma*, 469 U. S. 368 (1986)—evidence of a juvenile defendant's deprived background must be considered as a mitigating factor before death sentence can be imposed].

(4) **Verdict on lesser included offense permitted:** A jury may not impose a death sentence if it is not allowed to return a verdict of guilty to a lesser included offense which the evidence supports [*Beck v. Alabama*, 447 U.S. 625 (1980)]. However, *Beck* does not require a state court to instruct the jury on offenses that, under state law, are not considered lesser included offenses of crime charged [*Hopkins v. Reeves*, 118 S.Ct. 1895 (1998)].

(5) **Parole ineligibility:** Where a capital defendant's future dangerousness is at issue, and the only sentencing alternative to death is life imprisonment without possibility of parole, due process entitles the defendant to tell the jury that he is ineligible for parole [*Kelly v. South Carolina*, 122 S.Ct. 726 (2002)].

b. **Rape cases:** *Imposition of the death penalty for the crime of raping an adult woman is grossly disproportionate to the offense and unconstitutional* under the Eighth Amendment [*Coker v. Georgia*, 433 U.S. 584 (1977)].

c. **Specific examples:**

(1) **Execution of youth:** "Execution of individuals who were under 18 years of age at time of their capital crimes is prohibited by Eighth and Fourteenth Amendments" [*Roper v. Simmons*, 125 S.Ct. 1183 (2005)].

(2) Incidentally, a disproportionate use of capital punishment on one race does not violate the clause.

(3) **Execution of mentally retarded defendants:** Execution of mentally retarded defendants is cruel and unusual punishment under the Eighth Amendment [*Atkins v. Virginia*, 122 S.Ct. 2242 (2002)].

C. APPEAL

1. **No Constitutional Basis:** There is no right to an appeal guaranteed by the federal constitution. States may therefore provide such a right by statute, provided access to appellate review is afforded in a nondiscriminatory manner between the rich and the poor [*Griffin v. Illinois*, 351 U.S. 12 (1956)].

2. **Appeal as a Matter of Right:** Where a state grants a first appeal to all individuals (i.e., as a matter of right), ***indigents*** must be provided with appointed counsel to satisfy equal protection requirements [*Douglas v. California*, 372 U.S. 353 (1963)].

   a. **Free transcripts:** Indigents are entitled on appeal to be provided free transcripts of trial proceedings [*Mayer v. City of Chicago*, 404 U.S. 189 (1971)].

   b. **Reimbursement for court costs:** Recovery of defense costs is constitutional, provided it is achieved in a nondiscriminatory manner. A state can recover legal costs from an indigent who is convicted on appeal and is subsequently able to pay [*Fuller v. Oregon*, 417 U.S. 40 (1974)—allowing indigents who are acquitted on appeal not to pay for legal fees, on the other hand, does not violate equal protection since the prosecution itself was a restraint on the individual].

3. **Discretionary Appeals:** Following an automatic first appeal (as a matter of right), some jurisdictions provide a second avenue of appeal, a discretionary appeal. No right to counsel for indigents attaches during this proceeding, nor for a (discretionary) petition for certiorari before the U.S. Supreme Court [*Ross v. Moffitt*, 417 U.S. 600 (1974)].

4. **Effect of Reversal on Appeal:** Following a reversal of a conviction on appeal, a defendant can be retried; however, on retrial it is prejudicial error and a violation of both due process and double jeopardy to be tried for any crime more serious than the crime for which she was convicted [*Price v. Georgia*, 398 U.S. 323 (1970)].

D. HABEAS CORPUS

1. **Basis of Collateral Attack:** Following an unsuccessful appeal, a defendant may, in certain instances, collaterally attack the lawfulness of his detention in a civil suit by filing a writ of habeas corpus.

2. **Procedural Considerations:**

   a. **Burden of proof:** The defendant/petitioner must prove an unlawful detention by a preponderance of the evidence.

   b. **No right to counsel:** Indigents have no right to appointed counsel.

   c. **Relationship with double jeopardy:** The state may appeal the granting of a writ and the defendant may be retried for the same offense without violating the prohibition against double jeopardy.

   d. **Standing of petitioner:** To bring a timely writ of habeas corpus the petitioner must be in *custody* (including out on bail, or on probation or parole). State prisoners may seek a writ in either state or federal court, whereas federal prisoners may proceed only in federal court. In seeking federal habeas corpus, a federal prisoner must show both cause as to why an earlier objection was not made and a resulting actual prejudice [*United States v. Frady*, 103 S.Ct. 1584 (1982)].

3. **Federal Habeas Corpus for State Prisoners:** Certain requirements must be satisfied before a state prisoner can bring a writ for habeas corpus in a federal court.

   a. **Violation of federal rights:** The petitioner must show that the state detention is in violation of federal constitutional rights.

   b. **Compliance with state procedures:** Absent a showing of cause for noncompliance and resulting prejudice, a state petitioner must have followed all state procedural rules at trial or be denied relief [*Francis v. Henderson*, 425 U.S. 536 (1976)].

   c. **No state remedies available:** A writ will be denied (and the petitioner may return to state court) where it is shown at the time of filing the writ that all available state remedies have not been exhausted [*Fay v. Noia*, 372 U.S. 391 (1963)].

   d. **State findings of fact generally upheld:** The petitioner must show clear and convincing evidence of error before the federal court will review factual findings of the state court [*Sumner v. Mata*, 449 U.S. 539 (1981)].

   e. **No Fourth Amendment claims relitigated:** A major restriction on the availability of habeas corpus is that a petitioner who had a full and fair opportunity to raise a Fourth Amendment violation previously in state court will not be permitted to seek a writ in federal court [*Stone v. Powell*, 428 U.S. 465 (1976)—costs of allowing collateral attack on the basis of the exclusionary rule outweighed defendant's Fourth Amendment rights].

(1) **Examples of valid claims:**

    (a) Claims challenging *sufficiency of the evidence* may be reviewed to satisfy due process, if it is found that no rational trier of fact could have found the defendant guilty after viewing the evidence as favorably as possible for the prosecution [*Jackson v. Virginia*, 443 U.S. 307 (1979)].

    (b) Claims of grand jury racial discrimination are recognized in federal habeas corpus proceedings [*Rose v. Mitchell*, 443 U.S. 545 (1979)].

    (c) Claims of ineffective assistance of counsel will be heard on habeas [*Strickland v. Washington, supra*].

Example:

    Convict was found guilty of conspiring to commit armed robbery at Arrowhead National Park. He was convicted and sentenced under an appropriate federal conspiracy statute.

    At a subsequent habeas corpus proceeding, which of the following claims is most likely to be recognized in his behalf?

    (A) Evidence obtained in an unconstitutional search and seizure was introduced at Convict's trial.

    (B) Convict's counsel failed to interview any potential witnesses prior to trial.

    (C) New evidence relevant to Convict's innocence has been discovered.

    (D) A confession made under coercion was introduced at Convict's trial.

Answer:

(C) Based upon the decision in *Arizona v. Fulminante, supra*, choice (D) is not the best answer. As such, *coerced confessions do not result in automatic reversal*. In *Watts v. Indiana*, 338 U.S. 49, 69 S.Ct. 1347 (1949), the U.S. Supreme Court held that coerced confessions were "constitutionally obnoxious" and were the "only instances of the general requirement that States in their prosecutions respect certain decencies of civilized conduct." Since coerced confessions no longer offend the Court's sense of fair play and decency, choice (C) is thus correct.

VI. RIGHTS OF PRISONERS AND JUVENILES

A. PRISONERS' RIGHTS

1. **In General:** Prisoners' constitutional rights are more limited in scope than those held by individuals in society at large [*Shaw v. Murphy*, 121 S.Ct. 1475 (2001)]. The usual test is whether restrictions are reasonably related to legitimate penological interests [*Turner v. Safley*, 482 U.S. 78 (1987)].

2. **Right to Parole and Probation:** No federal constitutional right to parole or probation exists. Nevertheless, where state law provides for a right to parole, a prisoner who is denied parole must be granted an opportunity to be heard and notice of the reasons for denial [*Greenholtz v. Inmates of Nebraska*, 442 U.S. 1 (1979)].

3. **Parole and Probation Revocation:** Revocation of probation entitles the prisoner to the right to counsel if a new sentence is imposed [*Mempa v. Rhay*, 389 U.S. 128 (1967)]; otherwise, the right to counsel is substantially limited and determined on a case-by-case basis. Due process affords a prisoner with the right to both a pre-revocation hearing and a revocation hearing. At this latter hearing evidence may be presented and confrontation of witnesses is allowed subject to discretion of the court [*Morrissey v. Brewer*, 408 U.S. 471 (1972)].

4. **Examples of Other Specific Rights:**

   a. Reasonable access to the courts and to legal counsel must be afforded [*Bounds v. Smith*, 430 U.S. 817 (1977)], as well as some form of communication with the press [*Pell v. Procunier*, 417 U.S. 817 (1974)—personal interviews with the media may be prohibited, however, where other channels of communication exist].

   b. Prisoners have no right to unionize [*Jones v. North Carolina Prisoners' Labor Union, Inc.*, 443 U.S. 119 (1977)].

   c. Mail may be censored subject to strict guidelines [*Procunier v. Martinez*, 416 U.S. 396 (1974)], and letters to inmates from their attorneys may be opened by prison authorities but not read [*Wolff v. McDonnell*, 418 U.S. 539 (1974)].

   d. The state may not refuse to provide prisoners with medical care [*Estelle v. Gamble*, 429 U.S. 97 (1976)—such a refusal would amount to cruel and unusual punishment].

   e. Inmates do not have a First Amendment right to provide legal assistance to fellow inmates [*Shaw v. Murphy*, 121 S.Ct. 1475 (2001)].

   f. Where a private corporation operates a correctional facility through a contract with the Bureau of Prisons, such corporation is not subject to suit under *Bivens* for allegedly violating prisoner's constitutional rights [*Correctional Services Corp. v. Malesko*, 122 S.Ct. 515 (2001)].

g. When a prisoner is given notice of forfeiture of property through a certified letter addressed to him at the facility where he is confined, such a system is reasonably calculated to give him actual notice and satisfies the Fifth Amendment [*Dusenbery v. United States*, 122 S.Ct. 694 (2002)].

h. Visiting regulations are usually viewed as reasonably related to legitimate penological interests and are therefore constitutional [*Overton v. Bazzetta*, 123 S.Ct. 2162 (2003)].

B. JUVENILES' RIGHTS

1. **Constitutional Rights Extended to Juvenile Proceedings:** To afford due process to juvenile offenders, the Court has recognized the following procedural safeguards [*In re Gault*, 387 U.S. 1 (1967); *In re Winship*, 397 U.S. 358 (1970)]:

   a. *Right to written notice of the charges;*

   b. *Right to counsel;*

   c. *Right to confront and cross-examine witnesses;*

   d. *Privilege against self-incrimination;*

   e. *Right to have guilt proved beyond a reasonable doubt; and*

   f. *Right not to be placed twice in jeopardy for the same offense once a juvenile has been adjudicated a delinquent* [*Breed v. Jones*, 421 U.S. 519 (1975)].

2. **Constitutional Rights Not Extended to Juvenile Proceedings:**

   a. *Right to jury trial* [*McKeiver v. Pennsylvania*, 403 U.S. 528 (1971)];

   b. *Right to bail; and*

   c. *Right to public trial.*

C. ALIENS' RIGHTS

1. **Indefinite Detention of Aliens:** Under the Constitution, an alien's detention is limited to the time reasonably necessary to accomplish that alien's removal from the United States. Indefinite detention is not allowed [*Zadvydas v. Davis*, 121 S.Ct. 2491 (2001)].

VII. DOUBLE JEOPARDY

The Double Jeopardy Clause is intended to prevent undue harassment and expense by eliminating the risk of a defendant twice being punished for the same offense. The Fifth Amendment provision "... nor shall any person be subject for the same offense to be twice put in jeopardy of life or limb" has been made applicable to the states through the

Due Process Clause of the Fourteenth Amendment [*Benton v. Maryland,* 395 U.S. 784 (1969)].

A. WHEN JEOPARDY ATTACHES

1. **Nonjury Trial:** When the first witness is sworn and the court begins to hear the evidence jeopardy attaches.

2. **Jury Trial:** Jeopardy attaches when the jury is impaneled and sworn [*Christ v. Bretz,* 437 U.S. 28 (1978)].

B. "SAME OFFENSE"

1. **General Rule:** Two crimes are considered the same offense, unless one of them requires proof of ***an additional element*** not contained in the other [*Brown v. Ohio,* 432 U.S. 161; *Blockburger v. United States,* 284 U.S. 299 (1932)].

   a. **Examples of separate offenses (jeopardy does not attach):**

      (1) *burglary and conspiracy to commit burglary;*

      (2) *kidnapping and felony murder;*

      (3) *driving while intoxicated and involuntary manslaughter; or*

      (4) *murder of more than one victim* [*Ciucci v. Illinois,* 356 U.S. 571 (1958)— the murder of multiple victims constituted separately triable and punishable offenses for each victim].

2. **Lesser Included Offenses:** When all elements of one offense (i.e., larceny) are contained in another offense which contains additional elements (i.e., robbery), ***then the first offense is a lesser included offense.***

   a. **Rule:** Once jeopardy has attached for the lesser included offense retrial is barred for the greater offense [*Brown v. Ohio, supra*]. Likewise, once jeopardy has attached for the greater offense, retrial is barred for the lesser included offense [*Harris v. Oklahoma,* (1977)]. The order of trials is irrelevant, as is the determination of whether the defendant was acquitted or convicted for the first offense.

3. **Exceptions:**

   a. **Incomplete offense:** Where, at the time jeopardy attaches for the first offense are all the elements of the second offense have not occurred, a later trial for the greater offense is permitted—that is, if the defendant is tried for assault and battery and then the victim succumbs, a later trial for murder is allowed.

b. **Waiver:** If the prosecution wishes to try closely related charges together, the defendant may make a motion for separate trials, but if her request is granted, she has waived any claim to double jeopardy [*Jeffers v. United States*, 432 U.S. 137 (1977)].

4. **Separate Crimes from One Act:** Separate trial and separate punishment does not violate double jeopardy and is proper where one unlawful act produces more than one separate criminal offense.

   a. **Examples:**

   (1) ***Imposition of consecutive sentences*** does not violate double jeopardy where a single conspiracy produces multiple crimes, as long as each separate crime requires proof of a fact which the other does not [*Albernaz v. Rodriguez*, 450 U.S. 333 (1981)—conspiracy to (a) import and (b) distribute marijuana constitute separate offenses punishable by consecutive sentences]. But note: if a civil fine is truly a punishment (not merely restitution) then the Double Jeopardy Clause is implicated [*United States v. Halper*, 109 S.Ct. 1892 (1989)].

   (2) No violation of double jeopardy occurred where ***cumulative sentences for two offenses*** were imposed for conduct arising from one criminal act [*Missouri v. Hunter*, 74 L.Ed.2d 535 (1983)—sentences of ten years for robbery and fifteen years for "armed criminal action" upheld].

   Example:

   > Julie was employed as a cocktail waitress at the Lenapee Inn. When she got off work at 2:00 A.M. one night, she was accosted by Josie in the parking lot. Josie, who was a transient, pulled out a knife and ordered Julie into her car. Grabbing her pocketbook, he took Julie's wallet which contained about $35. Josie then directed Julie to drive to an isolated wooded area where he raped her repeatedly. Before leaving, he stabbed her to death. Josie was subsequently arrested and indicted separately for the crimes of armed robbery, rape and felony murder with the underlying felony being the rape.
   >
   > With respect to double jeopardy, which of the following statements is most accurate?
   >
   > (A) Josie may be tried for each offense separately and may be convicted of each with sentences running consecutively.
   >
   > (B) Josie may be tried for the two separate offenses of armed robbery and felony murder and may be convicted of both with sentences running consecutively.
   >
   > (C) Josie may be tried for the two separate offenses of armed robbery and felony murder and may be convicted of both with the

armed robbery sentence running consecutively with concurrent sentences for the felony murder and rape.

(D) Josie may be tried for the single offense of felony murder and sentenced for that crime only.

Answer:

(C) The Fifth Amendment double jeopardy provision provides, "nor shall any person be subject for the same offense to be twice put in jeopardy of life or limb." Where, in a single transaction, the same act or transaction constitutes a violation of two distinct statutory provisions each requiring different elements, multiple or cumulative punishments for those several offenses do *not* offend the prohibition against double jeopardy [*see Gore v. United States*, 78 S.Ct. 1280 (1958)]. The test to be applied to determine whether there are two offenses, or only one, is whether each crime requires proof of a fact which the other does not [*see Blockburger v. United States*, 52 S.Ct. 180 (1931)]. Thus, *cumulative sentences of ten years for robbery and fifteen years for "armed criminal action," which arose from the same act, were upheld in* Missouri v. Hunter, 74 L.Ed.2d 535 (1983).

C. SEPARATE SOVEREIGNTIES DOCTRINE

1. **Rule:** The double jeopardy prohibition does not prevent dual prosecution by separate sovereigns. Therefore, a *defendant may be prosecuted for the same criminal conduct by a federal court and then by a state court* (or vice versa), or by two separate state courts [*Bartkus v. Illinois*, 359 U.S. 121 (1959)—federal prosecution followed by state prosecution; *Abbate v. United States*, 359 U.S. 187 (1959)—state trial followed by federal trial].

2. **Municipalities:** Since a municipality is not considered a separate sovereign, a local conviction would bar a state prosecution for the same offense [*Waller v. Florida*, 397 U.S. 387 (1970)].

D. RETRIAL AFTER JEOPARDY ATTACHES

There are two major exceptions to the double jeopardy prohibition. Retrial is permitted in these situations.

1. **Successful Appeal by Defendant**: A successful appeal by the defendant may be based on either an error made at trial or insufficiency of the evidence. In the former situation retrial is generally permitted, whereas in the latter situation double jeopardy bars retrial.

   a. **Appeal based on error at trial:** A defendant can be retried where a prior conviction is reversed on appeal due to an error committed at trial. In this situation, the appeal by the defendant is viewed as a waiver of a double jeopardy claim [*Burks v. United States*, 437 U.S. 1 (1978)].

    (1) **Limitation:**

        (a) Retrial for a greater offense is unconstitutional after a conviction for a lesser included offense, since the conviction of the lesser crime implies acquittal of the greater [*Price v. Georgia*, 398 U.S. 323 (1970)—following appeal of a manslaughter conviction, defendant cannot be retried for murder].

  b. **Appeal based on insufficiency of the evidence:** Evidence is insufficient as a matter of law where, viewed most favorable toward the prosecution, no reasonable trier of fact could have found the defendant guilty. Retrial following reversal of a conviction due to insufficient evidence is prohibited by the Double Jeopardy Clause [*Hudson v. Louisiana*, 450 U.S. 40 (1981)]. However, retrial following reversal due to the *weight* of the evidence is not barred (i.e., where the court disagrees with the jury's findings) [*Tibbs v. Florida*, 457 U. S. 31 (1982)].

2. **Reprosecution After Mistrial**

  a. **Based on defendant's consent:** Retrial is permitted in situations where a mistrial has been granted on defendant's motion [*United States v. Dinitz*, 424 U.S. 600 (1976)—mistrial granted due to prosecutorial misconduct].

  b. **Based on "manifest necessity":** Retrial is not permitted when the defendant objects to a mistrial, ***unless*** in the discretion of the court a "manifest necessity" exists such that the ends of justice can only be served by declaring a mistrial [*Illinois v. Somerville*, 410 U.S. 458 (1973)—retrial permitted when judge declared a mistrial due to indictment which the prosecution defectively drafted].

    (1) **Examples:**

        (a) **Hung jury:** A jury which fails to agree on a verdict is a proper basis to find "manifest necessity" and permit retrial. **Note:** If a judge grants an ***acquittal instead of a mistrial*** following a hung jury, retrial is not permitted [*United States v. Martin Linen Supply*, 430 U.S. 564 (1977)].

        (b) **Misconduct by defense:** Improper conduct by the defendant or improper remarks by defense counsel is sufficient grounds to declare a mistrial and permit retrial [*Arizona v. Washington*, 434 U.S. 497 (1978)].

        (c) **Illness:** Illness or death of the judge, jurors, or the defendant may result in mistrial without double jeopardy barring retrial [*United States v. Sanford*, 429 U.S. 14 (1976)].

(d) **Caveat:** Necessity caused by the prosecution may be invalid grounds to declare a mistrial [*Downum v. United States,* 372 U.S. 734 (1963)— double jeopardy will attach and prevent retrial where the prosecution requested a mistrial due to the inability to locate one of its witnesses].

E. APPEAL BY THE PROSECUTION

The right of the prosecution to appeal an adverse ruling is more limited than that of the defendant. Two situations arise where the prosecution may appeal without the bar of double jeopardy.

1. **Appeal of Acquittal Not Based on the Merits:** When the defendant has been acquitted on the merits, the Double Jeopardy Clause prohibits the prosecution from appealing. However, when the judge ***grants an acquittal on an issue not related to the guilt or innocence*** of the defendant, the prosecution may appeal the dismissal [*United States v. Scott,* 437 U.S. 82 (1978)—retrial of defendant not in violation of double jeopardy where dismissal was ordered for failure to grant a speedy trial].

2. **Where Successful Appeal Would Not Require a New Trial:** The prosecution is allowed to appeal whenever the appeal can be decided without subjecting the defendant to a second trial. When the judge sets aside a jury's guilty verdict ***as a matter of law***, the prosecution may appeal [*United States v. Wilson,* 420 U.S. 332 (1975)—a new trial could not possibly result since the appeal will either affirm the judge's decision or overrule it and thereby reinstate the jury's verdict]. Similarly, following a guilty verdict, an appeal by the prosecution challenging the leniency of the sentence, was found not to be in violation of the Double Jeopardy Clause [*United States v. DiFrancesco,* 449 U.S. 117 (1980)].

F. APPLICATION OF DOUBLE JEOPARDY IN SENTENCING

1. **Imposition of Harsher Sentence in Nonjury Situation:** When a defendant appeals his conviction, receives a new trial, and is then reconvicted for the same offense, double jeopardy is not an absolute bar to the imposition of a harsher sentence; however, due process requires that a more severe sentence can be given upon reconviction only where the judge makes an affirmative showing of new information on the record [*North Carolina v. Pearce,* 395 U.S. 711 (1969)].

2. **Sentencing Upon Reconviction in Jury Situation and Trial *de Novo:*** The limitation preventing more serious punishment upon resentencing is inapplicable both following a jury sentence [*Chaffin v. Stynchcombe,* 412 U.S. 17 (1973)—no vindictive punishment likely since the jury would be unaware of the original sentencing] and following a trial *de novo* [*Colten v. Kentucky,* 407 U.S. 104 (1972)—two-tier system allows sentencing in a separate, higher court].

3. **Can Reduce Sentence on Appeal to the Sentence of a Nonjeopardy Barred Crime** [*Jones v. Thomas*, 109 S.Ct. 2522 (1989)]

G. COLLATERAL ESTOPPEL

1. **Application to Double Jeopardy Clause:** The doctrine of collateral estoppel, which precludes relitigation between the same parties of issues actually determined at an earlier trial, is embodied in the guarantee against double jeopardy [*Ashe v. Swenson*, 397 U.S. 436 (1970)—following defendant's acquittal of being *the criminal* who robbed one of six persons, all of whom were robbed (i.e., final determination on the issue of identity established), he cannot thereafter be prosecuted for robbery of any of the other persons (i.e., different offenses)].

2. **Limitation:** Collateral estoppel will only be applicable where *the very issue sought to be precluded in the later prosecution has been necessarily determined* in the earlier trial.

    a. **Example:** By reviewing the pleadings and the evidence at trial, the court in *Ashe* found that the *defendant's identity was the issue determined,* yet had the acquittal been based upon lack of one of the elements of robbery, such as "taking by force or fear," then collateral estoppel would not have barred reprosecution for the separate offense of robbery of one of the victims.

H. "AS APPLIED" CIVIL STATUTES

1. An act found to be civil in nature cannot be deemed punitive "as applied" to a single individual in violation of the Double Jeopardy and Ex Post Facto Clauses and provide cause for release [*Seling v. Young*, 121 S.Ct. 727 (2001)].

VIII. MISCELLANEOUS PROCEDURAL CONSIDERATIONS

A. RETROACTIVITY OF NEW DECISIONS: A U.S. Supreme Court case creating a new constitutional right is fully retroactive to all defendants pretrial, at trial, or in the process of direct appeal. However, a collateral petitioner (habeas corpus) will receive the benefit of a new decision only if:

1. His crime is, itself, decriminalized or

2. Prosecution is fundamentally unfair and the new rule maximizes the truth-finding function of trial [*Trague v. Lane*, 109 S.Ct. 1060 (1989); *Saffle v. Parks*, 110 S.Ct. 1257 (1990)].

    a. Examples: Thus, since flag burning is considered to be protected speech, all petitioners would receive the benefit of the new case so holding [*Cf. United States v. Eichman*, 110 S.Ct. 2404 (1990)]. However, it is a rare case now where a collateral petitioner will receive the benefit of a new decision.

B. EX POST FACTO CRIMES: A crime must be written at the time of the offense in order to punish the defendant. The basic ex post facto protections include prohibition of the following:

1. *Retroactive* criminal statutes;

2. Increasing the punishment after the commission of the offense;

3. Removing a defense which was viable at the time of the offense; and

4. Applying rules of procedure or evidence retroactively if those rules would make it easier to convict a defendant.

   [*Collins v. Youngblood*, 110 S.Ct. 2715 (1990); *but see Smith v. Doe*, 123 S.Ct. 1140 (2003)—law requiring sex offenders to register with authorities and allowing authorities to post registry on Internet is not unconstitutional under the *ex post facto* clause, even as applied to those who committed sex offenses before the law's enactment, because it does not impose punishment].

   Furthermore, a state may not enact a statute that extends the limitations period for a crime when the previously applicable limitations period has already expired [*Stogner v. California*, 123 S.Ct. 2446 (2003)].

C. INDEPENDENT STATE GROUNDS:

In accord with the 10th Amendment, all powers not expressly given to the federal government by the Constitution reside in the States. Thus, state courts, pursuant to their own constitutions and cases interpreting their constitutions, can give to the criminally accused greater procedural protections than are federally required. However, if they so proceed they must indicate such a decision to be based on "adequate and independent state grounds" and they must not entangle state and federal cases—otherwise there will be federal jurisdiction [*Michigan v. Long*, 463 U.S. 1032 (1983)].

1. Thus in any state prosecution, a competent defense will make a separate set of solely state constitutional arguments.

D. ENTRAPMENT: A long line of U.S. Supreme Court cases indicate entrapment is a valid defense only when the origin of intent was in the police. Thus, *if the defendant was personally predisposed to commit the crime, entrapment is not a defense.*

QUESTION TOPIC LIST

1. Application of *Miranda* to Confessions

2. Jailhouse Confessions

3. Grand Jury Proceedings—Exclusionary Rule

4. Effect of *Miranda* on Subsequent Search Warrant

5. Appeal—Grounds for New Trial

6. Conspiracy and Murder

7. *Miranda* Waiver

8. *Massiah v. United States*

9. Jury Verdicts

10. Plain View Doctrine

11. Prejudicial Error

12. Burden of Production and Persuasion

13. Sixth Amendment Right to Counsel

14. Interrogations

15. Lineups

16. Dual Representation

17. Waiver of Right to Counsel

18. Involuntary Manslaughter

19. Disclosure Requirements

20. Legislatively Protected Classes

21. Burden of Persuasion

22. Third-Party Consensual Search

23. Warrant Requirements/Informants

24. Prosecutorial Comment

25. Coconspirator Standing

26. Demonstrative Evidence

KAPLAN) *pmbr*

Question 1 is based on the following fact situation.

Smelson was employed by the B&O Railroad Company as a watchman at its crossing, to give warning to the public of approaching trains. Late one evening he fell asleep in his shanty, and failed to warn of the approach of an oncoming train. Fishbone, who was driving his car, knew of the usual presence of the watchman. As he approached the crossing, he received no warning. Driving onto the track, Fishbone's car was struck and crushed by the train. Fishbone died instantly.

A few minutes after the accident, Police Officer Rose arrived at the crossing and walked into the shanty. As he entered, Smelson then awoke. Rose asked him, "What happened here?" Smelson made incriminating statements.

1. Smelson is subsequently charged with involuntary manslaughter. His motion to prevent the introduction of his incriminating statements into evidence will *MOST* likely be

    (A) granted, because Police Officer Rose failed to give Smelson his *Miranda* warnings
    (B) granted, because Police Officer Rose's conduct in questioning Smelson immediately after he awoke was unfairly prejudicial to the defendant
    (C) denied, because the exchange took place in a noncustodial setting and the question was investigatory in nature
    (D) denied, because Smelson's incriminating statements were volunteered

Question 2 is based on the following fact situation.

Kent was convicted of assault of a federal officer and imprisoned in a federal penitentiary in West Virginia. While in prison, federal authorities began investigating the murder of Kent's 11-year-old stepdaughter who was murdered in Arizona two years earlier. Believing that Kent was responsible for this killing, federal agents decided to plant an informer at the West Virginia prison to befriend Kent and possibly obtain evidence about the crime.

In accord with this plan, the F.B.I. hired Norris to be a paid informant and placed him in the prison as a fellow inmate, masquerading as an organized crime figure. Norris soon befriended Kent and learned that he was being threatened by other inmates because of a rumor that he had killed a child in Arizona. Norris then raised the subject in several conversations, but Kent repeatedly denied any such involvement. After Kent started receiving tough treatment from other inmates because of the rumor, Norris offered to protect Kent but told him, "You have to tell me the truth about what really happened … you know if you want me to help you." Believing that Norris would protect him from the other inmates, Kent then admitted to Norris that he had driven his stepdaughter to the desert where he killed her.

Based upon this confession, Kent was then indicted in Arizona for the first-degree murder of his stepdaughter. Prior to trial, Kent moves to suppress the statement given to Norris.

2. Kent's motion to suppress will *MOST* likely be

(A) granted, because the confession was coerced by the threat of physical violence, absent protection from the government agent, that motivated Kent to confess

(B) granted, because Norris was a "false friend" and Kent was tricked into making the confession

(C) denied, because the confession was voluntary

(D) denied, because under the "totality of circumstances" Norris' conduct was not inherently coercive

Question 3 is based on the following fact situation.

Late one evening the San Diego Police Department received a telephone call from an unidentified woman who reported hearing loud shrieks and screams from a neighboring home. The caller furnished the police with the address where the disturbance was taking place. When the police arrived at the home, they discovered the owner, a Mrs. Cynthia Garver, bludgeoned to death. The murder weapon was a blood-stained baseball bat found near the victim's body.

A subsequent investigation revealed that Mrs. Garver had recently been separated from her husband, Stevie, who had since moved to Los Angeles. After questioning several of the victim's friends and relatives, the police concluded that Stevie was a prime suspect in the murder. Thus, two San Diego detectives went to Los Angeles to question Stevie about the killing. When they arrived at his apartment, the detectives persuaded the landlord to let them into his flat. Finding no one inside, they searched the apartment. Before leaving, the detectives took a box of Wheaties which they planned to use for a fingerprint comparison. The prints from the Wheaties box matched those found on the baseball bat. The police provided the grand jury investigating the murder with the fingerprint comparison.

3. Stevie is subsequently subpoenaed to testify before the grand jury. Before his scheduled appearance, Stevie files a motion to suppress evidence of the fingerprint comparison contending that the evidence was illegally obtained. His motion should be

(A) granted, because the warrantless search of Stevie's apartment was unconstitutional

(B) granted, because the grand jury is barred from considering illegally obtained evidence

(C) denied, because the exclusionary rule has not been extended to grand jury hearings

(D) denied, because the landlord had the apparent authority to authorize the search of Stevie's apartment

Question 4 is based on the following fact situation.

Cruz was suspected of having burglarized his neighbor Alou's apartment. Alou reported that his apartment had been ransacked and several items of clothing had been stolen. During the course of their investigation, two police detectives went to Cruz's place of work to interview him. After being advised of his *Miranda* rights, Cruz requested permission to call his attorney. Although his attorney was unavailable, the attorney's receptionist admonished him not to say anything. Cruz told the detectives he would have nothing further to say unless his attorney was present. The detectives then asked him if he would accompany them to the police station to answer some questions about an unrelated robbery incident. Cruz agreed.

As they were driving to the police station, he was asked where he had purchased the boots that he was wearing. He refused to answer. When they arrived at the police station, the detectives requested that he sign a waiver of his right to counsel. Cruz replied that he would not sign anything in the absence of his attorney. He was then placed in an interrogation room. Shortly thereafter, he was told that he could leave if he would be willing to say where he purchased his boots. Cruz admitted that he bought the boots and some shirts from Sanchez. From this information, the detectives obtained a search warrant and went to Cruz's home, where they found the stolen clothing.

4. Cruz is charged with burglarizing Alou's apartment. At trial, the court should

(A) admit both the confession because it was volunteered and the clothing because it was obtained pursuant to a valid search warrant

(B) suppress the confession because it was obtained in violation of his Sixth Amendment right to counsel, but admit the clothing because it was obtained pursuant to a valid search warrant

(C) suppress the confession because Cruz failed to sign the waiver, but admit the clothing because it was obtained pursuant to a valid search warrant

(D) suppress both the confession because it was obtained in violation of his Fifth Amendment right to counsel and the clothing because the search warrant was secured as a result of the confession

Question 5 is based on the following fact situation.

Swane, a junior criminology major at the University of Michigan, was a member of Eta Beta Pi fraternity. While new members were pledging the fraternity, Swane had a reputation for initiating pranks and hazing the pledges. Late one night after a fraternity party, Swane decided to "kidnap" one of the pledges named Jimbo. Enlisting the help of his friend, Harper, they grabbed Jimbo, tied him up, and locked him in the trunk of Swane's car. They then drove from Ann Arbor to Detroit, where they dropped Jimbo at a street corner in an inner-city neighborhood. While Jimbo was wandering around and trying to find a telephone booth, a gang of youths saw his predicament and attacked him. Jimbo, who was severely beaten, suffered a broken nose, multiple lacerations, and contusions.

When Jimbo finally returned to Ann Arbor, he filed a criminal complaint against Swane who was charged with violating Michigan Penal Law Section 324, which provides:

> "Every person who hazes a student and thereby is responsible for causing bodily harm to said student is guilty of a felony punishable by three years in prison."

At trial, the prosecuting attorney called Harper, Swane's alleged accomplice, as a witness. Harper refused to answer any questions and was cited for contempt. After Harper left the witness stand, the prosecutor offered into evidence a transcript of Harper's testimony given at Swane's preliminary hearing. At the preliminary hearing, Harper testified under oath that he and Swane were responsible for hazing Jimbo and driving the victim against his will to Detroit. During the preliminary hearing, Harper was also cross-examined by Swane's defense counsel. Over defense objections, the trial court admitted the transcript of Harper's testimony at the preliminary hearing. Thereafter, Swane was convicted of violating the aforementioned hazing statute.

5. Swane appeals the conviction and contends that the admission of the transcript of Harper's testimony at the preliminary hearing violated his Sixth Amendment right of confrontation. As to this claim, Swane's appeal will *MOST* likely be

(A) granted, because there was no opportunity to cross-examine the witness at trial

(B) granted, because in order to admit prior testimony the witness must be shown to be unavailable

(C) denied, because the witness was unavailable and there was adequate opportunity for cross-examination at the preliminary hearing

(D) denied, because the testimony was a statement by a coconspirator, and therefore admissible as a recognized exception to the hearsay rule

Question 6 is based on the following fact situation.

Lionel, a construction worker, was injured in a job-site accident at Ft. Polk, Louisiana, a federal enclave. Lionel sued Clapper Concrete Company for negligence in federal district court in Louisiana claiming that a Clapper employee permitted one of the company's trucks to roll backward and pin him against some construction equipment. Lionel invoked his Seventh Amendment right to a trial by jury.

During *voir dire*, Clapper used two of its three peremptory challenges authorized by statute to remove black persons from the prospective jury. Clapper's challenges were exercised under 28 U.S.C. Section 1870. The federal law provides:

"In civil cases, each party shall be entitled to three peremptory challenges. Several defendants or several plaintiffs may be considered as a single party for the purposes of making challenges, or the court may allow additional peremptory challenges and permit them to be exercised separately or jointly."

Lionel, who is black, requested that the court require Clapper to articulate a race-neutral explanation for the peremptory strikes. The district court judge denied the request on the ground that a private litigant in a civil case can exercise peremptory challenges without accountability for alleged racial classifications.

As impaneled, the jury included 11 white persons and 1 black person. In this judicial district, blacks comprise 50 percent of the population. The jury subsequently returned the verdict in favor of Clapper.

6. Lionel appeals the district court ruling to the U.S. Court of Appeals. He bases his appeal on the ground that the trial court judge erred in failing to have Clapper offer a race-neutral explanation for its peremptory challenges. Lionel's appeal will be

(A) successful, if Clapper used its peremptory challenges to exclude jurors on account of race

(B) successful, because Lionel did not receive a fair trial since the jury was not drawn from a representative cross-section of the community

(C) unsuccessful, because a civil litigant may not raise the equal protection claim of a person whom the opposing party has excluded from jury service on account of race

(D) unsuccessful, because Clapper's peremptory challenges were authorized by statute, it is not required to articulate a race-neutral explanation for striking the two jurors

Question 7 is based on the following fact situation.

Under which of the following fact situations would Defendant's *Miranda* waiver *MOST* likely be *ineffective*?

(A) Defendant recently graduated from Georgetown Law Center. At her graduation party, Defendant became highly intoxicated after drinking a pint of Southern Comfort. Following the party, Defendant attempted to drive home in her auto. She fell asleep at the wheel and crashed into another vehicle, seriously injuring the driver. Shortly after the accident, a police officer came on the scene and arrested Defendant, charging her with D.U.I. The Defendant was then given her *Miranda* warnings and transported to the police station. Upon questioning, Defendant, who was still highly intoxicated, waived her *Miranda* rights and elicited an incriminating statement.

(B) Defendant stabbed victim after a violent argument. Following the stabbing death, the police arrested Defendant and charged him with murder. He was transported to the station house where *Miranda* warnings were given. Afterwards the Defendant was interrogated and proceeded to waive his *Miranda* rights. He then confessed to committing the crime. At trial, a psychiatrist testified that Defendant was mentally ill and his confession was not the result of a knowing and intelligent waiver.

(C) Defendant was a 15 year-old boy who was a high school sophomore. He possessed normal intelligence and experience for a youth of his age. One night he and two friends attended a Simon and Garfunkle concert in Central Park. After the concert, Defendant and his friends went on a "wilding" spree assaulting and robbing a number of victims in the park. The next day Defendant was arrested and received proper *Miranda* warnings. After being subjected to persistent questioning for two hours, Defendant waived his *Miranda* rights and made a confession. At trial, Defendant claims that he did not make a knowing and intelligent waiver.

(D) Defendant was a 16 year-old juvenile who was in police custody on suspicion of murder. He was given his *Miranda* warnings and then requested to have his probation officer present. He had been on probation for a series of juvenile offenses. His request was denied. During a brief interrogation, Defendant proceeded to waive his *Miranda* rights and made incriminating statements that linked him with the crime. At trial Defendant's lawyer claims that his waiver was ineffective because his request to see the probation officer was the equivalent of asking for a lawyer.

Question 8 is based on the following fact situation.

Gilley was arrested and charged with conspiracy to receive stolen property. At his arraignment Gilley was represented by counsel. He was then released after posting bond. Following his release, Gilley resumed his job as a bartender at The Lone Star Saloon. Three weeks before Gilley's scheduled trial, Gatlin entered the bar. After a few drinks, Gatlin began conversing with Gilley, who was on duty at the time. Unknown to Gilley, Gatlin was a paid police informant. During the course of their conversation, Gatlin told Gilley that he had read about his arrest in the newspapers and questioned Gilley about the names of his accomplices. Unsuspectingly, Gilley made some admissions which Gatlin then passed on to the prosecuting attorney.

8. At trial, the prosecution tried to introduce into evidence Gilley's admissions. The defendant's motion to exclude this offer of proof will *MOST* likely be

(A) denied, because Gilley's statements were voluntary

(B) denied, because Gilley assumed the risk that his confidence in Gatlin was not misplaced

(C) granted, because Gilley's Sixth Amendment right to counsel was violated

(D) granted, because Gilley's Fifth Amendment privilege against self-incrimination was violated

Question 9 is based on the following fact situation.

One evening Glover set fire to Horsey's occupied house. As a result of the blaze, Horsey's daughter was burned to death. Glover was charged with felony murder on the first count and arson on the second count of the two-count indictment. The jury found the defendant guilty on the first count, but returned an innocent verdict on the second count.

9. Glover's attorney's motion to set aside the guilty verdict on the felony murder charge will *MOST* probably be

(A) granted, because the guilty verdict is plain error that adversely affects Glover's constitutional rights

(B) granted, because the verdicts are legally inconsistent and should lead to an acquittal of both charges

(C) denied, because the verdicts do not amount to a reversible error

(D) denied, because Glover's proper remedy is to seek an appellate review for a nonconstitutional error

Question 10 is based on the following fact situation.

Leech lived at 789 Mesa Drive in a residential section of Tucson. The police received reliable information that Leech had a stolen Yamaha stereo in his possession. Tucson detectives then submitted an affidavit to a neutral magistrate setting forth sufficient underlying circumstances for the issuance of a search warrant. Making a determination of probable cause, the magistrate issued a warrant for the Yamaha stereo at "the premises on 789 Mesa Drive."

The police arrived at Leech's dwelling, showed him the warrant and came inside. In the living room, they noticed a Sanyo stereo which had the serial number removed. Upon further inspection, the police determined that the Sanyo stereo had been stolen from a local Federated Store during a recent burglary. Thereupon, the police placed Leech under arrest and instructed him to remain seated in the living room while they searched the rest of the home. One of the officers proceeded to the basement where she found the stolen Yamaha stereo. She then decided to search the upstairs and came upon a stolen Marantz stereo in Leech's second-floor bedroom.

10. Leech was subsequently prosecuted for receiving stolen property. At trial, Leech moves to prevent introduction of the stereos in evidence. His motion should be granted with respect to

(A) the Sanyo stereo

(B) the Marantz stereo

(C) the Marantz and the Sanyo stereos

(D) none of the stereos

Question 11 is based on the following fact situation.

Loggins was prosecuted for murder. At trial, the prosecutor called Messina, a police detective, to testify. Messina, who questioned Loggins at the station house after his arrest, testified that Loggins declared his innocence and initially wanted to take a lie detector test. Messina further testified, however, that when the time came to take the lie detector test, Loggins refused. Loggins's attorney did not object to Messina's testimony. Loggins was convicted and sentenced to prison.

11. Loggins, who is now represented by a new attorney, appeals claiming that it was error to admit Messina's testimony. The appellate court should find

    (A) plain error because the trial court should have acted on its own motion to order reference to the lie detector test stricken
    (B) error because admission of Messina's testimony violated Loggins's privilege against self-incrimination
    (C) no error because Loggins's trial attorney failed to preserve the argument by timely objection
    (D) no error because Loggins's statements were admissions by a party

Question 12 is based on the following fact situation.

12. Major is charged with murder in the shooting death of his brother-in-law Minor. In the jurisdiction in which Major is on trial for murder, the defense of insanity is an affirmative defense. Major pleads insanity as his defense. At the trial in order to prove his defense of insanity, Major has

    (A) the burden of production only
    (B) the burden of persuasion only
    (C) both the burden of production and the burden of persuasion
    (D) neither the burden of production nor the burden of persuasion

Question 13 is based on the following fact situation.

Defendant was arrested and charged with statutory rape. At trial, Defendant took the stand to testify in his own behalf. In brief, Defendant testified on direct that late one Friday night he was at a tavern when Victim, who appeared to be in her early twenties, approached him. They had a couple of drinks together and Defendant invited Victim back to his apartment, whereupon he spent the weekend with her engaging in marathon sex. During this time Victim told Defendant that she was a sophomore in college. Subsequently, Defendant was arrested and found out for the first time that victim was only 12 years old.

Defendant's direct examination continued until 7:30 P.M. when it finally concluded. At this time, the trial court judge adjourned the proceedings for the evening. The judge then instructed the Defendant not to speak with anyone during the night and scheduled cross-examination to begin in the morning.

13. The judge's instruction to Defendant was

   (A) proper, because a judge has broad discretion to instruct witnesses in such a manner
   (B) proper, because it would have the same effect as permitting cross-examination to continue after direct was concluded
   (C) improper, because it violates Defendant's Sixth Amendment right to counsel
   (D) improper, because it violates the attorney-client privilege

Questions 14–16 are based on the following fact situation.

Morris Morgan was arrested one morning by a police officer for the attempted murder of Harry Hamilton. Morris and his brother Mike had allegedly fired three shots at Harry, a physical education teacher, on the schoolyard of Doobie Elementary School.

Immediately after the arrest, the arresting officer advised Morris of his *Miranda* rights. Morris responded that he would not make any statement until he consulted with his attorney.

Within minutes, a patrol car arrived, and Morris was taken into the car to be transported to the police station. The arresting officer sat in the front, next to the driver, and Morris sat alone in the backseat, with his hands cuffed.

On the way to the station, the driver stated to the arresting officer, "I hope that the shotgun involved in this crime doesn't get into the hands of those small children, because one of them could be seriously injured, to say the least." Morris interrupted the officers and told them where to look in the schoolyard for the abandoned shotgun. As a result of this information, the police found the gun where Morris said it was.

At the police station, Morris was placed in a lineup. Harry observed the lineup, and after each of the six participants stated, "I'm going to get you" (the same phrase that the shooter allegedly said to Harry before he fired), Harry identified Morris as the perpetrator.

Subsequently Mike was also arrested, and Mike and Morris were tried together. Both were represented by their family's trusted attorney, Janis Purclon. At trial, Mike's defense was that Morris forced him to go to the schoolyard on the day of the crime and that he did not know that Morris was armed with a shotgun until he saw Morris take it out of a bag that day.

14. The state's best rebuttal to Morris's argument that the gun was illegally seized is that

   (A) Morris was not entitled to be rewarned of his *Miranda* rights in the patrol car
   (B) Morris was not interrogated in the patrol car
   (C) Morris waived his right to consult with counsel
   (D) the seizure of the gun was not the fruit of Morris's statement

15. The police requirement that Morris state at the lineup, "I'm going to get you"

   (A) invalidated the lineup
   (B) violated Morris's right against self-incrimination
   (C) tainted Harry's identification of Morris
   (D) would not prohibit Harry's lineup identification from being introduced at trial

16. If appropriate objections are made by Mike and/or Morris, the court should rule Janis's representation of Mike and Morris at trial

    (A) violated Mike's Sixth Amendment right to counsel
    (B) constituted an impermissible conflict of interest
    (C) violated Mike's constitutional rights, but did not infringe on Morris's constitutional rights
    (D) did not violate Morris's constitutional rights, if he separately paid for her representation

Question 17 is based on the following fact situation.

On October 30, 1984, riots broke out in the city of Cucamonga. Many shops had been looted and some had been burned during the riots. Goods of all kinds were in piles or strewn about the sidewalk. In mid-afternoon on October 30, Lightfoot was walking along the street when he paused in front of Wilson's Appliance Store. He picked up a portable television set that was lying on the sidewalk, and started to walk off quickly. A police officer who was standing in front of the shop rushed after Lightfoot and arrested him.

Lightfoot, an indigent, was charged with grand larceny, a felony carrying the maximum penalty of six months imprisonment and $1,000 fine. At his arraignment, the judge advised Lightfoot of his right to have counsel appointed for him. Lightfoot, however, told the judge that he wanted to represent himself and waive his right to a jury trial. The judge then questioned Lightfoot at length about his demands. Lightfoot indicated that he had no previous legal experience. He told the judge that the reason he didn't want a court-appointed attorney to represent him was because he didn't trust lawyers. The judge did not find Lightfoot's reasons for representing

himself to be persuasive and appointed an attorney to represent him.

Thereafter, Gordon was appointed by the court to represent Lightfoot. Gordon told the court that Lightfoot wanted a nonjury trial. However, at the prosecution's request, the court impaneled a jury. Lightfoot was subsequently convicted by the jury and sentenced to six months imprisonment. In addition, Lightfoot was ordered to reimburse the state $450 to cover the cost of his attorney. This reimbursement order was made pursuant to a relevant statute in effect at the time of Lightfoot's arrest.

17. Lightfoot appeals both the conviction and the reimbursement order. The appellate court should

    (A) affirm both the conviction and the reimbursement order
    (B) affirm the conviction, but not the reimbursement order
    (C) reverse the conviction because he was denied the right to a nonjury trial, but not the reimbursement order
    (D) reverse both the conviction and the reimbursement order because Lightfoot was denied the right to represent himself

Questions 18–19 are based on the following fact situation.

The state of Newton has the following hit-and-run statute in effect:

"Any driver of a motor vehicle (including but not limited to automobiles, trucks, buses, or motorcycles) involved in an accident or collision resulting in injury or death to a human being shall immediately stop his or her vehicle at the scene of such accident or collision, render necessary aid to the injured

victim, and furnish the police or other person(s) at the scene with his or her name, address and driver's license. Any violation or noncompliance with said statute shall be punished by imprisonment for not less than three years nor more than seven years."

At 3:30 P.M. on the afternoon of January 13, 1997, nine-year-old Goldie Hand was riding her bicycle along Pacific Coast Highway. As Goldie swerved into the southbound lane, her bicycle was struck by a car driven by Ellen Brennan. Goldie was knocked off her bike and thrown onto the sidewalk adjacent to the highway. Although Goldie received some minor scrapes and bruises, she was not seriously injured. Following the accident, the car driven by Brennan sped away.

Moments later, however, a tractor-trailer crashed into the rear of a Ford Pinto about thirty feet from where Goldie was lying. The Pinto almost instantly caught fire as its gas tank exploded. Goldie, who was engulfed in the flaming wreckage, burned to death.

18. If Brennan is charged with involuntary manslaughter for the death of Hand, the defendant should be found

    (A) guilty, because she unlawfully fled the scene of an accident in violation of her statutory duty

    (B) guilty, because her failure to render aid to Hand would make Brennan criminally responsible for the victim's death

    (C) not guilty, because under the circumstances her failure to aid Hand cannot be a basis for imposing criminal responsibility for the victim's death

    (D) not guilty, because there was not a sufficient causal connection between her actions and Hand's death to impose criminal responsibility

19. Assume for the purposes of this question only that Brennan is charged with violating the aforementioned statute. She files a motion to dismiss on the grounds that the disclosure requirement of the statute violates her privilege against self-incrimination. Her motion should be

    (A) granted, because the statute makes no provision for *Miranda* warnings concerning her right to remain silent

    (B) granted, because the statute requires her to provide incriminating information that can be used against her in a criminal prosecution

    (C) denied, because the legislative intent in enacting the statute was designed to require disclosure of information to be used primarily in civil litigation

    (D) denied, because in accordance with public policy considerations the required disclosures are insufficiently testimonial

Question 20 is based on the following fact situation.

At 9:00 P.M. on the evening of April 12, 1998, Agent Erving of the FBI's Office of Narcotics and Dangerous Drugs (with the help of a confidential informant) met one Ervin Johnson. The latter took Agent Erving to the home of Marcus Barnes, who sold Erving four pounds of hashish (a hemp that is smoked, chewed, or drunk as a narcotic and intoxicant). At trial, Barnes claimed the defense of entrapment and demanded that the informant's identity be disclosed and that he be produced. At no time prior to trial did Barnes seek to subpoena Johnson. However, Johnson was a fugitive from justice the whole time, and no subpoena could have been served. The government claims a right to protect the informant's identity.

20. Should the government's claim be honored?

    (A) yes, because an informant has a Fifth Amendment privilege against self-incrimination
    (B) yes, because informants would not assist in crime prevention unless they were reasonably certain that their identities would be kept secret
    (C) no, because under the Fifth Amendment a defendant has the right to be confronted by witnesses against him
    (D) no, because under the Sixth Amendment a defendant has the right to a fair trial

Questions 21–22 are based on the following fact situation.

Lois, a divorcee, was on the first day of her new secretarial job when her boss, Pete, called her into his office. Pete directly suggested that if Lois did not grant him certain sexual favors, she would be fired in one week. Every day during the remainder of the week, Pete approached Lois with his demands, and Lois refused to cooperate.

At the end of the week, when Pete called Lois into his office and again tried to pressure her to engage in sexual relations, Lois knocked him unconscious with a giant stapler and choked him to death.

Lois is tried for murder. In accordance with the following statute, the state relies at trial on the presumption of malice:

"When the act of killing another is proved, malice aforethought shall be presumed, and the burden shall rest upon the party who committed the killing to show that malice did not exist."

21. If Lois is convicted of first-degree murder and challenges her conviction on the grounds of the above statute, on appeal she will

    (A) win, because the statute is unconstitutional
    (B) win, because the statute violates due process
    (C) lose, unless she was denied the opportunity to overcome the presumption
    (D) lose, since the presumption may be rebutted

22. Assume for the purposes of this question only that Lois shot, rather than choked, Pete to death. After the shooting, Lois left on a two-day trip to the mountains to get the week's events off her mind. She called her teenage neighbor, Judy, to take care of her apartment while she was gone and to look after her four-year-old daughter. That night, after Lois left, the police came to the apartment and asked Judy if they could search the apartment and Judy gave them permission. The police found in Lois's bedroom the pistol used to kill Pete. At a motion to suppress the pistol prior to trial, which of the following facts would Lois's attorney be LEAST likely to attempt to prove:

    (A) Lois gave Judy the keys to her apartment.
    (B) The police did not have a search warrant.
    (C) Lois told Judy not to answer the door for anyone.
    (D) The police told Judy she would be taken to the police station if she refused permission to search.

Question 23 is based on the following fact situation.

23. Detective received information from Informant, who had given reliable information many times in the past, that Harry was a narcotics dealer. Specifically, Informant said that, two months before, he had visited Harry's apartment with Bill and that on that occasion he saw Harry sell Bill some heroin. Detective knew that Informant, Harry, and Bill were friends. Thereafter, Detective put all this information into affidavit form, appeared before a magistrate, and secured a search warrant for Harry's apartment. The search turned up a supply of heroin. Harry's motion to suppress introduction of the heroin into evidence will *MOST* probably be

(A) granted, because a search warrant cannot validly be issued solely on the basis of an informant's information
(B) granted, because the information supplied to Detective concerned an occurrence too remote in time to justify a finding of probable cause at the time of the search
(C) granted, because a search for "mere evidence" alone is improper and illegal
(D) denied, because Informant had proven himself reliable in the past and the information he gave turned out to be correct

Question 24 is based on the following fact situation.

During the murder trial of Slick Savage, the prosecution presented four witnesses to the brutal slaying of Melody Mercy. The evidence pointed to the fact that Slick beat her about the head and neck with a thirty-two inch baseball bat, causing severe injuries to her brain and her ultimate death.

The prosecution rested, and Slick presented two witnesses—his brother and his girlfriend—who testified that Slick was dining at an elegant French restaurant on the other side of town at the time of the alleged murder. Slick presented no other witnesses.

During his closing argument to the jury, the assistant district attorney, Don Dandee, called attention to the fact that the prosecution witnesses had no apparent reason to have any bias toward the prosecution or against the defendant. He then noted that Slick's witnesses had clear motives to falsify their testimony and favor Slick. Dandee added, "If Slick was on the other side of town, why didn't he tell us himself? Why didn't he get on the stand? What was he hiding? Those are questions for you, the jury, to answer."

Slick was convicted of first-degree murder and sentenced to life imprisonment.

24. On appeal his conviction should be

(A) reversed, because the prosecutor improperly referred to the possible motives or interests of the defense witness
(B) reversed, because Slick's constitutional rights were violated in Dandee's closing argument
(C) reversed, because Dandee referred to Slick's failure to testify
(D) reversed, because Dandee's argument violated Slick's rights under the Fifth and Fourteenth Amendments

Question 25 is based on the following fact situation.

Benny Blade and Cullen Clovis were arrested and charged with robbery and conspiracy to commit robbery. Following their arrest, Benny and Cullen were taken to the police station and given *Miranda* warnings. They both expressed a desire to remain silent until they could consult with an attorney. At the station house Benny and Cullen were booked and placed in separate jail cells.

The following day, Van Dyke, a police detective, went to Cullen's cell and began interrogating him. Van Dyke told Cullen if he cooperated in their investigation, the prosecuting attorney would drop charges against him. Cullen then reluctantly confessed and implicated Benny in the commission of the crime. Cullen also told the police where Benny had hidden the stolen property. Based on this information, the police retrieved the stolen property which included a pearl-studded diamond necklace.

Thereafter, the police went to Benny's jail cell and showed him the diamond necklace that they had recovered. They also told Benny that Cullen had confessed and implicated him in the perpetration of the crime. Confronted by this evidence, Benny confessed.

25. Benny was then prosecuted for conspiracy and robbery. At Benny's trial, the prosecution sought to introduce into evidence the necklace and Benny's confession. Defendant's motion to exclude these offers of proof will be

   (A) denied to both the necklace and the confession
   (B) denied to the necklace but granted to the confession
   (C) granted to the necklace but denied to the confession
   (D) granted to both the necklace and the confession

Question 26 is based on the following fact situation.

Wayne Wilson was arrested at Kansas City Municipal Airport when the small satchel he was carrying was found to contain cocaine. Wilson, who did not challenge the legality of the airport search, was subsequently prosecuted for possession of cocaine.

At trial, Wilson testified in his own behalf and said that the satchel belonged to his girlfriend, Jerri Martin, who was accompanying Wilson when he was arrested. (Martin died in a skydiving accident two weeks before Wilson's trial.) Moreover, Wilson testified that although he was a former cocaine addict, he had not used any drugs in the past three years. On cross-examination, the prosecuting attorney asked Wilson to roll up the sleeves of his shirt and exhibit his arms to see if there were any needle marks.

26. This request is

   (A) objectionable, because Wilson has a privilege against self-incrimination
   (B) objectionable, because the probative value is substantially outweighed by the danger of unfair prejudice
   (C) permissible, because Wilson waived his privilege against self-incrimination by taking the stand
   (D) permissible, because such evidence is relevant to Wilson's credibility

Questions 27–28 are based on the following fact situation.

Fernando Callousenza attended a weight reduction clinic in Rooksville, but as part of his self-prescribed program to assist himself in the loss of several inches around the waist, Fernando smoked three marijuana cigarettes, or "joints," daily. He decided to smoke his first joint of the day as he headed home in his car from the clinic one afternoon.

A police officer approached him on the San Rolando Freeway and stopped the car to issue a citation for speeding, that is, traveling in excess of the speed limit. As Fernando handed the officer his driver's license, the officer smelled burnt marijuana, saw the joint, and saw an open envelope on the seat next to Fernando containing a substance that appeared like marijuana. The officer ordered Fernando out of the car, arrested him for unlawful possession of marijuana, and searched Fernando.

He then searched the passenger compartment of the car and found a sealed envelope under the backseat. Without asking Fernando's permission, the officer opened the envelope and discovered that it contained cocaine. He also found a jacket lying on the rear seat. The officer unzipped one of the jacket pockets and found more cocaine, and arrested Fernando for possession of cocaine.

Fernando was taken to the police station and immediately escorted to an interrogation room. He was given his *Miranda* warnings, waived his rights and gave a statement admitting to possession of cocaine and marijuana.

27. Which of the following is a correct statement of the applicable legal principles regarding the search of Fernando's automobile?

  (A) When a police officer has made a lawful custodial arrest of an occupant of an automobile, he may, as a contemporaneous incident of that arrest, search the passenger compartment of that automobile.
  (B) The exclusionary rule requires that if an officer conducts an unconstitutional search, the evidence acquired in the course of the officer's subsequent activities is inadmissible.
  (C) If the owner-occupant of an automobile effectively consents to a search of the automobile, the evidence gathered during the search is admissible.
  (D) One who drives an automobile on a public highway does not have a legitimate expectation of privacy.

28. Assuming Fernando's facts are accurate, which of the following allegations would be *LEAST* helpful in suppressing his statement?

  (A) Before Fernando gave the statement he was refused permission to use the bathroom.
  (B) Fernando had a private lawyer on retainer at the time he gave his statement.
  (C) Fernando's arrest was not based on probable cause.
  (D) Fernando could not speak English, and the warnings were given in English.

Question 29 is based on the following fact situation.

Defendant was arrested and prosecuted for the crime of confidence game (which in several states is a form of aggravated false pretenses). At trial, Defendant testified that she dressed up as a gypsy and prophesied Victim's imminent death. Defendant admitted that she told Victim she could save him if he brought a large sum of money wrapped in a handkerchief to a ritual. After the ritual, Defendant returned the handkerchief to Victim filled with waste paper rather than the money. After Defendant was convicted of confidence game, she moved for a new trial and offered the affidavits of several jurors who sat on the case.

29. An affidavit containing which of the following facts will most likely furnish Defendant's *BEST* basis for securing a new trial?

    (A) A juror misunderstood the judge's instructions regarding the burden of proof.
    (B) A juror in violation of the court's instructions read a newspaper article implicating Defendant in several other confidence game schemes.
    (C) A juror fell asleep during defense counsel's closing argument.
    (D) A juror admittedly stated during deliberations that he had a personal animosity toward Defendant.

Question 30 is based on the following fact situation.

While on routine patrol, police officers observed McAdoo make an illegal U-turn across Broad Street. After stopping McAdoo's car, they observed him reach under the driver's seat. They ordered him out of the car and saw a cellophane package protruding from under the seat. The package contained a white powdery substance which the officers suspected to be cocaine.

The officers placed McAdoo under arrest and put him in the rear of their patrol car. They then proceeded to search the rest of McAdoo's car. In the trunk they found an Uzi, a submachine gun that was later determined to be the weapon used in a liquor store robbery. Charged with that robbery, McAdoo moved to suppress the Uzi as evidence on the ground that the police did not have a warrant to search the trunk.

30. The best theory that the prosecution can use in support of the admissibility of the Uzi as evidence is that

    (A) the police conducted an automobile search
    (B) the police conducted an inventory search
    (C) the search was incident to a lawful arrest
    (D) the search was made under exigent circumstances

Question 31 is based on the following fact situation.

31. Defendant sold heroin to Morgan. Morgan was later stopped by police for speeding. The police searched Morgan's car and found the heroin concealed under the rear seat. Defendant is charged with illegally selling heroin.

    Defendant's motion to prevent introduction of the heroin into evidence will *MOST* probably be

    (A) granted, because the heroin was not in plain view
    (B) granted, because the scope of the search was excessive
    (C) denied, because Defendant has no standing to object to the search
    (D) denied, because the search was proper as incident to a valid full custodial arrest

Questions 32–33 are based on the following fact situation.

At about 2:00 P.M. a reliable police informant telephoned the police to report seeing two men in a red van selling narcotics outside a local high school. The informant gave a detailed description of the two men and the license number of the vehicle. A patrol car was immediately dispatched to the high school location. A few minutes later, the police saw a van matching the description parked about two blocks from the high school location. When the police approached, they saw one man fitting the description as provided and also saw a woman in the backseat of the van. Then they saw the woman leave the van and walk across the street to a bus stop.

The police proceeded to the van and opened the doors of the vehicle. The police then pried open a locked toolcase that was situated in the rear of the vehicle. Inside the police found an envelope which contained about one gram of cocaine. They then placed the driver of the vehicle under arrest. Immediately thereafter, the police opened the glove compartment and found a small amount of marijuana.

Thereupon, one of the officers walked across the street to where the woman (who was seen leaving the van) was standing. The officer went ahead and took her purse and looked inside. There he found a packet containing a gram of cocaine. The woman was then placed under arrest and charged with possession of a controlled dangerous substance.

32. The driver of the van was subsequently prosecuted and charged with two counts of possession of controlled dangerous substances. He filed a motion to exclude the cocaine and marijuana from evidence. His motion will *MOST* likely be granted with respect to

(A) the cocaine only
(B) the marijuana only
(C) both the cocaine and the marijuana
(D) neither the cocaine nor the marijuana

33. The woman was thereafter prosecuted and charged with illegal possession of a controlled dangerous substance based upon the cocaine confiscated from her pocketbook. She, too, filed a motion to exclude the cocaine from evidence. Her motion will *MOST* likely be

(A) granted, because the police did not have probable cause to conduct the search of her pocketbook
(B) granted, because the police did not secure a warrant before conducting the search
(C) denied, because the search was justified under "hot pursuit" since she was about to leave the scene of the crime
(D) denied, because she was sufficiently close or proximate to the crime scene to justify the warrantless search

Question 34 is based on the following fact situation.

The Bridgeport Police Department filed a complaint charging Bruce Gray with the sale of narcotic drugs in violation of a state statute and obtained a valid warrant for his arrest. Two police officers went to Gray's house, a two-story colonial, located at 2501 Bancroft Drive. After knocking at the door, they were admitted by a man who identified himself as Lloyd Gray. One of the policemen, Officer Brown, showed the man the arrest warrant and asked if he were Bruce Gray. He replied that he was Bruce's brother, Lloyd Gray, and that he was staying at Bruce's house while Bruce was away on a business trip. Officer Brown then asked the man for some identification. He was only able to produce an out-of-state driver's license in the name of Lloyd Gray. The other policeman, Officer Sawyer, then became suspicious and proceeded to frisk Lloyd. During the pat-down, Officer Sawyer found the following letter which read:

"Dear Lloyd,
If you could get rid of Bruce permanently, we could be together forever.

With love,
Jennifer"

Nervously, Lloyd then agreed to allow the policemen to search the house. The officers conducted an extensive two-hour search of the house and found nothing of interest to them.

As they were leaving, Officer Sawyer walked over to a parked car in the driveway of the house and noticed that the car's trunk was slightly open. When he looked in the trunk, Officer Sawyer discovered the body of Bruce Gray.

34. If Lloyd Gray's attorney files a motion to suppress the introduction of the letter into evidence, the court should rule that the evidence is

(A) admissible, because it was on the person, or in the presence of the person, who was later arrested
(B) admissible, because it was obtained pursuant to a valid search
(C) inadmissible, because the letter was obtained as a result of a non-consensual search and seizure
(D) inadmissible, because the letter was the fruit of an illegal search and seizure

Question 35 is based on the following fact situation.

Ken Klinger was arrested and charged with burglarizing Young's Pharmacy. The break-in allegedly occurred late one evening after the store had closed for business. Klinger was identified as the perpetrator of the crime by a film that was recorded during the burglary from a hidden camera. When Klinger was apprehended, he denied involvement in the crime and told the arresting officers that he had been out of town when the burglary occurred.

Prior to trial, Klinger's court-appointed attorney filed a motion requesting discovery of the videotape film that was recorded during the perpetration of the crime. The trial judge granted the defense request and ordered a duplicate copy of the videotape be sent to Klinger's attorney. Following the judge's ruling, the prosecuting attorney, pursuant to state law, then filed a discovery motion specifically asking Klinger whether he planned to raise an alibi defense. The prosecuting attorney also sought discovery of the identity of such an alibi witness.

35. Assume that the judge requires Klinger to respond as to whether the defendant intends to raise an alibi defense. Should the judge also require Klinger to disclose the identity of the alibi witness?

(A) yes, because if the defendant is constitutionally required to give notice of an alibi, then the disclosure order only affects the time of disclosure of the witness's identity

(B) yes, because the defendant waived any claim of privilege *ab initio* when he sought discovery of the film from the prosecution

(C) no, because by requiring the defendant to reveal information before he is tactically ready to do so substantially impairs his ability to successfully defend himself

(D) no, because such disclosure constitutes an implied representation that is testimonial in character, and thus violates the defendant's privilege against self-incrimination

Question 36 is based on the following fact situation.

Tito was driving his van along a public road one night. Police Officer Fuentes, who was driving behind Tito, decided to make a random stop of Tito's vehicle to check his license and registration. Officer Fuentes pulled Tito's van over to the side of the road and then walked up to the driver's side of the vehicle. When he came alongside the driver's window, Fuentes asked Tito for his identification. As Tito was thumbing through his wallet, the officer shined his flashlight into the van and spotted a plastic bag containing marijuana lying on the floor under the backseat. Officer Fuentes then arrested Tito and charged him with possession of marijuana.

36. At his trial for illegal possession of narcotics, Tito moved to suppress the use of the marijuana as evidence. His motion should be

(A) granted, because under the "poisonous tree" doctrine the marijuana was a fruit of an illegal search

(B) granted, because the police officer did not have probable cause or a reasonable suspicion to believe that Tito's van contained narcotics

(C) denied, because the marijuana was in plain view when the police officer shined his flashlight inside the van

(D) denied, because the seizure of the marijuana was made pursuant to a lawful investigatory stop

Question 37 is based on the following fact situation.

The state of Marlboro has recently enacted the following anti-smoking statute:

"It shall be a misdemeanor for any person to smoke a cigarette, cigar, or pipe in any restaurant, bar, cafe, or other establishment within the state that serves food, beer, wine, or liquor. Whoever violates this ordinance shall be fined not more than five hundred dollars, or imprisoned not more than thirty days, or both."

Nick O'Teen was tried in state court for violating the anti-smoking statute. The prosecution's evidence consisted of the testimony of Philip Morris, a patron of Chesterfield's Bar and Grill, who was disturbed by O'Teen's cigar smoking at the restaurant. At the close of all the evidence, O'Teen's lawyer moved for a dismissal of the charge on the ground that applying the statute to smoking at a public restaurant would violate the defendant's equal protection rights. The trial judge agreed and granted the motion.

The state prosecutor appealed the ruling under a statute that permitted prosecutorial appeals in such circumstances. The state won the appeal, but the prosecutor decided not to reprosecute O'Teen. However, the city attorney in the city in which Chesterfield's was located then sought to prosecute O'Teen for the same incident under the city's anti-smoking ordinance, which was identical to the state statute. The city attorney planned to call as her only witness Philip Morris, who testified at O'Teen's first trial. O'Teen moved to dismiss on the ground that the prosecution of the city charge would violate his rights against double jeopardy.

37. The court should

   (A) grant the motion, because jeopardy attached in the first prosecution
   (B) grant the motion, because the law and the evidence will be identical at the second trial
   (C) deny the motion, because the city and the state are separate sovereigns
   (D) deny the motion, because the granting of O'Teen's motion to dismiss was not a judgment of acquittal since it did not resolve any factual elements of the statutory offense

Question 38 is based on the following fact situation.

While parked on a downtown street in Brownsville at 7 P.M. on Monday, Officer Stork noticed a man sauntering down the street whistling. As the man came under a street light, Stork recognized him as Hendricks, a conviction parole from a neighboring state. Stork got out, stood in front of Hendricks, and asked him to give an account of himself. Hendricks replied, "I'm Ronnie Reagan, you dope … get out of my way or the Secret Service will gun you down," and reached into his coat pocket to bring something out, which he held in his clenched fist. Stork forced Hendricks's hand open and found a number of diamond rings therein. Just then the police radio in Stork's car announced that the burglar alarm of Rodeo's Jewelry Store had rung in police headquarters. Believing that Hendricks was responsible for burglarizing the jewelry store, Officer Stork arrested him and took him to the police station where he was booked and fingerprinted. After he was given his *Miranda* warnings, Hendricks requested to speak to Alzado, his attorney. Officer Stork led Hendricks to a telephone and asked him if he knew Alzado's telephone number. Hendricks responded, "Yes, it's 523-0777." Stork dialed the number and waited until a voice answered, "Law offices." The officer then handed the telephone receiver to Hendricks. As Stork was walking out the room, he heard Hendricks say, "Hello, Alzado, it's me Hendricks. I just got arrested after robbing Rodeo's Jewelry Store."

38. At trial, Officer Stork is called to testify to what Hendricks told Alzado during their telephone conversation. Upon proper objection by Hendricks's attorney, Stork's proposed testimony should be

   (A) admitted, because Hendricks's confession was not coerced
   (B) admitted, because the statement was not the product of interrogation
   (C) excluded, because Officer Stork's conduct violated Hendricks's Sixth Amendment right to counsel
   (D) excluded, because Officer Stork's conduct violated the confidentiality of Hendricks's attorney-client privilege

Question 39 is based on the following fact situation.

Billy Butler was booked on a commercial airplane flight from San Antonio to Phoenix. When Billy arrived at the airport, two undercover police narcotics agents observed him. His appearance and actions led the police to believe that he fit the description of a predetermined profile of a drug courier. The officers approached Billy and told him they wanted to detain him for questioning. Billy asked, "What for?" The police explained that they were narcotics agents assigned to the airport and that he fit the profile of a drug dealer. They then asked Billy to hand over his overnight bag. Billy refused. The officers then explained that he wouldn't be permitted to board the plane unless they inspected the contents of his bag. Billy told the officers that he changed his mind and decided not to fly to Phoenix after all. The officers still requested that Billy turn his overnight bag over to them. Billy did so and then he was given permission to leave the airport.

The next day, the police had a dog sniff Billy's bag for narcotics. The results of this search gave police suspicion to believe that the bag contained narcotics. They opened Billy's bag and found a cache of heroin inside. Billy was subsequently arrested and charged with unlawful possession of narcotics.

39. At trial, Billy's attorney moves to prevent introduction of the heroin into evidence. This motion will *MOST* likely be

   (A) granted, because the police did not have probable cause to hold the bag overnight for the search
   (B) granted, because the heroin was discovered as a result of an unlawful airport detection
   (C) denied, because since Billy fit the predetermined profile of a narcotics courier, the police had probable cause to conduct the search of his bag
   (D) denied, because the search resulted from a lawful airport detention

Question 40 is based on the following fact situation.

Smirk was standing on the street corner at South and Broad when Police Officer Eckerk approached him. Officer Eckerk gently grabbed Smirk's arm and said, "Hey, I want to talk to you." Smirk responded, "About what ... I'm in a hurry to go home and watch the Phillies game on TV." Officer Eckerk then remarked, "Listen, what were you doing at Lefty's Liquor Store last Saturday night?" Smirk stated, "All right, man, I was there during the robbery." Whereupon, Officer Eckerk placed Smirk under arrest and charged him with robbery.

Smirk was taken to police headquarters where he was booked. For the first time, he was given his *Miranda* warnings. He then waived his rights and confessed to being an accessory during the liquor store robbery. Afterwards, the court appointed an attorney to represent Smirk. The attorney moved to suppress both statements Smirk gave to the police. The trial court granted the motion with respect to the first statement. Smirk's attorney now moves to suppress the second statement given at the police headquarters.

40. This motion should be

   (A) granted, because statement two was a fruit of statement one
   (B) granted, because since statement one was excluded, statement two must also be tainted
   (C) not granted, if Officer Eckerk reasonably believed that he was not required to give Smirk *Miranda* warnings when he initially detained him
   (D) not granted, because statement two was volunteered after a knowing *Miranda* waiver

Question 41 is based on the following fact situation.

On May 3,1984, two men held up Uribe's Liquor Store in the city of Southland. During the robbery, one of the participants shot and killed Uribe, the proprietor. On February 3,1985, Southland police detectives arrested Gonzalez after obtaining reliable information that Gonzalez was the robber who was responsible for killing Uribe. Afterwards Gonzalez was taken to the station house where he was "booked" for the crime and then incarcerated. The next day, the prosecuting attorney made a decision to delay indictment until he could discover the identity of Gonzalez's accomplice. Gonzalez was then released from police custody. In this jurisdiction the statute of limitations for murder is five years.

Five months later the prosecuting attorney, after unsuccessfully attempting to secure information on Gonzalez's cohort, indicted Gonzalez, charging him with felony murder. Shortly before trial, the only eyewitness to the crime died. He would have testified that Gonzalez did not participate in the robbery.

41. Gonzalez's motion to dismiss the indictment because of the delay between the date of the crime and the date of the indictment will *MOST* probably be

    (A) granted, because the prosecutor is constitutionally required to press charges, if at all, within a reasonable time after probable cause is established
    (B) granted, because the delay in prosecuting Gonzalez actually prejudiced him
    (C) denied, because preindictment delay does not violate the Constitution as long as it does not exceed an applicable statute of limitations
    (D) denied, because the delay was not excessive and was for a permissible purpose

Question 42 is based on the following fact situation.

The Commonwealth of Josephina has adopted a system of bifurcated trials in cases in which a defendant's insanity is in issue. According to the bifurcated trial system, whenever a defendant pleads not guilty to an offense by reason of insanity, two trials will be held. The first one will simply determine whether the defendant has committed the offense for which she is charged. This trial will not address the issue of insanity. In the event that it is found that the defendant has, in fact, committed the offense, then a second trial will be conducted to determine whether she should be exculpated for the criminal action by reason of insanity.

Regina was arrested and charged with the murder of Crawford. She pleaded not guilty by reason of insanity. At her first trial, the state introduced evidence showing that Regina was having an affair with Crawford. When Crawford tried to break off their relationship, Regina shot and killed him during a lover's quarrel. Regina was then called to testify in her own behalf. She testified that she had been living with Crawford for two years prior to the time of his death. During that period she had undergone psychiatric treatment and was diagnosed as being schizophrenic. She further testified that at the time Crawford was killed, she was under the influence of LSD. While she was hallucinating, she remembered perceiving Crawford as Satan and shot at this satanic figure in order to free herself from his evil spell. She then testified that she didn't believe shooting Satan was morally wrong. The prosecuting attorney objected to Regina's testimony. Over such objections, the trial judge admitted Regina's testimony.

42. Was the trial judge correct in admitting Regina's testimony?

(A) no, because proof of mental disease requires the use of expert testimony
(B) no, because testimony relating to her belief that she didn't know what she was doing was wrong, is not relevant until the second trial
(C) yes, because her testimony is relevant to the mental state necessary for the commission of the crime
(D) yes, because her testimony is relevant to the issue of self-defense

Question 43 is based on the following fact situation.

Defendant is arrested and charged with shoplifting. He claims he intended to pay for the item he took and requests an attorney and a jury trial. Both requests are denied by the judge and Defendant is found guilty. The maximum penalty for shoplifting is a $500 fine and six months in jail. Defendant is sentenced to three months in jail which he is allowed to serve on weekends in the county detention center.

43. Defendant claims his constitutional rights have been violated. Is he correct?

(A) no, because his actual sentence was only three months
(B) yes, because Defendant was denied the right to counsel
(C) yes, because Defendant was denied the right to a jury trial
(D) yes, because defendant was denied both the right to counsel and the right to a jury trial

Question 44 is based on the following fact situation.

Herman was a senior pre-med student at Slippery Rock University. Before a big football game with arch rival Transylvania Tech, Herman attended a pep rally at the university football field. During the pep rally, the students drank beer, sang songs, and gave members of the football team fervent cheers. After the rally ended, Herman was walking toward his car when he felt the need to take a "leak." He then strutted across the street to a municipal park and urinated against a tree. In this jurisdiction, urinating in public is a misdemeanor.

Unknown to Herman, a meter maid who was ticketing cars in the area witnessed the incident and wrote down the license number of Herman's vehicle as he drove off. She immediately gave the information to the police, who did a DMV check and learned Herman's identity and home address. Within an hour, the police went to Herman's house and forcibly entered the dwelling without a search warrant. While searching his home, they found Herman studying in an upstairs bedroom. After giving him his *Miranda* warnings, Herman confessed to the crime.

44. Herman was thereafter prosecuted for the misdemeanor of urinating in public. If Herman moves to suppress evidence of the statement that he made to the police when he was apprehended, the motion should be

(A) denied, because Herman received *Miranda* warnings and was not compelled to incriminate himself
(B) denied, because Herman volunteered the confession
(C) sustained, because the police lacked probable cause to search Herman's home
(D) sustained, because Herman's statement was the product of a warrant-less entry of his home

Question 45 is based on the following fact situation.

Reefer, an indigent, had hitchhiked to California from Arkansas. The day Reefer arrived in California he was arrested and charged with possession of less than one ounce of marijuana. Under the relevant California statute, possession of less than one ounce of marijuana is a misdemeanor, punishable by a maximum of one year in jail and/or a fine of $500. At trial, Reefer pleaded not guilty and requested that an attorney be appointed to represent him. The trial judge refused to honor Reefer's request for an attorney.

45. If Reefer is subsequently found guilty, which of the following is the *MOST* severe sentence that can constitutionally be imposed?

    (A) $500 fine
    (B) six months in jail
    (C) one year in jail
    (D) no sentence because Reefer was denied the right to counsel

Question 46 is based on the following fact situation.

Mary Ann was a 14 year-old girl who attended St. Patrick's parochial school in Elizabeth, New Jersey. One afternoon after school, Mary Ann went into Lee's Drug Store. While browsing, she picked up a Snickers candy bar and placed it in her coat pocket. She left the store without paying for it.

Unknown to Mary Ann, the store security guard, Bob, saw what she had done. He immediately ran outside, grabbed her arm, and said, "Hey, girl, do you like being a thief?" Mary Ann broke down and started crying. She then told Bob that she was hungry because she hadn't eaten any lunch.

46. At a juvenile delinquency court hearing, Bob proposes to testify to what Mary Ann said. Upon objection by Mary Ann's attorney, the *STRONGEST* reason for admitting her statement will be because

    (A) *Miranda* warnings need not be given to juveniles
    (B) Bob's remark was an accusation not an interrogation
    (C) Bob was not employed by an agency of the government
    (D) Mary Ann was not in custody

Question 47 is based on the following fact situation.

Julie was employed as a cocktail waitress at the Lenapee Inn. When she got off work at 2:00 A.M. one night, she was accosted by Josie in the parking lot. Josie, who was a transient, pulled out a knife and ordered Julie into her car. Grabbing her pocketbook, he took Julie's wallet which contained about $35. Josie then directed Julie to drive to an isolated wooded area where he raped her repeatedly. Before leaving, he stabbed her to death. Josie was subsequently arrested and indicted separately for the crimes of armed robbery, rape, and felony murder with the underlying felony being the rape.

47. With respect to double jeopardy, which of the following statements is *MOST* accurate?

   (A) Josie may be tried for each offense separately and may be convicted of each with sentences running consecutively.
   (B) Josie may be tried for the two separate offenses of armed robbery and felony murder and may be convicted of both with sentences running consecutively.
   (C) Josie may be tried for the two separate offenses of armed robbery and felony murder and may be convicted of both with the armed robbery sentence running consecutively with concurrent sentences for the felony murder and rape.
   (D) Josie may be tried for the single offense of felony murder and sentenced for that crime only.

Question 48 is based on the following fact situation.

Elvis and his girlfriend Priscilla broke into Bobby's house late at night with the intent to steal Bobby's stereo system. Although they believed that Bobby was away on a business trip, actually he was asleep in an upstairs bedroom. While they were inside the house, Priscilla announced that she had changed her mind and urged Elvis to leave.

Bobby, who was awakened by the noise downstairs, descended the staircase to investigate. Upon seeing Bobby, Priscilla again urged Elvis to flee. Instead Elvis attacked Bobby and then tied him up with rope. Thereupon, Elvis and Priscilla departed with Bobby's stereo equipment. After they left, Bobby choked to death from the ropes while trying to free himself.

Priscilla and Elvis were charged with burglary but were acquitted. Thereafter, Priscilla and Elvis were apprehended and prosecuted for felony murder with the underlying felony being burglary.

48. With respect to Priscilla and Elvis's criminal liability for felony murder, which of the following is *MOST* correct?

   (A) The burglary acquittal precludes any subsequent prosecution under the doctrine of *res judicata*.
   (B) The burglary acquittal precludes any subsequent prosecution under the doctrine of collateral estoppel.
   (C) The burglary acquittal precludes any subsequent prosecution under the doctrine of double jeopardy.
   (D) The burglary acquittal does not preclude subsequent prosecution for felony murder.

Question 49 is based on the following fact situation.

Parker, a suspected drug dealer, was arrested after selling three grams of "angel dust," a controlled dangerous substance, to undercover police agents. He was subsequently convicted in state court of possession with intent to distribute narcotics. Following his conviction, Parker was sentenced to a prison term of ten years. After being sentenced, Parker's attorney, Ball, appealed the conviction citing jury misconduct. While his appeal was pending, Parker was then indicted by both a federal and a state grand jury for conspiracy to distribute the same "angel dust."

49. Parker's attorney filed motions to dismiss each of the new indictments on the ground that they violate the Double Jeopardy Clause. In all likelihood, the Double Jeopardy Clause requires the dismissal of

   (A) both indictments
   (B) the state indictment but not the federal indictment
   (C) the federal indictment but not the state indictment
   (D) neither of the indictments

Question 50 is based on the following fact situation.

The police received an anonymous tip informing them that Cracker, a pharmacist, was engaged in the illegal manufacture of synthetic cocaine. As part of its investigation, the police placed an electronic tracking device on Cracker's car. The "beeper" device was attached to the underbody of Cracker's car while it was parked outside his home. The police did not secure a warrant before installing the "beeper."

By means of the "beeper," the police were able to trail Cracker's movements. The police followed Cracker every day for almost a month. Finally, one day the police tracked Cracker's car to a vacant warehouse on the outskirts of town. While Cracker was inside the building, the police peered in the window and saw drug paraphernalia and equipment used in the manufacture of synthetic cocaine.

Based on these observations, the police secured a search warrant and gained entry into the building. Once inside, the police arrested Cracker and confiscated a large quantity of synthetic cocaine that had just been produced.

50. At his trial for illegal possession and manufacture of a controlled dangerous substance, Cracker moves to suppress the cocaine confiscated by the police. Cracker's motion will *MOST* likely be

   (A) granted, because the information upon which the search warrant was based was illegally obtained by means of the "beeper" device
   (B) granted, because the seizure must be suppressed as the "fruit" of an antecedent illegal search
   (C) denied, because the police could have discovered the location of the warehouse simply by following Cracker's car
   (D) denied, but only if the electronic surveillance of Cracker's car did not exceed 30 days

CRIMINAL PROCEDURE EXPLANATORY ANSWERS

1. (C) With *Miranda,* the Fifth Amendment privilege against compelled self-incrimination became the basis for ruling upon the admissibility of a confession. It should be noted that *Miranda* warnings (and a valid waiver) are prerequisites to the admissibility of any statement made by the accused *during a custodial interrogation.* Generally speaking, an interrogation will be considered custodial if the individual is *not* free to leave. According to *Orozco v. Texas,* 394 U.S. 324, 89 S.Ct. 1095, (1969), the U.S. Supreme Court held that a person is in "custody" if he is not free to leave, even if the questioning occurs in the individual's bedroom. In the present example, the facts do not indicate that Smelson was in police "custody" for *Miranda* purposes. Therefore, choice (C) is the best answer because Smelson's statements were not made during a custodial interrogation. Note that choice (C) is a better answer than (D) because the issue here is whether the police questioning was "on the scene" or "custodial."

2. (A) Under the voluntariness standard, the issue of whether a defendant's confession will be admissible is determined by a "totality of circumstances" approach which examines both (1) the nature of the defendant, that is, age, sex, race, mental condition, physical condition, history of drug or alcohol abuse, and (2) the nature of the police conduct. These factors help determine the extent to which the defendant's ability to submit to external pressures has been affected. Confessions obtained under conditions where the defendant's free choice is significantly impaired are likely to be found coercive. However, where the police employ a "false friend," such as a jail cell "plant," and by deception the defendant is unaware that the person with whom he is conversing is a police officer or agent, a confession thereby obtained will not necessarily be involuntary, even if the defendant mistakenly believed the person could be trusted. LaFave, **Criminal Procedure**, p. 268. Choice (B) is incorrect. Nevertheless, where actual or threatened physical harm or brutality is involved, the Court has readily found there to be coercion sufficient to negate the defendant's free will. In *Arizona v. Fulminante,* 59 LW 4235 (1991) under similar facts regarding the murder of defendant's stepdaughter, the Court held that a credible threat of physical violence is sufficient to support a finding of coercion. By intimidating Kent with the threat of physical violence from other inmates unless he sought Norris's protection, the government employed coercive tactics in obtaining Kent's confession. Therefore, choice (A) is correct.

3. (C) In *United States v. Calandra,* 414 U.S. 338, 94 S.Ct. 613 (1974), the United States Supreme Court refused to extend the exclusionary rule to grand jury proceedings. A divided Supreme Court (6–3) noted that "in deciding whether to extend the exclusionary rule to grand jury proceedings, we must weigh the potential injury to the historic role and functions of the grand jury against the potential benefits of the rule as applied in this context. *It is evident that this extension of the exclusionary rule would seriously impede the grand jury.*"

4. (D) In *Miranda* the U.S. Supreme Court said "if the individual states that he wants an attorney, the interrogation must cease until an attorney is present." In addition, the Court stated that "if the interrogation continues without the presence of an attorney and a statement is taken, a heavy burden rests on the government to demonstrate that the defendant knowingly and intelligently waived his privilege against self-incrimination and his right to retained or appointed counsel." In the present example, Cruz told the police he would have nothing to say unless his attorney was present. Thereafter, the police drove him to the stationhouse, placed him in an interrogation room, and resumed questioning *(without* further *Miranda advisement)*. Since Cruz's statement was the product of renewed questioning, there is a virtually irrebuttable presumption of compulsion. Furthermore, in *Commonwealth v.* White, 371 N.E.2d 777 (1977), affirmed by an equally divided court 439 U.S. 280, 99 S.Ct. 712, it was held that statements obtained in violation of *Miranda* cannot be used for the purpose of establishing probable cause to obtain a valid search warrant. As a consequence, choice (D) is correct.

5. **(C)** Former testimony under **F.R.E.** 804(b)(1) is defined as "testimony given as a witness at another hearing of the same or a different proceeding, or in a deposition taken in compliance with law in the course of the same or another proceeding, if the party against whom the testimony is now offered, or, in a civil action or proceeding, a predecessor in interest, had an opportunity and similar motive to develop the testimony by direct, cross, or redirect examination." The transcript of Harper's testimony at the preliminary hearing will be admissible as former testimony and Swane's claim will be denied. Similarly, in *California v. Green,* 399 U.S. 149 (1969), the use of preliminary hearing testimony of a witness who was unavailable at trial was held not to violate the defendant's constitutional right of confrontation. Choice (C) is thus correct. Choice (A) is incorrect because the opportunity to cross-examine Harper at trial is unnecessary since he was already cross-examined by Swane's attorney at the preliminary hearing concerning the testimony given at that time. Choice (B) is incorrect because under **F.R.E.** 804(a)(2), refusal to testify constitutes unavailability. Finally, choice (D) is incorrect because it mixes two different rules. First, under **F.R.E.** 804(b)(3), a declaration against interest must be against the declarant's (penal) interest at the time when made. Harper's statement incriminated Swane as the perpetrator, not himself. Second, a coconspirator's admission under **F.R.E.** 801 (d)(2)(e) is defined as nonhearsay—not as a hearsay exception—under the Federal Rules.

6. **(A)** In the case of *Edmondson v. Leesville Concrete Co.,* 59 LW 4574 (1991), the Court held a ***private litigant in a civil case may not use peremptory challenges to exclude jurors on account of race.*** Race-based exclusion of potential jurors in a civil case violates the excluded person's equal protection rights. If Clapper used its peremptory challenge to exclude jurors on account of race, Lionel's appeal will be successful. Choice (A) is correct. Choice (B) is incorrect even though it addressed a possible claim by Lionel. Lionel's appeal is based on failure to offer a race-neutral explanation for the peremptory challenges, rather than a denial of right to a fair trial, therefore Choice (A) is the better response. Choice (D) is incorrect because the *Edmondson* holding forbids race-based exclusion of potential civil jurors. Choice (C) is incorrect. The *Edmondson* case addressed ***the issue of third-party standing***

and concluded that a private civil litigant may raise the equal protection claim of a person whom the opposing party has excluded from jury service on account of race.

7. (C) The *Miranda* right to silence can be waived either expressly or impliedly. *Miranda* waiver is based on **voluntariness** as determined by the "totality of circumstances." To determine if a knowing and intelligent waiver has occurred, the Court views both the (1) **competence of the defendant,** i.e., age, experience, intelligence, and ability to fully understand the warnings, and (2) **the conduct of the police,** namely as to whether there has been overreaching. In the present example, choice (A) is wrong because defendants have generally been **un**successful in claiming that their *Miranda* waivers should be held invalid because they were either intoxicated or under the influence of drugs or medication at that time. Likewise, choice (B) is wrong inasmuch as the "personal characteristics of the defendant existing at the time of the purported waiver are relevant only as they relate to police overreaching." See *Colorado v. Connelly*, 107 S.Ct. 515 (1986), where the Court rejected a state court ruling that a defendant's *Miranda* waiver was not voluntary because he suffered from a psychosis that interfered with his ability to make free and rational choices. The Court concluded that "*Miranda* protects defendants against government coercion but goes no further than that." As a result, choice (C) is the best answer because Defendant was subjected to persistent questioning for two hours before waiving his *Miranda* rights. According to LaFave, courts have held waivers invalid where the defendant had been held in custody an extended period of time before being given the warnings, or where the defendant had first been subjected to persistent questioning. Lastly, choice (D) is incorrect because in *Fare v. Michael C.*, 442 U.S. 707 (1979), the Court held that **a juvenile's request to have his probation officer present was not a per se invocation of Miranda rights.**

8. (C) The clear rule in *Massiah v. United States*, 377 U.S. 201, 84 S.Ct. 1199 (1964), is that **once adversary proceedings have been commenced against an individual, he (or she) has a right to legal representation when the government interrogates him (or her).** As in *Brewer v. Williams*, 430 U.S. 387, 97, S.Ct. 1232 (1977), the critical issue in this example is whether, after judicial proceedings have been initiated against the defendant, a police informant elicited information from him in the absence of defense counsel. According to *Brewer v. Williams*, proof of formal interrogation is unnecessary to invoke the protection of the Sixth Amendment. A conversation that is tantamount to interrogation is sufficient. Similarly, since Gilley was under arraignment, Gatlin could not effectively "interrogate" (i.e., attempt to obtain information reasonably calculated to induce conversations relative to the crime) him in the absence of defense counsel.

9. (B) Students should note that in order for one to be found guilty of murder under the felony murder rule, he must also be found guilty of the underlying felony. Thus, as in the present example, if a defendant is found innocent of the underlying felony, he cannot be found guilty of felony murder. Briefly, the felony murder rule provides that one whose conduct brought about an unintended death in the commission or attempted commission of a felony was guilty of murder.

Multistate Nuance Chart:

CRIMINAL PROCEDURE

MIRANDA	MASSIAH	HOFFA
1. *custodial* interrogation 2. Once a defendant is in police custody, he must be advised of his *Miranda* rights: (a) right to remain silent; (b) any statement he does make may be used against him; (c) he has the right to have an attorney present; and (d) if he cannot afford an attorney, one will be appointed for him. 3. Only the defendant in custody must be warned. 4. *Miranda* does not apply to spontaneous, unsolicited confessions (as when a defendant blurts out incriminating statements or voluntarily confesses without prodding).	1. *post-indictment* interrogation 2. A defendant has the right to counsel when the police seek to interrogate him. 3. interrogation by police informant 4. Interrogation results when the police (or its informants) seek to elicit incriminating statements from the defendant.	1. defendant *not* in police custody 2. The government did *not* "plant" or encourage informant to interrogate (or elicit incriminating information from the defendant). 3. Eavesdropping was committed by the defendant's "friend," who later volunteered to become an informer. 4. Eavesdropping is permissible because there is no constitutional right to protect misplaced confidences. 5. Each party to a conversation must assume the risk that the other will reveal the substance of the conversation.

10. (C) With the new distribution of Criminal Law/Procedure questions as of the July 1997 MBE, Criminal Procedure will be more heavily tested than in previous years. Of the 33 questions in this area, approximately 19 will deal with Criminal law and 14 will cover Criminal Procedure. In this regard, **students should anticipate at least four or five search and seizure questions.** A search made under authority of a search warrant may extend to the entire area covered by the warrant's description. For example, if the warrant authorizes a search of "premises" at a certain described geographical location, buildings standing on that land may be searched. If the place is identified by street number, the search may extend to those buildings within the curtilage and the yard within the curtilage. LaFave points out that the **permissible intensity of the search within the described premises is determined by the description of the things to be seized.** Here, the warrant covered the seizure of a stolen "Yamaha at 789 Mesa Drive." When the police arrived at the defendant's home, they noticed a Sanyo stereo in the living room. The first question is whether the police under the "plain view" doctrine were permitted to seize the Sanyo which also turned out to be stolen. In *Coolidge v. New Hampshire*, the Supreme Court held that the "plain view" doctrine is legitimate only where it is immediately apparent to the police that they have evidence before them; the "plain view" doctrine may not be used to extend a general exploratory search from one object to another. In fact, in *Arizona v. Hicks* it was held that full probable cause was needed to pick up an item of stereo equipment to ascertain its serial number (which revealed it was stolen). Based on *Hicks*, the Sanyo was unlawfully seized since the police needed to "further inspect" it to determine its stolen status. By the same token, the police did not have authority to continue to search Leech's home after discovering the stolen Yamaha (specified in the warrant). When the ***purpose(s) of the warrant have been carried out, the authority to search is at an end.*** Choice (C) is correct because the defendant's motion to exclude the Sanyo and the Marantz stereos will be granted.

11. **(A)** Another distinction frequently tested on the MBE is between ***"harmless error" and "plain error." If an error has not resulted in damage to the complaining party, it may be deemed harmless and a new trial need not be had.*** For an example of "harmless error" see *U.S. v. Shepard*, 538 F.2d 107 (1976): permitting psychiatrist who examined defendant to determine competency to stand trial and to testify about alibi related to him by defendant. On the other hand, even where no timely objection is made, ***if a grave injustice might result from a serious trial error, the Appellate Court may still order a new trial.*** For example, in *U.S. v. Sisto*, 534 F.2d 616 (1976), it was held to be "plain error" where the judge failed to instruct the jury that an undercover agent's statements (concerning what an alleged accomplice said about defendant's activities) should be considered only as impeachment evidence and not for its truth. Choice (A) is a better answer than (B) because it addresses the issue that "plain error" affects substantial rights to such a serious degree that a new trial can be given (even though Loggins's attorney did not object to Messina's testimony).

12. **(A)** Major has the ***burden of production of proving his insanity*** at the time of the offense. On the issue of lack of responsibility because of insanity, the ***initial burden of going forward (the production burden) is placed upon the defendant*** in every jurisdiction in the United States. The burden of persuasion, on the other hand, after the issue of insanity has been raised, is upon the prosecution. LaFave and Scott, in **Criminal Law**, p. 312, note that the defendant's production burden is often stated in terms of a presumption of sanity; most people are sane, and thus the defendant in the particular case is presumed to be sane until some amount of evidence to the contrary is produced. Students should note that the Model Penal Code takes the view as to the affirmative defenses—the accused has the first burden of producing evidence.

13. **(C)** In *Geders v. United States*, 425 U.S. 80 (1976), the trial court ordered the defendant not to consult with his attorney during an overnight recess which separated the direct examination and the cross-examination of the defendant. The court of appeals affirmed the conviction because the defendant made no

claim of prejudice from the order. The Supreme Court reversed, holding the 17-hour denial of counsel, regardless of demonstrated evidence, constituted a deprivation of the effective assistance of counsel. LaFave and Israel, **Criminal Procedure**, p. 511. This "evidence" question is obviously very difficult since it involves knowledge of a specific "criminal procedure" case. In light of *Geders*, choice (C) is correct, since the judge's instruction to the defendant denied him his Sixth Amendment right to counsel.

14. (B) The state's best rebuttal to Morris's argument of illegal seizure of the gun would be that Morris was not being interrogated in the police car when he revealed the location of the gun to the police officers. The United States Supreme Court in *Rhode Island v. Innis*, 446 U.S. 21 (1980), held that where a suspect in crimes committed with a shotgun told police of the gun's location after hearing police talk of a handicapped child's possibility of finding a gun (when the suspect was being transported to a police station), it was not an interrogation in violation of the suspect's *Miranda* rights. In the *Innis* case, as in our factual presentation, the suspect upon arrest was advised of his *Miranda* rights and refused to make any statements without an attorney present. Furthermore, neither suspect was questioned or interrogated by the police officers during the ride to the police station. Rather, the suspect acted voluntarily when he heard the police officers mention the possibility of children being injured by the gun. It is important to note that the Supreme Court has held that "interrogation" under *Miranda* refers not only to express questioning, but also to any words or actions on the part of the police that the police should know or should have known are reasonably likely to elicit an incriminating response from the suspect. In our factual presentation, nothing suggests that the police were aware that Morris was particularly susceptible to an appeal to his conscience concerning the safety of small children.

15. (D) Morris's statement during the line-up would not be testimonial in nature. Therefore, Harry's line-up identification may be introduced by the prosecution at trial. Students should note that appearing in a line-up and being required to make statements during the line-up procedure are not testimonial activities, but demonstrative in nature. Thus, a suspect does not have a right under the Fifth Amendment privilege against self-incrimination to refuse to appear or make a statement during a line-up. See *U.S. v. Wade*, 388 U.S. 218, 87 S.Ct. 1926 (1967), where the U.S. Supreme Court held that an accused's privilege against self-incrimination was not violated by the line-up itself or by requiring the accused to speak the words allegedly uttered by the robber.

16. (A) The Sixth Amendment, which is applicable to the states through the Fourteenth Amendment, guarantees an accused the right to be represented by counsel. In our factual situation, Janis's dual representation of both Mike and Morris created a conflict of interest which violated Mike's Sixth Amendment rights. The U.S. Supreme Court in *Cuyler v. Sullivan*, 446 U.S. 335 (1980), held that multiple representation in the sense that the same counsel actively represented two defendants charged with the same crime does not violate the Sixth Amendment unless it gives rise to a conflict of interest. The court further stated that since a conflict of interest inheres in almost every instance of multiple representation, a defendant who objects to it must have the opportunity to show a potential conflict which imperils his right to a fair trial. It should be noted that Mike's incriminating testimony about Morris at trial should have been sufficient for the court to inquire as to whether or not a conflict of interest existed over Janis's dual representation of Morris and Mike. In other words, the trial court more or less had a duty to inquire as to whether there was a conflict of interest as a result of Mike's defense. Although choice (B) provides a correct statement of fact, choice (A) is the better or more preferable alternative since it provides a correct statement of law.

17. **(D)** Here's another classic Multistate example dealing with waiver of right to counsel. Students must be cognizant that a defendant may waive his constitutional right to assistance of counsel provided he does so "knowingly and intelligently," which means it must have been the product of a reasoned and deliberate choice based upon adequate knowledge of what the assistance of counsel encompasses. A defendant who acts knowingly and intelligently in waiving his right to counsel has a right to proceed pro se since he (or she) must be free to decide if counsel will be to his (or her) advantage in the case. In the present case, Lightfoot had the right to waive representation by counsel [*Faretta v. California*, 422 U.S. 806 (1975)]. Although this right of waiver may be denied if a defendant is not competent to represent himself, there is no evidence that Lightfoot was incompetent. Therefore, his conviction should be overturned since he was not given the right to represent himself. In addition, Lightfoot should not be required to reimburse the state for his lawyer fees due to the fact that counsel was imposed upon him in violation of his constitutional rights. Note, however, that a state can recover legal costs from an indigent who is convicted and is subsequently able to pay [*Fuller v. Oregon*, 417 U.S. 40 (1974)].

18. **(D)** As a general rule, most crimes require the following elements: (1) an act, (2) mental fault (or "guilty mind"), (3) concurrence (or act plus mental state), (4) harm, and (5) causation. With crimes so defined as to require not merely conduct but also a specified result of conduct, the defendant's conduct must be the "legal" or "proximate" cause of the result. In the example provided herein, the fact that Brennan fled the scene of the accident (in violation of the hit-and-run statute) was not the "legal" cause of Hand's death. Rather, Hand's death resulted from the Pinto's gas tank exploding, which was caused by the collision with the tractor-trailer. Note that although choice (C) is also conceivably correct, alternative (D) is preferred because it refers to the requirement of a *causal connection,* which is a material element in both criminal and tort law.

19. **(D)** The facts in this hypothetical are taken from *California v. Byers*, 402 U.S. 424, 91 S.Ct. 1535 (1971), in which the U.S. Supreme Court held that a statute requiring a motorist involved in an accident to stop and give his name and address did not involve self-incrimination in a constitutional sense. Students should be aware that choice (C), is wrong because violation of the statute results in a (criminal) sentence of imprisonment. Therefore, clearly, the legislative intent was not directed for the disclosure requirement to be used primarily in civil litigation.

20. (B) In the present fact situation, the government's claim should be honored. See *McCray v. Illinois*, 386 U.S. 300 (1967). Note that choice (A) is incorrect because an unidentified informant has not been extended a Fifth Amendment privilege against self-incrimination. In the *McCray* case, the court held that it may in the exercise of its power to formulate evidentiary rules for federal criminal cases decline to disclose an informer's identity.

21. (B) Lois will win on the appeal of her murder conviction under the state murder statute since the statute placed the burden on the defendant to prove or disprove the element of malice. The United States Supreme Court in *In re Winship*, 397 U.S. 358, 90 S.Ct. 068 (1910), held that the **Due Process Clause protects an accused in a criminal case against conviction except upon proof "beyond a reasonable doubt"** of every fact necessary to constitute the crime for which the defendant is charged. In other words, the court in the *Winship* case held that proof of a criminal charge beyond a reasonable doubt is constitutionally required. Consequently, the murder statute in our hypothetical is unconstitutional, since the burden of proving the various elements of the offense (murder) is on the defendant, and not on the prosecution as required in all jurisdictions.

22. (A) Choice (B) is incorrect since Lois's attorney would attempt to prove that the search of her apartment was illegal and thus violative of the Fourth Amendment's protection against unreasonable searches and seizures. Choice (C) is wrong because if Lois told Judy not to answer the door for anyone, Judy could not exercise apparent authority and thus consent to a search of Lois's apartment. Choice (D) is also wrong since Lois's attorney would attempt to prove that Judy was coerced into granting consent for the search, thus deeming it an illegal search and seizure. Consequently, choice (A) is the least likely fact which Lois's attorney would attempt to prove at the suppression hearing. It is important to note that consent searches are one of the exceptions of the Fourth Amendment requirement of a search warrant. However, for a consent search to be valid three factors must be considered: (1) the person consenting must have the authority to consent to a search of the premises; (2) the person's consent to the search must be voluntary; and (3) the police may not exceed their search into areas for which consent to search has not been given.

23. (B) The Fourth Amendment states, in part, "… and no warrants shall issue but on probable cause supported by oath or affirmation … " Searches conducted pursuant to a warrant must be based on an adequate and reasonable showing of probable cause when a *police officer* provides information to a neutral and detached magistrate by affidavit or by testimony under oath. However, when an *informant* uses an affidavit to provide information, the rigid Aguilar-Spinelli Test has been used to establish 1) probable cause for issuing the warrant as well as 2) reliability of the informant. More recently, a "totality of the circumstances" approach has been adopted [*Illinois v. Gates*, 386 U.S. 300] to determine whether there is a *"fair probability"* or *"substantial basis"* to conclude that contraband will be found at the particular time and place. In question 23, the fact that Informant saw Harry sell heroin *two months before* is critical because it is too remote in time to justify a present finding of probable cause. Choice (B) is correct. Choice (D) is incorrect because reliability of the informant *without probable cause* to search is an insufficient basis to issue a warrant.

24. (D) In *Griffin v. California,* 380 U.S. 609, 85 S.Ct. 1229 (1965), the U.S. Supreme Court held that the self-incrimination guarantee of the Fifth Amendment, as applicable to the states under the Fourteenth Amendment, forbids either comment by the prosecution of an accused's silence or instructions by the court that such silence is evidence of guilt. The comments by the prosecutor during his closing argument that Slick failed to take the stand would be violative of the defendant's right against self-incrimination. *Examination Tip:* Note that choice (D) is a better answer than (C) *because a correct statement of law is generally preferred over a correct statement of fact.*

25. (B) This identical issue dealing with "derivative standing" was tested two consecutive administrations of the MBE. Many students will be "suckered" into choosing (D), erroneously believing that the "fruits of the poisonous tree" doctrine will exclude both offers of evidence. However, *a conspirator does not have automatic standing to challenge the seizure of illegally obtained evidence from a coconspirator.* In fact, in *Alderman v. United States,* the Court held that "Fourth Amendment rights are personal rights" and concluded that there was "no necessity to exclude evidence against one defendant in order to protect the rights of another." **Criminal Procedure**, pg. 470.

26. (D) Students must be aware that choice (A) is wrong because *the privilege against self-incrimination only applies to evidence that is testimonial in nature.* Here, choice (D) is correct because the prosecuting attorney is attempting to attack Wilson's credibility. According to **F.R.E.** 806, "When a hearsay statement, or a statement defined in Rule 801(d)(2), (C), (D), or (E), has been admitted in evidence, the credibility of the declarant may be attacked, and if attacked may be supported, by any evidence which would be admissible for those purposes if declarant had testified as a witness." In our case, Wilson testified that he "had not used any drugs for the past three years." Consequently, it is proper for the prosecution to attack his credibility by seeing if there are any needle marks on his arms.

27. (A) In a 1981 United States Supreme Court case, *New York v. Belton,* 453 U.S. 454 (1981), based on facts similar to our hypothetical situation, the Supreme Court held that when a police officer has made a lawful custodial arrest of the occupant of an automobile, the police officer may, as a contemporaneous incident of that arrest, search the passenger compartment of that automobile. Thus, the search of Fernando's automobile, after the police officer issued the speeding citation, would not be violative of the Fourth or Fourteenth Amendments. First of all, the arrest was lawful as a result of Fernando's violation of the speed limit. Secondly, the police officer had a probable cause to search Fernando as incident to the arrest on the charge of unlawful possession of marijuana. Lastly, the search of the inside of the automobile was lawful since the sealed envelope found under the backseat and the jacket lying on the rear seat were "within the arrestee's immediate control" in accordance with the meaning of *Chimel v. California*, 395 U.S. 752 (1969). Students should note the importance of *Chimel v. California* with regard to frequent MBE questions in the area of search and seizure. In the *Chimel* case, the Supreme Court defined the limits of the area in which a police officer may search incident to a lawful arrest as "the area into which an arrestee might reach in order to grab a weapon or evidentiary item (the lunge test)."

28. (B) Choice (B) would be least helpful to Fernando in suppressing his statements to the police in which he admitted possessing the marijuana and cocaine. If students refer back to the hypothetical, the facts tell us that Fernando waived his rights to remain silent. In accordance with *Miranda*, a suspect may waive his rights as long as the waiver was knowingly, voluntarily, and intelligently made by the suspect. Consequently, the mere fact that one has retained an attorney does not preclude him from waiving his *Miranda* rights.

29. (B) The right to a fair and impartial trial is required by the concept of due process and the Sixth Amendment's guarantee of an *impartial jury*. Based upon the decision in *Sheppard v. Maxwell*, 384 U.S. 333 (1966), choice (B) would provide the best grounds to justify a showing that a juror was biased and not impartial. In *Sheppard*, the U.S. Supreme Court held that the judge should act "where there is a reasonable likelihood the prejudicial news" would prevent a fair trial.

30. (A) This Criminal Procedure question deals with the highly tested area of **warrantless searches.** By process of elimination, choice (A) furnishes the best grounds to justify the search of McAdoo's vehicle. A warrantless search and seizure of items from an automobile may be permitted where there is probable cause to believe the vehicle contains contraband (or where the vehicle could be moved before there is time to obtain a warrant). In accordance with the holding in *United States v. Ross*, 456 U.S. 798 (1982), once probable cause to search exists, the police can search the entire vehicle *including closed containers.* Note that choice (B) is not a strong answer since an inventory search is one which is made either at the police station or at a police impounding. In either case, such a warrantless search is made well *after* the initial stopping of the vehicle. By the same token, choice (C) presents a weak argument because *a search incident to a lawful arrest extends only to the area within the immediate control of the defendant (i.e., his "wingspan").* Also, choice (D) is not the best answer because "exigent circumstances" only applies in *emergency situations* where the evidence may be lost or destroyed before a warrant can be obtained.

31. (C) A commonly tested area on the Multistate Exam is that of **standing,** both in Constitutional Law, as well as in Criminal Procedure. In *Rakas v. Illinois*, 439 U.S. 128 (1978), a passenger who had no property interest in an automobile was held not to have standing to challenge a search of the vehicle as to items seized from it. This decision is founded on the principle of *no reasonable expectation of privacy.* To have Fourth Amendment standing, a person must show that *his own rights* were violated. **Standing is proper if a person owns or has a right to**

possession of the place or thing searched, or if the place searched is the person's home. Since Morgan, not Defendant, owned the car, Defendant has no standing to object to the search. Choice (C) is therefore correct. Students should note further that *Rakas* held that being "legitimately on the premises" is insufficient grounds to assert standing by itself, without proof of some possessory interest. Also, note that testimony given by the defendant to assert standing may not be admitted substantively against him at trial [*Simmons v. United States*, 390 U.S. 377 (1968)].

32. **(D)**   In *United States v. Chadwick*, 97 S.Ct. 2476 (1977), three persons were arrested for transportation of marijuana, following which the police seized and later searched without a warrant a double-locked footlocker which had just been put into the trunk of a car belonging to one of the defendants. The Court declined to uphold the search, reasoning that vehicles have a "diminished expectation of privacy" but that the footlocker did not because it was not open to public view and it was "intended as a repository of personal effects." However, in *California v. Acevedo,* 59 LW 4559 (1991), the Supreme Court limited the breadth of *Chadwick* and held that police may search an automobile and the containers within where they have probable cause to believe contraband or evidence is contained. Accordingly in *United States v. Ross*, 102 S.Ct. 2157 (1982), the Court held that if ***"probable cause justifies the search of a lawfully stopped vehicle, it justifies the search of every part of the vehicle and its contents that may conceal the object of the search."*** Based upon the given facts, since the police had probable cause to search the entire vehicle for drugs, the police may lawfully search both the toolcase and the glove compartment.

33. **(A)**   This is a "tricky" Multistate question which requires a careful reading of the facts. The police informant reported seeing ***two men*** in the red van engaging in the sale of narcotics. Consequently, the police did ***not*** have probable cause to suspect that the woman was engaged in the commission of a crime. In this regard, it is important to point out that "a person's expectations of privacy in personal luggage are substantially greater than in an automobile." The rule for automobiles does not extend to personal belongings. Rather, when the circumstances are sufficiently "exigent" to allow the police to make a warrantless seizure of personal items, this does not permit the "far greater intrusion" of examining the contents thereof but only the continued possession of the personal effects while a warrant is sought. **Criminal Procedure**, pg. 152.

34. **(D)**   Choice (D) is correct since the letter was the "fruit" of an illegal search. The Fourth Amendment prohibition against unreasonable search and seizure, as applicable to the States by the Fourteenth Amendment, would be invoked since the officers neither had "probable cause " to search Lloyd nor had a valid search warrant. Although "probable cause" is not required to justify an investigatory field stop (e.g., "stop and frisk"), the police still must have some objective basis for believing that the person was about to engage, or already had engaged, in criminal activity. Choices (A) and (B) are clearly incorrect. Choice (C), though correct, is the less preferred choice since the basis for excluding the letter from

evidence is that it is the "fruit" or product of an illegal search, rather than the result of a nonconsensual search.

35. (A) Here is a truly *classic* Multistate example where the correct answer is derived from a footnote in McCormick's hornbook on **Evidence**. McCormick points out that a "1963 study indicated that 14 states required a defendant to give advance notice of intent to assert an alibi and to furnish specific information as to the place where he claims to have been at the time of the crime. Seven states require a list of witnesses who will be called to support the defense." [McCormick, **Law of Evidence,** p 284, footnote 63] In a similar case, the Florida requirement was upheld against constitutional attack in [*Williams v. Florida,* 399 U.S. 916 (1970)]. In this PMBR example, since the prosecuting attorney's discovery motion was pursuant to state law, choice (A) is correct.

36. (A) A random stopping of a vehicle on the highway where the officer has no suspicion of wrongdoing is unconstitutional because it leaves too much discretion in the police officer [*Delaware v. Prouse,* 440 U.S. 648 (1979)]. And, applying the *"fruits of the poisonous tree" doctrine,* no evidence seized as a result of a Fourth Amendment violation may be admitted at trial [*Wong Sun v. United States,* 371 U.S. 471 (1963)]. CAVEAT: Be cognizant that the rule suppressing fruits of an illegal search applies not only to objects found, but also to verbal statements obtained because of the original tainted search, or as a result of an illegal arrest. See *Brown v. Illinois,* 422 U.S. 590 (1975).

37. (D) The Fifth Amendment right to be free from double jeopardy for the same offense prohibits retrial after a determination on the merits. In *United States v. Scott,* 437 U.S. 82 (1978), the Court held that "the defendant, by deliberately choosing to seek termination of the proceedings against him on a basis unrelated to factual guilt or innocence of the offense of which he is accused, suffers no injury cognizable under the Double Jeopardy Clause if the Government is permitted to appeal from such a ruling of the trial court in favor of the defendant." [LaFave and Israel, **Criminal Procedure,** p. 910]. Thus, the general rule is that *reprosecution following dismissal by the judge upon the defendant's motion which does not constitute an acquittal on the merits is not prohibited by the double jeopardy clause.* In these facts, O'Teen's motion for dismissal at the first trial was granted by the judge based on an equal protection violation, not on any factual element of the statutory offense charged. Hence, no jeopardy has attached to bar O'Teen's municipal prosecution. Choice (A) is incorrect and O'Teen's motion to dismiss at the second trial will be denied. Choice (D) properly states the correct rationale. Choice (B) is incorrect because *collateral estoppel* bars retrial of issues that have been *actually litigated.* O'Teen's first trial ended in a dismissal without litigating any factual issues not being raised at the second trial. Choice (C) is incorrect because the *separate sovereignties doctrine* does not apply to trials by a state and by its municipalities.

38. (B) There are four specific bases with which to attack the admissibility of a statement or confession—(1) the *Miranda* standard, (2) the right to counsel approach,

(3) the voluntariness approach, and (4) fruits of illegal conduct. The *Miranda* standard only applies once ***custodial interrogation*** has begun. Statements elicited once the right to remain silent has been requested or once counsel has been requested will be inadmissible. In this question, Hendricks was arrested and given his *Miranda* warnings. He requested counsel. However, his statements to his attorney, Alzado, were not made as a product of interrogation. Hendricks's statement was not violative of the *Miranda* standard once one ***assumes the risk*** that telephone conversation will be overheard. Therefore, Stork's testimony will be admitted under answer choice (B). Choice (A) is incorrect because Hendricks's remarks were inadvertent. He was not knowingly and voluntarily conferring, so lack of coercion is not the proper basis upon which to admit his statement. Choice (C) is incorrect. The Sixth Amendment right to counsel approach, which attaches to all "critical stages" of a criminal proceeding, operates to exclude any statements *deliberately elicited* once criminal charges have been filed. Hendricks's statements were ***volunteered***, not elicited. Finally, choice (D) is incorrect because Hendricks, as holder of the attorney-client privilege, waived confidentiality by speaking out over the telephone. Note: General on-the-scene questioning as to facts surrounding a crime or other general questioning of citizens in the fact-finding process is not considered custodial interrogation for *Miranda* purposes. [See LaFave, **Criminal Procedure,** p. 292].

39. **(A)**   Here's a *tricky* Criminal Procedure example dealing with airport searches. Generally, under federal law ***warrantless administrative searches are permitted at airports*** in order to protect passengers from weapons and explosives. Although narcotics-sniffing dogs may smell a passenger's luggage, *any resulting detention must be brief* and a seizure of the luggage is subject to Fourth Amendment limitations. [See *United States v. Place,* 77 L.Ed.2d 110 (1983)]. In this example, although the police may have been justified to temporarily detain Butler, they would not be permitted to confiscate his baggage and hold it overnight. Choice (A) is correct because such a seizure is violative of the Fourth Amendment based on the decision in the *Place* case.

40. **(D)**   In the case of *Oregon v. Elstad,* 470 U.S. 298 (1985), police officers picked up a burglary suspect who made an incriminating statement without being advised of his *Miranda* warnings. After he was taken to the stationhouse, he was given the warnings. He then waived his rights and confessed. The trial court excluded the first statement, but admitted the confession. After the appeals court reversed Elstad's conviction, the Supreme Court held that "the Self-Incrimination Clause of the Fifth Amendment does not require the suppression of a confession, made after proper *Miranda* warnings and a valid waiver of rights, solely because the police had obtained an earlier voluntary but unwarned admission from the suspect." In light of the *Elstad* decision, Smirk's motion to suppress his second statement given at the police station should not be granted. Choice (D) is correct because the second statement was volunteered after a knowing *Miranda* waiver. Students should be aware from this example that ***absent deliberate coercion or improper tactics, a thorough administration of* Miranda *warnings*** cures the condition that rendered the unwarned statement inadmissible. As to answer

choices (A) and (B), the *Elstad* Court noted that no further purpose is served by imputing "taint" to subsequent statements obtained pursuant to a voluntary and knowing waiver.

41. (D) Another area in Criminal Procedure commonly tested on the bar exam deals with *indictment delays* after arrest. When a defendant, after being arrested and released, is not indicted until a long time interval has passed, the Sixth Amendment right to a speedy trial does apply [*Dillingham v. United States*, 423 U.S. 64 (1975)]. However, the Court determines whether the delay is reasonable or unreasonable by balancing the following factors: (1) the length of the delay; (2) the good faith and justification of the delay; (3) the defendant's assertion of the right to a speedy trial; and (4) prejudice to the defendant. In the present example, the prosecution's delay in indicting Gonzalez was for a proper purpose (i.e., to obtain information about his accomplice). Moreover, a five-month delay (where the statute of limitations is five years for murder) does not appear to be unreasonably long. Therefore, choice (D) is correct.

42. (C) Students must be familiar with the area of "bifurcated trials." In a very few jurisdictions, most notably California, the defense of insanity is tried separately from the other issues in the case. Under California law, for example, a defendant may plead (1) not guilty, (2) not guilty and also not guilty by reason of insanity, or (3) merely not guilty by reason of insanity. If the second form of plea is entered, the guilty-stage of the trial is first concluded without any reference to the insanity defense, after which (if defendant was found guilty) a separate proceeding takes place before the same or a different jury for purposes of trying the insanity defense. According to LaFave, pp. 315-316, the purpose of the bifurcated trial procedure is to eliminate from the basic trial on the issue of whether the defendant engaged in the conduct a great mass of evidence having no bearing on that question and which may confuse the jury or be made the basis of appeals to the sympathy or prejudice of the jury. However, this objective has not been realized. As a result of the ruling in *People v. Wells*, 202 P.2d 53 (1949), *evidence of mental disease or defect is admissible on the issue of whether the defendant had the requisite mental state and is permitted at both the* guilty-stage *and insanity-stage of the trial.* Based on the decision in *People v. Wells,* choice (C) is correct.

43. (B) The Sixth Amendment provides that the accused shall have "the assistance of counsel for his defense." This right not only encompasses the right to hire private counsel, but also the right to be provided with counsel without charge if the accused is unable to afford counsel. Choice (B) is correct because in *Argersinger v. Hamlin,* 92 S.Ct. 2006 (1972), the U.S. Supreme Court held that "absent a knowing and intelligent waiver, no person may be imprisoned for any offense, whether classified as petty, misdemeanor, or felony unless he was represented by counsel." Note that choice (D) is not correct because *the right to jury exists whenever the accused faces a sentence of possibly more than six months* [*Baldwin v. New York*, 399 U.S. 66 (1970)]. In this example, since Defendant's maximum sentence was six months in jail (not more than six months imprisonment), he would not have the right to a jury trial.

44. (D) The exclusionary rule is a remedy for Fourth, Fifth, and Sixth Amendment violations by which all evidence obtained through illegal searches and seizures is inadmissible. The scope of the rule applies furthermore to exclude ***all evidence obtained or derived therefrom***. Such additional evidence is deemed to be tainted "fruit of the poisonous tree" [*Wong Sun v. U.S.*, 371 U.S. 471 (1963)]. The forcible entry and search by the police of Herman's home was illegal since they did not obtain a warrant when the law required them to do so. As a result of their illegal warrantless search of the home, Herman's confession will be properly excluded under the fruit of the poisonous tree doctrine. Choice (D) is correct. Choice (C) is incorrect because it gives the wrong justification for excluding Herman's confession. Regarding choices (A) and (B), which reach the wrong conclusion, note that even where the *Miranda* warnings are given after the illegal police conduct but before the confession, the confession is still regarded as inadmissible fruit [*Taylor v. Alabama*, 457 U.S. 687 (1982)].

45. (A) In *Argersinger v. Hamlin, 407* U.S. 25, 92 S.Ct. 2006 (1972) the U.S. Supreme Court held that "no person may be imprisoned for any offense, whether classified as petty, misdemeanor, or felony unless he was represented by counsel." Students should also be aware that in *Scott v. Illinois*, 440 U.S. 367, 99 S.Ct. 1158 (1979), the U.S. Supreme Court declined to extend *Argersinger* to a case where one is charged with an offense for which imprisonment upon conviction is authorized but not actually imposed. In *Scott,* the petitioner, an indigent, was charged with shoplifting merchandise valued at less than $150, punishable by as much as a $500 fine, or one year in jail, or both. He was not provided counsel. After a bench trial he was convicted of the offense and fined $50.

46. (C) Students should note that the Fourth Amendment generally protects only against governmental conduct, and not against searches by private persons. Be advised that government agents include only the publicly paid police and those citizens acting at their direction or behest, and not private security guards unless deputized as officers of the public police. Also, remember that the same requirement of governmental conduct in Fourth Amendment cases applies to confession cases as well. Since *Miranda* only applies to interrogation by the publicly paid police (or private citizens acting at their behest), choice (C) is the best answer.

47. (C) Although many students will undoubtedly choose (B) as correct, choice (C) is preferred. Although this is not an easy question to explain, here's why choice (C) is a better answer than (B). First, the double jeopardy rule prohibits multiple punishments for the same criminal offense. However, where a defendant is convicted of two separate criminal offenses (e.g., where each crime requires proof of a fact which the other does not), then consecutive sentences (or multiple punishments) may be imposed. That's why Josie may be convicted of the separate crimes of armed robbery and felony murder with sentences running consecutively. On the other hand, Josie could not receive consecutive sentences for rape and felony murder because rape is a lesser included offense inasmuch as rape was the underlying felony. However, the court could still impose concurrent sentences for rape and felony murder because concurrent sentences are not multiple sentences. Therefore, there is no violation of the double jeopardy rule.

48. (C) This is a tricky double jeopardy question concerning whether a defendant may be prosecuted and punished for both felony murder and the underlying felony. One double jeopardy issue concerns when multiple prosecutions may be undertaken, as to which the Supreme Court in *Brown v. Ohio*, 432 U.S. 161 (1977), adopted the longstanding *Blockburger* test, which originated as a device for determining congressional intent as to cumulative sentencing: "The applicable rule is that where the same act or transaction constitutes a violation of two distinct statutory provisions, the test to be applied to determine whether there are two offenses or one, is whether each provision requires proof of an additional fact which the other does not." This means, as the Supreme Court held in *Harris v. Oklahoma*, 433 U.S. 682 (1977), that except in extraordinary circumstances ***a defendant may not constitutionally be separately tried for felony murder and the underlying felony.*** [See **Criminal Law**, pg. 639]. Note that choice (B) is incorrect because although collateral estoppel has been an established rule of federal criminal law for more than 50 years, we are not dealing with issue preclusion (e.g., identity or motive) from a prior trial. Conversely, we are dealing with whether the burglary acquittal precludes subsequent prosecution for felony murder.

49. (D) In sum, the double jeopardy provision of the Fifth Amendment provides that no person shall be "twice put in jeopardy" for the "same offense." According to the prevailing view, it has been held that two crimes are not the "same offense" merely because they arose out of the same transaction. Note that choice (D) is correct because successive state and federal prosecutions for the same acts is constitutionally permissible, as each sovereign must be free to vindicate its own interests.

50. (C) Another search and seizure technique that has recently been tested on the MBE involves the use of an electronic tracking device, such as a beacon or "beeper." Such beepers are attached to a car, airplane, or container and the movements of that object are then tracked by the police. In *United States v. Karo*, 104 S.Ct. 3296 (1984), the Supreme Court concluded that "the mere installation of a beeper is **no search** because that act alone infringed no privacy interest." The Court reasoned that the surveillance objected to "amounted principally to the following of an automobile on public streets and highways, which if accomplished merely by visual surveillance would be no search because one travelling in an automobile on public thoroughfares has no reasonable expectations of privacy in his movements from one place to another."

SELECTED AMENDMENTS OF THE
UNITED STATES CONSTITUTION

AMENDMENT IV

The right of the people to be secure in their persons, houses, papers, and effects, against unreasonable searches and seizures, shall not be violated, and no Warrants shall issue, but upon probable cause, supported by Oath or affirmation, and particularly describing the place to be searched, and the persons or things to be seized.

AMENDMENT V

No person shall be held to answer for a capital, or otherwise infamous crime, unless on a presentment or indictment of a Grand Jury, except in cases arising in the land or naval forces, or in the Militia, when in actual service in time of War or public danger; nor shall any person be subject for the same offense to be twice put in jeopardy of life or limb; nor shall be compelled in any criminal case to be a witness against himself, nor be deprived of life, liberty, or property, without due process of law; nor shall private property be taken for public use, without just compensation.

AMENDMENT VI

In all criminal prosecutions, the accused shall enjoy the right to a speedy and public trial, by an impartial jury of the State and district wherein the crime shall have been committed, which district shall have been previously ascertained by law, and to be informed of the nature and cause of the accusation; to be confronted with the witnesses against him; to have compulsory process for obtaining Witnesses in his favor, and to have the Assistance of Counsel for his defense.

AMENDMENT VIII

Excessive bail shall not be required, nor excessive fines imposed, nor cruel and unusual punishments inflicted.

AMENDMENT XIV

SECTION 1. All persons born or naturalized in the United States and subject to the jurisdiction thereof, are citizens of the United States and of the State wherein they reside. No State shall make or enforce any law which shall abridge the privileges or immunities of citizens of the United States; nor shall any State deprive any person of life, liberty, or property, without due process of law; nor deny to any person within its jurisdiction the equal protection of the laws.

SECTION 2. Representatives shall be apportioned among the several States according to their respective numbers, counting the whole number of persons in each State, excluding Indians not taxed. But when the right to vote at any election for the choice of electors for President and Vice President of the United States, Representatives in Congress, the Executive and Judicial officers of a State, or the members of the Legislature thereof, is denied to any of the male inhabitants of such State, being twenty-one years of age, and citizens of the United States, or in any way abridged, except for participation in rebellion, or other crime, the basis of representation therein shall be reduced in the proportion which the number of such male citizens shall bear to the whole number of male citizens twenty-one years of age in such State.

SECTION 3. No person shall be a Senator or Representative in Congress, or elector of President and Vice President, or hold any office, civil or military, under the United States, or under any State, who, having previously taken an oath, as a member of Congress, or as an officer of the United States, or as a member of any State legislature, or as an executive or judicial officer of any State, to support the Constitution of the United States, shall have engaged in insurrection or rebellion against the same, or given aid or comfort to the enemies thereof. But Congress may by a vote of two-thirds of each House, remove such disability.

SECTION 4. The validity of the public debt of the United States, authorized by law, including debts incurred for payment of pensions and bounties for services in suppressing insurrection or rebellion, shall not be questioned. But neither the United States nor any State shall assume or pay any debt or obligation incurred in aid of insurrection or rebellion against the United States, or any claim for the loss or emancipation of any slave; but all such debts, obligations and claims shall be held illegal and void.

SECTION 5. The Congress shall have power to enforce, by appropriate legislation, the provisions of this article.

FEDERAL RULES OF CRIMINAL PROCEDURE

Effective March 21, 1946, as amended to December 1, 2006

TITLE I. APPLICABILITY

Rule 1. Scope; Definitions

(a) **Scope.**

   (1) *In General.* These rules govern the procedure in all criminal proceedings in the United States district courts, the United States courts of appeals, and the Supreme Court of the United States.

   (2) *State or Local Judicial Officer.* When a rule so states, it applies to a proceeding before a state or local judicial officer.

   (3) *Territorial Courts.* These rules also govern the procedure in all criminal proceedings in the following courts:

   (A) the district court of Guam;

   (B) the district court for the Northern Mariana Islands, except as otherwise provided by law; and

   (C) the district court of the Virgin Islands, except that the prosecution of offenses in that court must be by indictment or information as otherwise provided by law.

   (4) *Removed Proceedings.* Although these rules govern all proceedings after removal from a state court, state law governs a dismissal by the prosecution.

   (5) *Excluded Proceedings.* Proceedings not governed by these rules include:

   (A) the extradition and rendition of a fugitive;

   (B) a civil property forfeiture for violating a federal statute;

   (C) the collection of a fine or penalty;

   (D) a proceeding under a statute governing juvenile delinquency to the extent the procedure is inconsistent with the statute, unless Rule 20(d) provides otherwise;

   (E) a dispute between seamen under 22 U.S.C. §§256–258; and

   (F) a proceeding against a witness in a foreign country under 28 U.S.C. §1784.

(b) **Definitions.** The following definitions apply to these rules:

   (1) "Attorney for the government" means:

   (A) the Attorney General or an authorized assistant;

   (B) a United States attorney or an authorized assistant;

   (C) when applicable to cases arising under Guam law, the Guam Attorney General or other person whom Guam law authorizes to act in the matter; and

   (D) any other attorney authorized by law to conduct proceedings under these rules as a prosecutor.

   (2) "Court" means a federal judge performing functions authorized by law.

   (3) "Federal judge" means:

   (A) a justice or judge of the United States as these terms are defined in 28 U.S.C. §451;

(B) a magistrate judge; and

(C) a judge confirmed by the United States Senate and empowered by statute in any commonwealth, territory, or possession to perform a function to which a particular rule relates.

(4) "Judge" means a federal judge or a state or local judicial officer.

(5) "Magistrate judge" means a United States magistrate judge as defined in 28 U.S.C. §§631–639.

(6) "Oath" includes an affirmation.

(7) "Organization" is defined in 18 U.S.C. §18.

(8) "Petty offense" is defined in 18 U.S.C. §19.

(9) "State" includes the District of Columbia, and any commonwealth, territory, or possession of the United States.

(10) "State or local judicial officer" means:

(A) a state or local officer authorized to act under 18 U.S.C. §3041; and

(B) a judicial officer empowered by statute in the District of Columbia or in any commonwealth, territory, or possession to perform a function to which a particular rule relates.

(c) Authority of a Justice or Judge of the United States. When these rules authorize a magistrate judge to act, any other federal judge may also act.

(As amended Apr. 24, 1972, eff. Oct. 1, 1972; Apr. 28, 1982, eff. Aug. 1, 1982; Apr. 22, 1993, eff. Dec. 1, 1993; Apr. 29, 2002, eff. Dec. 1, 2002.)

Rule 2. Interpretation

These rules are to be interpreted to provide for the just determination of every criminal proceeding, to secure simplicity in procedure and fairness in administration, and to eliminate unjustifiable expense and delay.

(As amended Apr. 29, 2002, eff. Dec. 1, 2002.)

TITLE II. PRELIMINARY PROCEEDINGS

Rule 3. The Complaint

The complaint is a written statement of the essential facts constituting the offense charged. It must be made under oath before a magistrate judge or, if none is reasonably available, before a state or local judicial officer.

(As amended Apr. 24, 1972, eff. Oct. 1, 1972; Apr. 22, 1993, eff. Dec. 1, 1993; Apr. 29, 2002, eff. Dec. 1, 2002.)

Rule 4. Arrest Warrant or Summons on a Complaint

(a) Issuance. If the complaint or one or more affidavits filed with the complaint establish probable cause to believe that an offense has been committed and that the defendant committed it, the judge must issue an arrest warrant to an officer authorized to execute it. At the request of an attorney for the government, the judge must issue a summons, instead of a warrant, to a person authorized to serve it. A judge may issue more than one warrant or summons on the same complaint. If a defendant fails to appear in response to a summons, a judge may, and upon request of an attorney for the government must, issue a warrant.

(b) **Form.**

    (1) *Warrant.* A warrant must:

        (A) contain the defendant's name or, if it is unknown, a name or description by which the defendant can be identified with reasonable certainty;

        (B) describe the offense charged in the complaint;

        (C) command that the defendant be arrested and brought without unnecessary delay before a magistrate judge or, if none is reasonably available, before a state or local judicial officer; and

        (D) be signed by a judge.

    (2) *Summons.* A summons must be in the same form as a warrant except that it must require the defendant to appear before a magistrate judge at a stated time and place.

(c) **Execution or Service, and Return.**

    (1) *By Whom.* Only a marshal or other authorized officer may execute a warrant. Any person authorized to serve a summons in a federal civil action may serve a summons.

    (2) *Location.* A warrant may be executed, or a summons served, within the jurisdiction of the United States or anywhere else a federal statute authorizes an arrest.

    (3) *Manner.*

        (A) A warrant is executed by arresting the defendant. Upon arrest, an officer possessing the warrant must show it to the defendant. If the officer does not possess the warrant, the officer must inform the defendant of the warrant's existence and of the offense charged and, at the defendant's request, must show the warrant to the defendant as soon as possible.

        (B) A summons is served on an individual defendant:

            (i) by delivering a copy to the defendant personally; or

            (ii) by leaving a copy at the defendant's residence or usual place of abode with a person of suitable age and discretion residing at that location and by mailing a copy to the defendant's last known address.

        (C) A summons is served on an organization by delivering a copy to an officer, to a managing or general agent, or to another agent appointed or legally authorized to receive service of process. A copy must also be mailed to the organization's last known address within the district or to its principal place of business elsewhere in the United States.

    (4) *Return.*

        (A) After executing a warrant, the officer must return it to the judge before whom the defendant is brought in accordance with Rule 5. At the request of an attorney for the government, an unexecuted warrant must be brought back to and canceled by a magistrate judge or, if none is reasonably available, by a state or local judicial officer.

        (B) The person to whom a summons was delivered for service must return it on or before the return day.

(C) At the request of an attorney for the government, a judge may deliver an unexecuted warrant, an unserved summons, or a copy of the warrant or summons to the marshal or other authorized person for execution or service.

(As amended Feb. 28, 1966, eff. July 1, 1966; Apr. 24, 1972, eff. Oct. 1, 1972; Apr. 22, 1974, eff. Dec. 1, 1975; July 31, 1975, eff. Dec. 1, 1975; Mar. 9, 1987, eff. Aug. 1, 1987; Apr. 22, 1993, eff. Dec. 1, 1993; Apr. 29, 2002, eff. Dec. 1, 2002.)

Rule 5. Initial Appearance

(a) **In General.**
  (1) *Appearance Upon an Arrest.*
    (A) A person making an arrest within the United States must take the defendant without unnecessary delay before a magistrate judge, or before a state or local judicial officer as Rule 5(c) provides, unless a statute provides otherwise.
    (B) A person making an arrest outside the United States must take the defendant without unnecessary delay before a magistrate judge, unless a statute provides otherwise.
  (2) *Exceptions.*
    (A) An officer making an arrest under a warrant issued upon a complaint charging solely a violation of 18 U.S.C. §1073 need not comply with this rule if:
      (i) the person arrested is transferred without unnecessary delay to the custody of appropriate state or local authorities in the district of arrest; and
      (ii) an attorney for the government moves promptly, in the district where the warrant was issued, to dismiss the complaint.
    (B) If a defendant is arrested for violating probation or supervised release, Rule 32.1 applies.
    (C) If a defendant is arrested for failing to appear in another district, Rule 40 applies.
  (3) *Appearance Upon a Summons.* When a defendant appears in response to a summons under Rule 4, a magistrate judge must proceed under Rule 5(d) or (e), as applicable.
(b) **Arrest Without a Warrant.** If a defendant is arrested without a warrant, a complaint meeting Rule 4(a)'s requirement of probable cause must be promptly filed in the district where the offense was allegedly committed.
(c) **Place of Initial Appearance; Transfer to Another District.**
  (1) *Arrest in the District Where the Offense Was Allegedly Committed.* If the defendant is arrested in the district where the offense was allegedly committed:
    (A) the initial appearance must be in that district; and
    (B) if a magistrate judge is not reasonably available, the initial appearance may be before a state or local judicial officer.

(2) ***Arrest in a District Other Than Where the Offense Was Allegedly Committed.*** If the defendant was arrested in a district other than where the offense was allegedly committed, the initial appearance must be:

(A) in the district of arrest; or

(B) in an adjacent district if:

    (i)   the appearance can occur more promptly there; or

    (ii) the offense was allegedly committed there and the initial appearance will occur on the day of arrest.

(3) ***Procedures in a District Other Than Where the Offense Was Allegedly Committed.*** If the initial appearance occurs in a district other than where the offense was allegedly committed, the following procedures apply:

(A) the magistrate judge must inform the defendant about the provisions of Rule 20;

(B) if the defendant was arrested without a warrant, the district court where the offense was allegedly committed must first issue a warrant before the magistrate judge transfers the defendant to that district;

(C) the magistrate judge must conduct a preliminary hearing if required by Rule 5.1;

(D) the magistrate judge must transfer the defendant to the district where the offense was allegedly committed if:

    (i)   the government produces the warrant, a certified copy of the warrant, or a reliable electronic form of either; and

    (ii) the judge finds that the defendant is the same person named in the indictment, information, or warrant; and

(E) when a defendant is transferred and discharged, the clerk must promptly transmit the papers and any bail to the clerk in the district where the offense was allegedly committed.

(d) **Procedure in a Felony Case.**

(1) ***Advice.*** If the defendant is charged with a felony, the judge must inform the defendant of the following:

(A) the complaint against the defendant, and any affidavit filed with it;

(B) the defendant's right to retain counsel or to request that counsel be appointed if the defendant cannot obtain counsel;

(C) the circumstances, if any, under which the defendant may secure pretrial release;

(D) any right to a preliminary hearing; and

(E) the defendant's right not to make a statement, and that any statement made may be used against the defendant.

(2) ***Consulting with Counsel.*** The judge must allow the defendant reasonable opportunity to consult with counsel.

(3) ***Detention or Release.*** The judge must detain or release the defendant as provided by statute or these rules.

(4) ***Plea.*** A defendant may be asked to plead only under Rule 10.

(e) **Procedure in a Misdemeanor Case.** If the defendant is charged with a misdemeanor only, the judge must inform the defendant in accordance with Rule 58(b)(2).

(f) **Video Teleconferencing.** Video teleconferencing may be used to conduct an appearance under this rule if the defendant consents.

(As amended Feb. 28, 1966, eff. July 1, 1966; Apr. 24, 1972, eff. Oct. 1, 1972; Apr. 28, 1982, eff. Aug. 1, 1982; Oct. 12, 1984; Mar. 9, 1987, eff. Aug. 1, 1987; May 1, 1990, eff. Dec. 1, 1990; Apr. 22, 1993, eff. Dec. 1, 1993; Apr. 27, 1995, eff. Dec. 1, 1995; Apr. 29, 2002, eff. Dec. 1, 2002; Apr. 12, 2006, eff. Dec. 1, 2006.)

Rule 5.1. Preliminary Hearing

(a) **In General.** If a defendant is charged with an offense other than a petty offense, a magistrate judge must conduct a preliminary hearing unless:
   (1) the defendant waives the hearing;
   (2) the defendant is indicted;
   (3) the government files an information under Rule 7(b) charging the defendant with a felony;
   (4) the government files an information charging the defendant with a misdemeanor; or
   (5) the defendant is charged with a misdemeanor and consents to trial before a magistrate judge.

(b) **Selecting a District.** A defendant arrested in a district other than where the offense was allegedly committed may elect to have the preliminary hearing conducted in the district where the prosecution is pending.

(c) **Scheduling.** The magistrate judge must hold the preliminary hearing within a reasonable time, but no later than 10 days after the initial appearance if the defendant is in custody and no later than 20 days if not in custody.

(d) **Extending the Time.** With the defendant's consent and upon a showing of good cause—taking into account the public interest in the prompt disposition of criminal cases—a magistrate judge may extend the time limits in Rule 5.1(c) one or more times. If the defendant does not consent, the magistrate judge may extend the time limits only on a showing that extraordinary circumstances exist and justice requires the delay.

(e) **Hearing and Finding.** At the preliminary hearing, the defendant may cross-examine adverse witnesses and may introduce evidence but may not object to evidence on the ground that it was unlawfully acquired. If the magistrate judge finds probable cause to believe an offense has been committed and the defendant committed it, the magistrate judge must promptly require the defendant to appear for further proceedings.

(f) **Discharging the Defendant.** If the magistrate judge finds no probable cause to believe an offense has been committed or the defendant committed it, the magistrate judge must dismiss the complaint and discharge the defendant. A discharge does not preclude the government from later prosecuting the defendant for the same offense.

(g) **Recording the Proceedings.** The preliminary hearing must be recorded by a court reporter or by a suitable recording device. A recording of the proceeding may be made available to any party upon request. A copy of the recording and a transcript may be provided to any party upon request and upon any payment required by applicable Judicial Conference regulations.

    (h) **Producing a Statement.**

        (1) *General.* Rule 26.2(a)–(d) and (f) applies at any hearing under this rule, unless the magistrate judge for good cause rules otherwise in a particular case.

        (2) *Sanctions for Not Producing a Statement.* If a party disobeys a Rule 26.2 order to deliver a statement to the moving party, the magistrate judge must not consider the testimony of a witness whose statement is withheld.

(As added Apr. 24, 1972, eff. Oct. 1, 1972; amended Mar. 9, 1987, eff. Aug. 1, 1987; Apr. 22, 1993, eff. Dec. 1, 1993; Apr. 24, 1998, eff. Dec. 1, 1998; Apr. 29, 2002, eff. Dec. 1, 2002.)

TITLE III. THE GRAND JURY, THE INDICTMENT, AND THE INFORMATION

Rule 6. The Grand Jury

    (a) **Summoning a Grand Jury.**

        (1) *In General.* When the public interest so requires, the court must order that one or more grand juries be summoned. A grand jury must have 16 to 23 members, and the court must order that enough legally qualified persons be summoned to meet this requirement.

        (2) *Alternate Jurors.* When a grand jury is selected, the court may also select alternate jurors. Alternate jurors must have the same qualifications and be selected in the same manner as any other juror. Alternate jurors replace jurors in the same sequence in which the alternates were selected. An alternate juror who replaces a juror is subject to the same challenges, takes the same oath, and has the same authority as the other jurors.

    (b) **Objection to the Grand Jury or to a Grand Juror.**

        (1) *Challenges.* Either the government or a defendant may challenge the grand jury on the ground that it was not lawfully drawn, summoned, or selected, and may challenge an individual juror on the ground that the juror is not legally qualified.

        (2) *Motion to Dismiss an Indictment.* A party may move to dismiss the indictment based on an objection to the grand jury or on an individual juror's lack of legal qualification, unless the court has previously ruled on the same objection under Rule 6(b)(1). The motion to dismiss is governed by 28 U.S.C. §1867(e). The court must not dismiss the indictment on the ground that a grand juror was not legally qualified if the record shows that at least 12 qualified jurors concurred in the indictment.

    (c) **Foreperson and Deputy Foreperson.** The court will appoint one juror as the foreperson and another as the deputy foreperson. In the foreperson's absence, the deputy foreperson will act as the foreperson. The foreperson may administer oaths and affirmations and will sign all indictments. The foreperson—or another juror designated by the foreperson—will record the number of jurors concurring in every indictment and will file the record with the clerk, but the record may not be made public unless the court so orders.

(d) Who May Be Present.

   (1) *While the Grand Jury Is in Session.* The following persons may be present while the grand jury is in session: attorneys for the government, the witness being questioned, interpreters when needed, and a court reporter or an operator of a recording device.

   (2) *During Deliberations and Voting.* No person other than the jurors, and any interpreter needed to assist a hearing-impaired or speech-impaired juror, may be present while the grand jury is deliberating or voting.

(e) Recording and Disclosing the Proceedings.

   (1) *Recording the Proceedings.* Except while the grand jury is deliberating or voting, all proceedings must be recorded by a court reporter or by a suitable recording device. But the validity of a prosecution is not affected by the unintentional failure to make a recording. Unless the court orders otherwise, an attorney for the government will retain control of the recording, the reporter's notes, and any transcript prepared from those notes.

   (2) *Secrecy.*

   (A) No obligation of secrecy may be imposed on any person except in accordance with Rule 6(e)(2)(B).

   (B) Unless these rules provide otherwise, the following persons must not disclose a matter occurring before the grand jury:

   (i)   a grand juror;

   (ii) an interpreter;

   (iii) a court reporter;

   (iv) an operator of a recording device;

   (v)   a person who transcribes recorded testimony;

   (vi) an attorney for the government; or

   (vii) a person to whom disclosure is made under Rule 6(e)(3)(A)(ii) or (iii).

   (3) *Exceptions.*

   (A) Disclosure of a grand-jury matter—other than the grand jury's deliberations or any grand juror's vote—may be made to:

   (i)   an attorney for the government for use in performing that attorney's duty;

   (ii) any government personnel—including those of a state, state subdivision, Indian tribe, or foreign government—that an attorney for the government considers necessary to assist in performing that attorney's duty to enforce federal criminal law; or

   (iii) a person authorized by 18 U.S.C. §3322.

   (B) A person to whom information is disclosed under Rule 6(e)(3)(A)(ii) may use that information only to assist an attorney for the government in performing that attorney's duty to enforce federal criminal law. An attorney for the government must promptly provide the court that impaneled the grand jury with the names of all persons to whom a disclosure has been made, and must certify that the attorney has advised those persons of their obligation of secrecy under this rule.

(C) An attorney for the government may disclose any grand-jury matter to another federal grand jury.

(D) An attorney for the government may disclose any grand-jury matter involving foreign intelligence, counterintelligence (as defined in 50 U.S.C. §401a), or foreign intelligence information (as defined in Rule 6(e)(3)(D)(iii)) to any federal law enforcement, intelligence, protective, immigration, national defense, or national security official to assist the official receiving the information in the performance of that official's duties. An attorney for the government may also disclose any grand-jury matter involving, within the United States or elsewhere, a threat of attack or other grave hostile acts of a foreign power or its agent, a threat of domestic or international sabotage or terrorism, or clandestine intelligence gathering activities by an intelligence service or network of a foreign power or by its agent, to any appropriate federal, state, state subdivision, Indian tribal, or foreign government official, for the purpose of preventing or responding to such threat or activities.

    (i) Any official who receives information under Rule 6(e)(3)(D) may use the information only as necessary in the conduct of that person's official duties subject to any limitations on the unauthorized disclosure of such information. Any state, state subdivision, Indian tribal, or foreign government official who receives information under Rule 6(e)(3)(D) may use the information only in a manner consistent with any guidelines issued by the Attorney General and the Director of National Intelligence.

    (ii) Within a reasonable time after disclosure is made under Rule 6(e)(3)(D), an attorney for the government must file, under seal, a notice with the court in the district where the grand jury convened stating that such information was disclosed and the departments, agencies, or entities to which the disclosure was made.

    (iii) As used in Rule 6(e)(3)(D), the term "foreign intelligence information" means:

        (a) information, whether or not it concerns a United States person, that relates to the ability of the United States to protect against—

- actual or potential attack or other grave hostile acts of a foreign power or its agent;
- sabotage or international terrorism by a foreign power or its agent; or
- clandestine intelligence activities by an intelligence service or network of a foreign power or by its agent; or

        (b) information, whether or not it concerns a United States person, with respect to a foreign power or foreign territory that relates to—

- the national defense or the security of the United States; or
- the conduct of the foreign affairs of the United States.

(E) The court may authorize disclosure—at a time, in a manner, and subject to any other conditions that it directs—of a grand-jury matter:

    (i) preliminarily to or in connection with a judicial proceeding;

    (ii) at the request of a defendant who shows that a ground may exist to dismiss the indictment because of a matter that occurred before the grand jury;

    (iii) at the request of the government, when sought by a foreign court or prosecutor for use in an official criminal investigation;

    (iv) at the request of the government if it shows that the matter may disclose a violation of State, Indian tribal, or foreign criminal law, as long as the disclosure is to an appropriate state, state-subdivision, Indian tribal, or foreign government official for the purpose of enforcing that law; or

    (v) at the request of the government if it shows that the matter may disclose a violation of military criminal law under the Uniform Code of Military Justice, as long as the disclosure is to an appropriate military official for the purpose of enforcing that law.

(F) A petition to disclose a grand-jury matter under Rule 6(e)(3)(E)(i) must be filed in the district where the grand jury convened. Unless the hearing is ex parte—as it may be when the government is the petitioner—the petitioner must serve the petition on, and the court must afford a reasonable opportunity to appear and be heard to:

    (i) an attorney for the government;

    (ii) the parties to the judicial proceeding; and

    (iii) any other person whom the court may designate.

(G) If the petition to disclose arises out of a judicial proceeding in another district, the petitioned court must transfer the petition to the other court unless the petitioned court can reasonably determine whether disclosure is proper. If the petitioned court decides to transfer, it must send to the transferee court the material sought to be disclosed, if feasible, and a written evaluation of the need for continued grand-jury secrecy. The transferee court must afford those persons identified in Rule 6(e)(3)(F) a reasonable opportunity to appear and be heard.

(4) *Sealed Indictment.* The magistrate judge to whom an indictment is returned may direct that the indictment be kept secret until the defendant is in custody or has been released pending trial. The clerk must then seal the indictment, and no person may disclose the indictment's existence except as necessary to issue or execute a warrant or summons.

(5) *Closed Hearing.* Subject to any right to an open hearing in a contempt proceeding, the court must close any hearing to the extent necessary to prevent disclosure of a matter occurring before a grand jury.

(6) *Sealed Records.* Records, orders, and subpoenas relating to grand-jury proceedings must be kept under seal to the extent and as long as necessary to prevent the unauthorized disclosure of a matter occurring before a grand jury.

(7) *Contempt.* A knowing violation of Rule 6, or of any guidelines jointly issued by the Attorney General and the Director of National Intelligence under Rule 6, may be punished as a contempt of court.

(f) **Indictment and Return.** A grand jury may indict only if at least 12 jurors concur. The grand jury—or its foreperson or deputy foreperson—must return the indictment to a magistrate judge in open court. If a complaint or information is pending against the defendant and 12 jurors do not concur in the indictment, the fore-person must promptly and in writing report the lack of concurrence to the magistrate judge.

(g) **Discharging the Grand Jury.** A grand jury must serve until the court discharges it, but it may serve more than 18 months only if the court, having determined that an extension is in the public interest, extends the grand jury's service. An extension may be granted for no more than 6 months, except as otherwise provided by statute.

(h) **Excusing a Juror.** At any time, for good cause, the court may excuse a juror either temporarily or permanently, and if permanently, the court may impanel an alternate juror in place of the excused juror.

  (i) **"Indian Tribe" Defined.** "Indian tribe" means an Indian tribe recognized by the Secretary of the Interior on a list published in the Federal Register under 25 U.S.C. §479a–1.

(As amended Feb. 28, 1966, eff. July 1, 1966; Apr. 24, 1972, eff. Oct. 1, 1972; Apr. 26 and July 8, 1976, eff. Aug. 1, 1976; July 30, 1977, eff. Oct. 1, 1977; Apr. 30, 1979, eff. Aug. 1, 1979; Apr. 28, 1983, eff. Aug. 1, 1983; Oct. 12, 1984, eff. Nov. 1, 1987; Apr. 29, 1985, eff. Aug. 1, 1985; Mar. 9, 1987, eff. Aug. 1, 1987; Apr. 22, 1993, eff. Dec. 1, 1993; Apr. 26, 1999, eff. Dec. 1, 1999; Oct. 26, 2001; Apr. 29, 2002, eff. Dec. 1, 2002; Nov. 25, 2002; Dec. 17, 2004; Apr. 12, 2006, eff. Dec. 1, 2006.)

Rule 7. The Indictment and the Information

(a) **When Used.**

  (1) *Felony.* An offense (other than criminal contempt) must be prosecuted by an indictment if it is punishable:
  (A) by death; or
  (B) by imprisonment for more than one year.

  (2) *Misdemeanor.* An offense punishable by imprisonment for one year or less may be prosecuted in accordance with Rule 58(b)(1).

(b) **Waiving Indictment.** An offense punishable by imprisonment for more than one year may be prosecuted by information if the defendant—in open court and after being advised of the nature of the charge and of the defendant's rights—waives prosecution by indictment.

(c) **Nature and Contents.**

  (1) *In General.* The indictment or information must be a plain, concise, and definite written statement of the essential facts constituting the offense charged and must be signed by an attorney for the government. It need not contain a formal introduction or conclusion. A count may incorporate by reference

an allegation made in another count. A count may allege that the means by which the defendant committed the offense are unknown or that the defendant committed it by one or more specified means. For each count, the indictment or information must give the official or customary citation of the statute, rule, regulation, or other provision of law that the defendant is alleged to have violated. For purposes of an indictment referred to in section 3282 of title 18, United States Code, for which the identity of the defendant is unknown, it shall be sufficient for the indictment to describe the defendant as an individual whose name is unknown, but who has a particular DNA profile, as that term is defined in section 3282.

(2) *Criminal Forfeiture.* No judgment of forfeiture may be entered in a criminal proceeding unless the indictment or the information provides notice that the defendant has an interest in property that is subject to forfeiture in accordance with the applicable statute.

(3) *Citation Error.* Unless the defendant was misled and thereby prejudiced, neither an error in a citation nor a citation's omission is a ground to dismiss the indictment or information or to reverse a conviction.

(d) **Surplusage.** Upon the defendant's motion, the court may strike surplusage from the indictment or information.

(e) **Amending an Information.** Unless an additional or different offense is charged or a substantial right of the defendant is prejudiced, the court may permit an information to be amended at any time before the verdict or finding.

(f) **Bill of Particulars.** The court may direct the government to file a bill of particulars. The defendant may move for a bill of particulars before or within 10 days after arraignment or at a later time if the court permits. The government may amend a bill of particulars subject to such conditions as justice requires.

(As amended Feb. 28, 1966, eff. July 1, 1966; Apr. 24, 1972, eff. Oct. 1, 1972; Apr. 30, 1979, eff. Aug. 1, 1979; Mar. 9, 1987, eff. Aug. 1, 1987; Apr. 17, 2000, eff. Dec. 1, 2000; Apr. 29, 2002, eff. Dec. 1, 2002; Apr. 30, 2003.)

Rule 8. Joinder of Offenses or Defendants

(a) **Joinder of Offenses.** The indictment or information may charge a defendant in separate counts with two or more offenses if the offenses charged—whether felonies or misdemeanors or both—are of the same or similar character, or are based on the same act or transaction, or are connected with or constitute parts of a common scheme or plan.

(b) **Joinder of Defendants.** The indictment or information may charge two or more defendants if they are alleged to have participated in the same act or transaction, or in the same series of acts or transactions, constituting an offense or offenses. The defendants may be charged in one or more counts together or separately. All defendants need not be charged in each count.

(As amended Apr. 29, 2002, eff. Dec. 1, 2002.)

Rule 9. Arrest Warrant or Summons on an Indictment or Information

(a) **Issuance.** The court must issue a warrant—or at the government's request, a summons—for each defendant named in an indictment or named in an information if one or more affidavits accompanying the information establish probable cause to believe that an offense has been committed and that the defendant committed it. The court may issue more than one warrant or summons for the same defendant. If a defendant fails to appear in response to a summons, the court may, and upon request of an attorney for the government must, issue a warrant. The court must issue the arrest warrant to an officer authorized to execute it or the summons to a person authorized to serve it.

(b) **Form.**
   (1) *Warrant.* The warrant must conform to Rule 4(b)(1) except that it must be signed by the clerk and must describe the offense charged in the indictment or information.
   (2) *Summons.* The summons must be in the same form as a warrant except that it must require the defendant to appear before the court at a stated time and place.

(c) **Execution or Service; Return; Initial Appearance.**
   (1) *Execution or Service.*
      (A) The warrant must be executed or the summons served as provided in Rule 4(c)(1), (2), and (3).
      (B) The officer executing the warrant must proceed in accordance with Rule 5(a)(1).
   (2) *Return.* A warrant or summons must be returned in accordance with Rule 4(c)(4).
   (3) *Initial Appearance.* When an arrested or summoned defendant first appears before the court, the judge must proceed under Rule 5.

(As amended Apr. 24, 1972, eff. Oct. 1, 1972; Apr. 22, 1974, eff. Dec. 1, 1975; July 31, 1975, eff. Dec. 1, 1975; Dec. 12, 1975; Apr. 30, 1979, eff. Aug. 1, 1979; Apr. 28, 1982, eff. Aug. 1, 1982; Apr. 22, 1993, eff. Dec. 1, 1993; Apr. 29, 2002, eff. Dec. 1, 2002.)

TITLE IV. ARRAIGNMENT AND PREPARATION FOR TRIAL

Rule 10. Arraignment

(a) **In General.** An arraignment must be conducted in open court and must consist of:
   (1) ensuring that the defendant has a copy of the indictment or information;
   (2) reading the indictment or information to the defendant or stating to the defendant the substance of the charge; and then
   (3) asking the defendant to plead to the indictment or information.
(b) **Waiving Appearance.** A defendant need not be present for the arraignment if:
   (1) the defendant has been charged by indictment or misdemeanor information;

(2) the defendant, in a written waiver signed by both the defendant and defense counsel, has waived appearance and has affirmed that the defendant received a copy of the indictment or information and that the plea is not guilty; and

(3) the court accepts the waiver.

(c) **Video Teleconferencing.** Video teleconferencing may be used to arraign a defendant if the defendant consents.

(As amended Mar. 9, 1987, eff. Aug. 1, 1987; Apr. 29, 2002, eff. Dec. 1, 2002.)

Rule 11. Pleas

(a) **Entering a Plea.**

(1) *In General.* A defendant may plead not guilty, guilty, or (with the court's consent) nolo contendere.

(2) *Conditional Plea.* With the consent of the court and the government, a defendant may enter a conditional plea of guilty or nolo contendere, reserving in writing the right to have an appellate court review an adverse determination of a specified pretrial motion. A defendant who prevails on appeal may then withdraw the plea.

(3) *Nolo Contendere Plea.* Before accepting a plea of nolo contendere, the court must consider the parties' views and the public interest in the effective administration of justice.

(4) *Failure to Enter a Plea.* If a defendant refuses to enter a plea or if a defendant organization fails to appear, the court must enter a plea of not guilty.

(b) **Considering and Accepting a Guilty or Nolo Contendere Plea.**

(1) *Advising and Questioning the Defendant.* Before the court accepts a plea of guilty or nolo contendere, the defendant may be placed under oath, and the court must address the defendant personally in open court. During this address, the court must inform the defendant of, and determine that the defendant understands, the following:

(A) the government's right, in a prosecution for perjury or false statement, to use against the defendant any statement that the defendant gives under oath;

(B) the right to plead not guilty, or having already so pleaded, to persist in that plea;

(C) the right to a jury trial;

(D) the right to be represented by counsel—and if necessary have the court appoint counsel—at trial and at every other stage of the proceeding;

(E) the right at trial to confront and cross-examine adverse witnesses, to be protected from compelled self-incrimination, to testify and present evidence, and to compel the attendance of witnesses;

(F) the defendant's waiver of these trial rights if the court accepts a plea of guilty or nolo contendere;

(G) the nature of each charge to which the defendant is pleading;

(H) any maximum possible penalty, including imprisonment, fine, and term of supervised release;

(I) any mandatory minimum penalty;

(J) any applicable forfeiture;

(K) the court's authority to order restitution;

(L) the court's obligation to impose a special assessment;

(M) the court's obligation to apply the Sentencing Guidelines, and the court's discretion to depart from those guidelines under some circumstances; and

(N) the terms of any plea-agreement provision waiving the right to appeal or to collaterally attack the sentence.

(2) ***Ensuring That a Plea Is Voluntary.*** Before accepting a plea of guilty or nolo contendere, the court must address the defendant personally in open court and determine that the plea is voluntary and did not result from force, threats, or promises (other than promises in a plea agreement).

(3) ***Determining the Factual Basis for a Plea.*** Before entering judgment on a guilty plea, the court must determine that there is a factual basis for the plea.

(c) **Plea Agreement Procedure.**

(1) ***In General.*** An attorney for the government and the defendant's attorney, or the defendant when proceeding pro se, may discuss and reach a plea agreement. The court must not participate in these discussions. If the defendant pleads guilty or nolo contendere to either a charged offense or a lesser or related offense, the plea agreement may specify that an attorney for the government will:

(A) not bring, or will move to dismiss, other charges;

(B) recommend, or agree not to oppose the defendant's request, that a particular sentence or sentencing range is appropriate or that a particular provision of the Sentencing Guidelines, or policy statement, or sentencing factor does or does not apply (such a recommendation or request does not bind the court); or

(C) agree that a specific sentence or sentencing range is the appropriate disposition of the case, or that a particular provision of the Sentencing Guidelines, or policy statement, or sentencing factor does or does not apply (such a recommendation or request binds the court once the court accepts the plea agreement).

(2) ***Disclosing a Plea Agreement.*** The parties must disclose the plea agreement in open court when the plea is offered, unless the court for good cause allows the parties to disclose the plea agreement in camera.

(3) ***Judicial Consideration of a Plea Agreement.***

(A) To the extent the plea agreement is of the type specified in Rule 11(c)(1)(A) or (C), the court may accept the agreement, reject it, or defer a decision until the court has reviewed the presentence report.

(B) To the extent the plea agreement is of the type specified in Rule 11(c)(1)(B), the court must advise the defendant that the defendant has no right to withdraw the plea if the court does not follow the recommendation or request.

(4) ***Accepting a Plea Agreement.*** If the court accepts the plea agreement, it must inform the defendant that to the extent the plea agreement is of the type specified in Rule 11(c)(1)(A) or (C), the agreed disposition will be included in the judgment.

(5) *Rejecting a Plea Agreement.* If the court rejects a plea agreement containing provisions of the type specified in Rule 11(c)(1)(A) or (C), the court must do the following on the record and in open court (or, for good cause, in camera):

(A) inform the parties that the court rejects the plea agreement;

(B) advise the defendant personally that the court is not required to follow the plea agreement and give the defendant an opportunity to withdraw the plea; and

(C) advise the defendant personally that if the plea is not withdrawn, the court may dispose of the case less favorably toward the defendant than the plea agreement contemplated.

(d) **Withdrawing a Guilty or Nolo Contendere Plea.** A defendant may withdraw a plea of guilty or nolo contendere:

(1) before the court accepts the plea, for any reason or no reason; or

(2) after the court accepts the plea, but before it imposes sentence if:

(A) the court rejects a plea agreement under Rule 11(c)(5); or

(B) the defendant can show a fair and just reason for requesting the withdrawal.

(e) **Finality of a Guilty or Nolo Contendere Plea.** After the court imposes sentence, the defendant may not withdraw a plea of guilty or nolo contendere, and the plea may be set aside only on direct appeal or collateral attack.

(f) **Admissibility or Inadmissibility of a Plea, Plea Discussions, and Related Statements.** The admissibility or inadmissibility of a plea, a plea discussion, and any related statement is governed by Federal Rule of Evidence 410.

(g) **Recording the Proceedings.** The proceedings during which the defendant enters a plea must be recorded by a court reporter or by a suitable recording device. If there is a guilty plea or a nolo contendere plea, the record must include the inquiries and advice to the defendant required under Rule 11(b) and (c).

(h) **Harmless Error.** A variance from the requirements of this rule is harmless error if it does not affect substantial rights.

(As amended Feb. 28, 1966, eff. July 1, 1966; Apr. 22, 1974, eff. Dec. 1, 1975; July 31, 1975, eff. Aug. 1 and Dec. 1, 1975; Apr. 30, 1979, eff. Aug. 1, 1979, and Dec. 1, 1980; Apr. 28, 1982, eff. Aug. 1, 1982; Apr. 28, 1983, eff. Aug. 1, 1983; Apr. 29, 1985, eff. Aug. 1, 1985; Mar. 9, 1987, eff. Aug. 1, 1987; Nov. 18, 1988; Apr. 25, 1989, eff. Dec. 1, 1989; Apr. 26, 1999, eff. Dec. 1, 1999; Apr. 29, 2002, eff. Dec. 1, 2002.)

Rule 12. Pleadings and Pretrial Motions

(a) **Pleadings.** The pleadings in a criminal proceeding are the indictment, the information, and the pleas of not guilty, guilty, and nolo contendere.

(b) **Pretrial Motions.**

(1) *In General.* Rule 47 applies to a pretrial motion.

(2) *Motions That May Be Made Before Trial.* A party may raise by pretrial motion any defense, objection, or request that the court can determine without a trial of the general issue.

    (3) ***Motions That Must Be Made Before Trial.*** The following must be raised before trial:

        (A) a motion alleging a defect in instituting the prosecution;

        (B) a motion alleging a defect in the indictment or information—but at any time while the case is pending, the court may hear a claim that the indictment or information fails to invoke the court's jurisdiction or to state an offense;

        (C) a motion to suppress evidence;

        (D) a Rule 14 motion to sever charges or defendants; and

        (E) a Rule 16 motion for discovery.

    (4) ***Notice of the Government's Intent to Use Evidence.***

        (A) *At the Government's Discretion.* At the arraignment or as soon afterward as practicable, the government may notify the defendant of its intent to use specified evidence at trial in order to afford the defendant an opportunity to object before trial under Rule 12(b)(3)(C).

        (B) *At the Defendant's Request.* At the arraignment or as soon afterward as practicable, the defendant may, in order to have an opportunity to move to suppress evidence under Rule 12(b)(3)(C), request notice of the government's intent to use (in its evidence-in-chief at trial) any evidence that the defendant may be entitled to discover under Rule 16.

(c) **Motion Deadline.** The court may, at the arraignment or as soon afterward as practicable, set a deadline for the parties to make pretrial motions and may also schedule a motion hearing.

(d) **Ruling on a Motion.** The court must decide every pretrial motion before trial unless it finds good cause to defer a ruling. The court must not defer ruling on a pretrial motion if the deferral will adversely affect a party's right to appeal. When factual issues are involved in deciding a motion, the court must state its essential findings on the record.

(e) **Waiver of a Defense, Objection, or Request.** A party waives any Rule 12(b)(3) defense, objection, or request not raised by the deadline the court sets under Rule 12(c) or by any extension the court provides. For good cause, the court may grant relief from the waiver.

(f) **Recording the Proceedings.** All proceedings at a motion hearing, including any findings of fact and conclusions of law made orally by the court, must be recorded by a court reporter or a suitable recording device.

(g) **Defendant's Continued Custody or Release Status.** If the court grants a motion to dismiss based on a defect in instituting the prosecution, in the indictment, or in the information, it may order the defendant to be released or detained under 18 U.S.C. §3142 for a specified time until a new indictment or information is filed. This rule does not affect any federal statutory period of limitations.

(h) **Producing Statements at a Suppression Hearing.** Rule 26.2 applies at a suppression hearing under Rule 12(b)(3)(C). At a suppression hearing, a law enforcement officer is considered a government witness.

(As amended Apr. 22, 1974, eff. Dec. 1, 1975; July 31, 1975, eff. Dec. 1, 1975; Apr. 28, 1983, eff. Aug. 1, 1983; Mar. 9, 1987, eff. Aug. 1, 1987; Apr. 22, 1993, eff. Dec. 1, 1993; Apr. 29, 2002, eff. Dec. 1, 2002.)

Rule 12.1. Notice of an Alibi Defense

(a) **Government's Request for Notice and Defendant's Response.**
  (1) *Government's Request.* An attorney for the government may request in writing that the defendant notify an attorney for the government of any intended alibi defense. The request must state the time, date, and place of the alleged offense.
  (2) *Defendant's Response.* Within ten days after the request, or at some other time the court sets, the defendant must serve written notice on an attorney for the government of any intended alibi defense. The defendant's notice must state:
    (A) each specific place where the defendant claims to have been at the time of the alleged offense; and
    (B) the name, address, and telephone number of each alibi witness on whom the defendant intends to rely.

(b) **Disclosing Government Witnesses.**
  (1) *Disclosure.* If the defendant serves a Rule 12.1(a)(2) notice, an attorney for the government must disclose in writing to the defendant or the defendant's attorney:
    (A) the name, address, and telephone number of each witness the government intends to rely on to establish the defendant's presence at the scene of the alleged offense; and
    (B) each government rebuttal witness to the defendant's alibi defense.
  (2) *Time to Disclose.* Unless the court directs otherwise, an attorney for the government must give its Rule 12.1(b)(1) disclosure within 10 days after the defendant serves notice of an intended alibi defense under Rule 12.1(a)(2), but no later than 10 days before trial.

(c) **Continuing Duty to Disclose.** Both an attorney for the government and the defendant must promptly disclose in writing to the other party the name, address, and telephone number of each additional witness if:
  (1) the disclosing party learns of the witness before or during trial; and
  (2) the witness should have been disclosed under Rule 12.1(a) or (b) if the disclosing party had known of the witness earlier.

(d) **Exceptions.** For good cause, the court may grant an exception to any requirement of Rule 12.1(a)–(c).

(e) **Failure to Comply.** If a party fails to comply with this rule, the court may exclude the testimony of any undisclosed witness regarding the defendant's alibi. This rule does not limit the defendant's right to testify.

(f) **Inadmissibility of Withdrawn Intention.** Evidence of an intention to rely on an alibi defense, later withdrawn, or of a statement made in connection with that intention, is not, in any civil or criminal proceeding, admissible against the person who gave notice of the intention.

(As added Apr. 22, 1974, eff. Dec. 1, 1975; amended July 31, 1975, eff. Dec. 1, 1975; Apr. 29, 1985, eff. Aug. 1, 1985; Mar. 9, 1987, eff. Aug. 1, 1987; Apr. 29, 2002, eff. Dec. 1, 2002.)

Rule 12.2. Notice of an Insanity Defense; Mental Examination

(a) **Notice of an Insanity Defense.** A defendant who intends to assert a defense of insanity at the time of the alleged offense must so notify an attorney for the government in writing within the time provided for filing a pretrial motion, or at any later time the court sets, and file a copy of the notice with the clerk. A defendant who fails to do so cannot rely on an insanity defense. The court may, for good cause, allow the defendant to file the notice late, grant additional trial-preparation time, or make other appropriate orders.

(b) **Notice of Expert Evidence of a Mental Condition.** If a defendant intends to introduce expert evidence relating to a mental disease or defect or any other mental condition of the defendant bearing on either (1) the issue of guilt or (2) the issue of punishment in a capital case, the defendant must—within the time provided for filing a pretrial motion or at any later time the court sets—notify an attorney for the government in writing of this intention and file a copy of the notice with the clerk. The court may, for good cause, allow the defendant to file the notice late, grant the parties additional trial-preparation time, or make other appropriate orders.

(c) **Mental Examination.**

   (1) *Authority to Order an Examination; Procedures.*

      (A) The court may order the defendant to submit to a competency examination under 18 U.S.C. §4241.

      (B) If the defendant provides notice under Rule 12.2(a), the court must, upon the government's motion, order the defendant to be examined under 18 U.S.C. §4242. If the defendant provides notice under Rule 12.2(b) the court may, upon the government's motion, order the defendant to be examined under procedures ordered by the court.

   (2) *Disclosing Results and Reports of Capital Sentencing Examination.* The results and reports of any examination conducted solely under Rule 12.2(c)(1) after notice under Rule 12.2(b)(2) must be sealed and must not be disclosed to any attorney for the government or the defendant unless the defendant is found guilty of one or more capital crimes and the defendant confirms an intent to offer during sentencing proceedings expert evidence on mental condition.

   (3) *Disclosing Results and Reports of the Defendant's Expert Examination.* After disclosure under Rule 12.2(c)(2) of the results and reports of the government's examination, the defendant must disclose to the government the results and reports of any examination on mental condition conducted by the defendant's expert about which the defendant intends to introduce expert evidence.

   (4) *Inadmissibility of a Defendant's Statements.* No statement made by a defendant in the course of any examination conducted under this rule (whether conducted with or without the defendant's consent), no testimony by the expert based on the statement, and no other fruits of the statement may be admitted into

evidence against the defendant in any criminal proceeding except on an issue regarding mental condition on which the defendant:

(A) has introduced evidence of incompetency or evidence requiring notice under Rule 12.2(a) or (b)(1), or

(B) has introduced expert evidence in a capital sentencing proceeding requiring notice under Rule 12.2(b)(2).

(d) Failure to Comply.

    (1) *Failure to Give Notice or to Submit to Examination.* The court may exclude any expert evidence from the defendant on the issue of the defendant's mental disease, mental defect, or any other mental condition bearing on the defendant's guilt or the issue of punishment in a capital case if the defendant fails to:

        (A) give notice under Rule 12.2(b); or

        (B) submit to an examination when ordered under Rule 12.2(c).

    (2) *Failure to Disclose.* The court may exclude any expert evidence for which the defendant has failed to comply with the disclosure requirement of Rule 12.2(c)(3).

(e) Inadmissibility of Withdrawn Intention. Evidence of an intention as to which notice was given under Rule 12.2(a) or (b), later withdrawn, is not, in any civil or criminal proceeding, admissible against the person who gave notice of the intention.

(As added Apr. 22, 1974, eff. Dec. 1, 1975; amended July 31, 1975, eff. Dec. 1, 1975; Apr. 28, 1983, eff. Aug. 1, 1983; Oct. 12, 1984; Oct. 30, 1984, eff. Oct. 12, 1984; Apr. 29, 1985, eff. Aug. 1, 1985; Nov. 10, 1986; Mar. 9, 1987, eff. Aug. 1, 1987; Apr. 29, 2002, eff. Dec. 1, 2002; Apr. 25, 2005, eff. Dec. 1, 2005.)

Rule 12.3. Notice of a Public-Authority Defense

(a) Notice of the Defense and Disclosure of Witnesses.

    (1) *Notice in General.* If a defendant intends to assert a defense of actual or believed exercise of public authority on behalf of a law enforcement agency or federal intelligence agency at the time of the alleged offense, the defendant must so notify an attorney for the government in writing and must file a copy of the notice with the clerk within the time provided for filing a pretrial motion, or at any later time the court sets. The notice filed with the clerk must be under seal if the notice identifies a federal intelligence agency as the source of public authority.

    (2) *Contents of Notice.* The notice must contain the following information:

        (A) the law enforcement agency or federal intelligence agency involved;

        (B) the agency member on whose behalf the defendant claims to have acted; and

        (C) the time during which the defendant claims to have acted with public authority.

    (3) *Response to the Notice.* An attorney for the government must serve a written response on the defendant or the defendant's attorney within 10 days after receiving the defendant's notice, but no later than 20 days before trial. The response must admit or deny that the defendant exercised the public authority identified in the defendant's notice.

(4) *Disclosing Witnesses.*

(A) *Government's Request.* An attorney for the government may request in writing that the defendant disclose the name, address, and telephone number of each witness the defendant intends to rely on to establish a public-authority defense. An attorney for the government may serve the request when the government serves its response to the defendant's notice under Rule 12.3(a)(3), or later, but must serve the request no later than 20 days before trial.

(B) *Defendant's Response.* Within 7 days after receiving the government's request, the defendant must serve on an attorney for the government a written statement of the name, address, and telephone number of each witness.

(C) *Government's Reply.* Within 7 days after receiving the defendant's statement, an attorney for the government must serve on the defendant or the defendant's attorney a written statement of the name, address, and telephone number of each witness the government intends to rely on to oppose the defendant's public-authority defense.

(5) *Additional Time.* The court may, for good cause, allow a party additional time to comply with this rule.

(b) Continuing Duty to Disclose. Both an attorney for the government and the defendant must promptly disclose in writing to the other party the name, address, and telephone number of any additional witness if:

(1) the disclosing party learns of the witness before or during trial; and

(2) the witness should have been disclosed under Rule 12.3(a)(4) if the disclosing party had known of the witness earlier.

(c) Failure to Comply. If a party fails to comply with this rule, the court may exclude the testimony of any undisclosed witness regarding the public-authority defense. This rule does not limit the defendant's right to testify.

(d) Protective Procedures Unaffected. This rule does not limit the court's authority to issue appropriate protective orders or to order that any filings be under seal.

(e) Inadmissibility of Withdrawn Intention. Evidence of an intention as to which notice was given under Rule 12.3(a), later withdrawn, is not, in any civil or criminal proceeding, admissible against the person who gave notice of the intention.

(As added Nov. 18, 1988; amended Apr. 29, 2002, eff. Dec. 1, 2002.)

Rule 12.4. Disclosure Statement

(a) Who Must File.

(1) *Nongovernmental Corporate Party.* Any nongovernmental corporate party to a proceeding in a district court must file a statement that identifies any parent corporation and any publicly held corporation that owns 10 percent or more of its stock or states that there is no such corporation.

(2) *Organizational Victim.* If an organization is a victim of the alleged criminal activity, the government must file a statement identifying the victim. If the organizational victim is a corporation, the statement must also disclose the information required by Rule 12.4(a)(1) to the extent it can be obtained through due diligence.

(b) Time for Filing; Supplemental Filing. A party must:

    (1) file the Rule 12.4(a) statement upon the defendant's initial appearance; and

    (2) promptly file a supplemental statement upon any change in the information that the statement requires.

(As added Apr. 29, 2002, eff. Dec. 1, 2002.)

Rule 13. Joint Trial of Separate Cases

The court may order that separate cases be tried together as though brought in a single indictment or information if all offenses and all defendants could have been joined in a single indictment or information.

(As amended Apr. 29, 2002, eff. Dec. 1, 2002.)

Rule 14. Relief from Prejudicial Joinder

(a) Relief. If the joinder of offenses or defendants in an indictment, an information, or a consolidation for trial appears to prejudice a defendant or the government, the court may order separate trials of counts, sever the defendants' trials, or provide any other relief that justice requires.

(b) Defendant's Statements. Before ruling on a defendant's motion to sever, the court may order an attorney for the government to deliver to the court for in camera inspection any defendant's statement that the government intends to use as evidence.

(As amended Feb. 28, 1966, eff. July 1, 1966; Apr. 29, 2002, eff. Dec. 1, 2002.)

Rule 15. Depositions

(a) When Taken.

    (1) *In General.* A party may move that a prospective witness be deposed in order to preserve testimony for trial. The court may grant the motion because of exceptional circumstances and in the interest of justice. If the court orders the deposition to be taken, it may also require the deponent to produce at the deposition any designated material that is not privileged, including any book, paper, document, record, recording, or data.

    (2) *Detained Material Witness.* A witness who is detained under 18 U.S.C. §3144 may request to be deposed by filing a written motion and giving notice to the parties. The court may then order that the deposition be taken and may discharge the witness after the witness has signed under oath the deposition transcript.

(b) Notice.

    (1) *In General.* A party seeking to take a deposition must give every other party reasonable written notice of the deposition's date and location. The notice must state the name and address of each deponent. If requested by a party receiving the notice, the court may, for good cause, change the deposition's date or location.

    (2) *To the Custodial Officer.* A party seeking to take the deposition must also notify the officer who has custody of the defendant of the scheduled date and location.

(c) Defendant's Presence.
(1) *Defendant in Custody.* The officer who has custody of the defendant must produce the defendant at the deposition and keep the defendant in the witness's presence during the examination, unless the defendant:
(A) waives in writing the right to be present; or
(B) persists in disruptive conduct justifying exclusion after being warned by the court that disruptive conduct will result in the defendant's exclusion.
(2) *Defendant Not in Custody.* A defendant who is not in custody has the right upon request to be present at the deposition, subject to any conditions imposed by the court. If the government tenders the defendant's expenses as provided in Rule 15(d) but the defendant still fails to appear, the defendant—absent good cause—waives both the right to appear and any objection to the taking and use of the deposition based on that right.

(d) Expenses. If the deposition was requested by the government, the court may—or if the defendant is unable to bear the deposition expenses, the court must—order the government to pay:
(1) any reasonable travel and subsistence expenses of the defendant and the defendant's attorney to attend the deposition; and
(2) the costs of the deposition transcript.

(e) Manner of Taking. Unless these rules or a court order provides otherwise, a deposition must be taken and filed in the same manner as a deposition in a civil action, except that:
(1) A defendant may not be deposed without that defendant's consent.
(2) The scope and manner of the deposition examination and cross-examination must be the same as would be allowed during trial.
(3) The government must provide to the defendant or the defendant's attorney, for use at the deposition, any statement of the deponent in the government's possession to which the defendant would be entitled at trial.

(f) Use as Evidence. A party may use all or part of a deposition as provided by the Federal Rules of Evidence.

(g) Objections. A party objecting to deposition testimony or evidence must state the grounds for the objection during the deposition.

(h) Depositions by Agreement Permitted. The parties may by agreement take and use a deposition with the court's consent.

(As amended Apr. 22, 1974, eff. Dec. 1, 1975; July 31, 1975, eff. Dec. 1, 1975; Oct. 12, 1984; Mar. 9, 1987, eff. Aug. 1, 1987; Apr. 29, 2002, eff. Dec. 1, 2002.)

Rule 16. Discovery and Inspection

(a) Government's Disclosure.
(1) *Information Subject to Disclosure.*
(A) *Defendant's Oral Statement.* Upon a defendant's request, the government must disclose to the defendant the substance of any relevant oral statement made by the defendant, before or after arrest, in response to interrogation by a person the defendant knew was a government agent if the government intends to use the statement at trial.

(B) *Defendant's Written or Recorded Statement.* Upon a defendant's request, the government must disclose to the defendant, and make available for inspection, copying, or photographing, all of the following:
  (i)   any relevant written or recorded statement by the defendant if:
        • the statement is within the government's possession, custody, or control; and
        • the attorney for the government knows—or through due diligence could know—that the statement exists;
  (ii) the portion of any written record containing the substance of any relevant oral statement made before or after arrest if the defendant made the statement in response to interrogation by a person the defendant knew was a government agent; and
  (iii) the defendant's recorded testimony before a grand jury relating to the charged offense.

(C) *Organizational Defendant.* Upon a defendant's request, if the defendant is an organization, the government must disclose to the defendant any statement described in Rule 16(a)(1)(A) and (B) if the government contends that the person making the statement:
  (i)   was legally able to bind the defendant regarding the subject of the statement because of that person's position as the defendant's director, officer, employee, or agent; or
  (ii) was personally involved in the alleged conduct constituting the offense and was legally able to bind the defendant regarding that conduct because of that person's position as the defendant's director, officer, employee, or agent.

(D) *Defendant's Prior Record.* Upon a defendant's request, the government must furnish the defendant with a copy of the defendant's prior criminal record that is within the government's possession, custody, or control if the attorney for the government knows—or through due diligence could know—that the record exists.

(E) *Documents and Objects.* Upon a defendant's request, the government must permit the defendant to inspect and to copy or photograph books, papers, documents, data, photographs, tangible objects, buildings or places, or copies or portions of any of these items, if the item is within the government's possession, custody, or control and:
  (i)   the item is material to preparing the defense;
  (ii) the government intends to use the item in its case-in-chief at trial; or
  (iii) the item was obtained from or belongs to the defendant.

(F) *Reports of Examinations and Tests.* Upon a defendant's request, the government must permit a defendant to inspect and to copy or photograph the results or reports of any physical or mental examination and of any scientific test or experiment if:
  (i)   the item is within the government's possession, custody, or control;
  (ii) the attorney for the government knows—or through due diligence could know—that the item exists; and
  (iii) the item is material to preparing the defense or the government intends to use the item in its case-in-chief at trial.

(G) *Expert Witnesses.* At the defendant's request, the government must give to the defendant a written summary of any testimony that the government intends to use under Rules 702, 703, or 705 of the Federal Rules of Evidence during its case-in-chief at trial. If the government requests discovery under subdivision (b)(1)(C)(ii) and the defendant complies, the government must, at the defendant's request, give to the defendant a written summary of testimony that the government intends to use under Rules 702, 703, or 705 of the Federal Rules of Evidence as evidence at trial on the issue of the defendant's mental condition. The summary provided under this subparagraph must describe the witness's opinions, the bases and reasons for those opinions, and the witness's qualifications.

(2) ***Information Not Subject to Disclosure.*** Except as Rule 16(a)(1) provides otherwise, this rule does not authorize the discovery or inspection of reports, memoranda, or other internal government documents made by an attorney for the government or other government agent in connection with investigating or prosecuting the case. Nor does this rule authorize the discovery or inspection of statements made by prospective government witnesses except as provided in 18 U.S.C. §3500.

(3) ***Grand Jury Transcripts.*** This rule does not apply to the discovery or inspection of a grand jury's recorded proceedings, except as provided in Rules 6, 12(h), 16(a)(1), and 6.2.

(b) Defendant's Disclosure.

(1) ***Information Subject to Disclosure.***

(A) *Documents and Objects.* If a defendant requests disclosure under Rule 16(a)(1)(E) and the government complies, then the defendant must permit the government, upon request, to inspect and to copy or photograph books, papers, documents, data, photographs, tangible objects, buildings or places, or copies or portions of any of these items if:

(i) the item is within the defendant's possession, custody, or control; and

(ii) the defendant intends to use the item in the defendant's case-in-chief at trial.

(B) *Reports of Examinations and Tests.* If a defendant requests disclosure under Rule 16(a)(1)(F) and the government complies, the defendant must permit the government, upon request, to inspect and to copy or photograph the results or reports of any physical or mental examination and of any scientific test or experiment if:

(i) the item is within the defendant's possession, custody, or control; and

(ii) the defendant intends to use the item in the defendant's case-in-chief at trial, or intends to call the witness who prepared the report and the report relates to the witness's testimony.

(C) *Expert Witnesses.* The defendant must, at the government's request, give to the government a written summary of any testimony that the defendant intends to use under Rules 702, 703, or 705 of the Federal Rules of Evidence as evidence at trial, if—

(i) the defendant requests disclosure under subdivision (a)(1)(G) and the government complies; or

> (ii) the defendant has given notice under Rule 12.2(b) of an intent to present expert testimony on the defendant's mental condition.
>
> This summary must describe the witness's opinions, the bases and reasons for those opinions, and the witness's qualifications.

(2) ***Information Not Subject to Disclosure.*** Except for scientific or medical reports, Rule 16(b)(1) does not authorize discovery or inspection of:

    (A) reports, memoranda, or other documents made by the defendant, or the defendant's attorney or agent, during the case's investigation or defense; or

    (B) a statement made to the defendant, or the defendant's attorney or agent, by:

        (i) the defendant;

        (ii) a government or defense witness; or

        (iii) a prospective government or defense witness.

(c) **Continuing Duty to Disclose.** A party who discovers additional evidence or material before or during trial must promptly disclose its existence to the other party or the court if:

    (1) the evidence or material is subject to discovery or inspection under this rule; and

    (2) the other party previously requested, or the court ordered, its production.

(d) **Regulating Discovery.**

    (1) ***Protective and Modifying Orders.*** At any time the court may, for good cause, deny, restrict, or defer discovery or inspection, or grant other appropriate relief. The court may permit a party to show good cause by a written statement that the court will inspect ex parte. If relief is granted, the court must preserve the entire text of the party's statement under seal.

    (2) ***Failure to Comply.*** If a party fails to comply with this rule, the court may:

        (A) order that party to permit the discovery or inspection; specify its time, place, and manner; and prescribe other just terms and conditions;

        (B) grant a continuance;

        (C) prohibit that party from introducing the undisclosed evidence; or

        (D) enter any other order that is just under the circumstances.

(As amended Feb. 28, 1966, eff. July 1, 1966; Apr. 22, 1974, eff. Dec. 1, 1975; July 31, 1975, eff. Dec. 1, 1975; Dec. 12, 1975; Apr. 28, 1983, eff. Aug. 1, 1983; Mar. 9, 1987, eff. Aug. 1, 1987; Apr. 30, 1991, eff. Dec. 1, 1991; Apr. 22, 1993, eff. Dec. 1, 1993; Apr. 29, 1994, eff. Dec. 1, 1994; Apr. 11, 1997, eff. Dec. 1, 1997; Apr. 29, 2002, eff. Dec. 1, 2002; Nov. 2, 2002, eff. Dec. 1, 2002.)

Rule 17. Subpoena

(a) **Content.** A subpoena must state the court's name and the title of the proceeding, include the seal of the court, and command the witness to attend and testify at the time and place the subpoena specifies. The clerk must issue a blank subpoena—signed and sealed—to the party requesting it, and that party must fill in the blanks before the subpoena is served.

(b) Defendant Unable to Pay. Upon a defendant's ex parte application, the court must order that a subpoena be issued for a named witness if the defendant shows an inability to pay the witness's fees and the necessity of the witness's presence for an adequate defense. If the court orders a subpoena to be issued, the process costs and witness fees will be paid in the same manner as those paid for witnesses the government subpoenas.

(c) Producing Documents and Objects.

    (1) *In General.* A subpoena may order the witness to produce any books, papers, documents, data, or other objects the subpoena designates. The court may direct the witness to produce the designated items in court before trial or before they are to be offered in evidence. When the items arrive, the court may permit the parties and their attorneys to inspect all or part of them.

    (2) *Quashing or Modifying the Subpoena.* On motion made promptly, the court may quash or modify the subpoena if compliance would be unreasonable or oppressive.

(d) Service. A marshal, a deputy marshal, or any nonparty who is at least 18 years old may serve a subpoena. The server must deliver a copy of the subpoena to the witness and must tender to the witness one day's witness-attendance fee and the legal mileage allowance. The server need not tender the attendance fee or mileage allowance when the United States, a federal officer, or a federal agency has requested the subpoena.

(e) Place of Service.

    (1) *In the United States.* A subpoena requiring a witness to attend a hearing or trial may be served at any place within the United States.

    (2) *In a Foreign Country.* If the witness is in a foreign country, 28 U.S.C. §1783 governs the subpoena's service.

(f) Issuing a Deposition Subpoena.

    (1) *Issuance.* A court order to take a deposition authorizes the clerk in the district where the deposition is to be taken to issue a subpoena for any witness named or described in the order.

    (2) *Place.* After considering the convenience of the witness and the parties, the court may order—and the subpoena may require—the witness to appear anywhere the court designates.

(g) Contempt. The court (other than a magistrate judge) may hold in contempt a witness who, without adequate excuse, disobeys a subpoena issued by a federal court in that district. A magistrate judge may hold in contempt a witness who, without adequate excuse, disobeys a subpoena issued by that magistrate judge as provided in 28 U.S.C. §636(e).

(h) Information Not Subject to a Subpoena. No party may subpoena a statement of a witness or of a prospective witness under this rule. Rule 26.2 governs the production of the statement.

(As amended Dec. 27, 1948, eff. Oct. 20, 1949; Feb. 28, 1966, eff. July 1, 1966; Apr. 24, 1972, eff. Oct. 1, 1972; Apr. 22, 1974, eff. Dec. 1, 1975; July 31, 1975, eff. Dec. 1, 1975; Apr. 30, 1979, eff. Dec. 1, 1980; Mar. 9, 1987, eff. Aug. 1, 1987; Apr. 22, 1993, eff. Dec. 1, 1993; Apr. 29, 2002, eff. Dec. 1, 2002.)

Rule 17.1. Pretrial Conference

On its own, or on a party's motion, the court may hold one or more pretrial conferences to promote a fair and expeditious trial. When a conference ends, the court must prepare and file a memorandum of any matters agreed to during the conference. The government may not use any statement made during the conference by the defendant or the defendant's attorney unless it is in writing and is signed by the defendant and the defendant's attorney.

(As added Feb. 28, 1966, eff. July 1, 1966; amended Mar. 9, 1987, eff. Aug. 1, 1987; Apr. 29, 2002, eff. Dec. 1, 2002.)

TITLE V. VENUE

Rule 18. Place of Prosecution and Trial

Unless a statute or these rules permit otherwise, the government must prosecute an offense in a district where the offense was committed. The court must set the place of trial within the district with due regard for the convenience of the defendant and the witnesses, and the prompt administration of justice.

(As amended Feb. 28, 1966, eff. July 1, 1966; Apr. 30, 1979, eff. Aug. 1, 1979; Apr. 29, 2002, eff. Dec. 1, 2002.)

Rule 19. [Reserved]

Rule 20. Transfer for Plea and Sentence
  (a) **Consent to Transfer.** A prosecution may be transferred from the district where the indictment or information is pending, or from which a warrant on a complaint has been issued, to the district where the defendant is arrested, held, or present if:
    (1) the defendant states in writing a wish to plead guilty or nolo contendere and to waive trial in the district where the indictment, information, or complaint is pending, consents in writing to the court's disposing of the case in the transferee district, and files the statement in the transferee district; and
    (2) the United States attorneys in both districts approve the transfer in writing.
  (b) **Clerk's Duties.** After receiving the defendant's statement and the required approvals, the clerk where the indictment, information, or complaint is pending must send the file, or a certified copy, to the clerk in the transferee district.
  (c) **Effect of a Not Guilty Plea.** If the defendant pleads not guilty after the case has been transferred under Rule 20(a), the clerk must return the papers to the court where the prosecution began, and that court must restore the proceeding to its docket. The defendant's statement that the defendant wished to plead guilty or nolo contendere is not, in any civil or criminal proceeding, admissible against the defendant.
  (d) **Juveniles.**
    (1) *Consent to Transfer.* A juvenile, as defined in 18 U.S.C. §5031, may be proceeded against as a juvenile delinquent in the district where the juvenile is arrested, held, or present if:
      (A) the alleged offense that occurred in the other district is not punishable by death or life imprisonment;

> (B) an attorney has advised the juvenile;
>
> (C) the court has informed the juvenile of the juvenile's rights—including the right to be returned to the district where the offense allegedly occurred—and the consequences of waiving those rights;
>
> (D) the juvenile, after receiving the court's information about rights, consents in writing to be proceeded against in the transferee district, and files the consent in the transferee district;
>
> (E) the United States attorneys for both districts approve the transfer in writing; and
>
> (F) the transferee court approves the transfer.
>
> **(2)** *Clerk's Duties.* After receiving the juvenile's written consent and the required approvals, the clerk where the indictment, information, or complaint is pending or where the alleged offense occurred must send the file, or a certified copy, to the clerk in the transferee district.

(As amended Feb. 28, 1966, eff. July 1, 1966; Apr. 22, 1974, eff. Dec. 1, 1975; July 31, 1975, eff. Dec. 1, 1975; Apr. 28, 1982, eff. Aug. 1, 1982; Mar. 9, 1987, eff. Aug. 1, 1987; Apr. 29, 2002, eff. Dec. 1, 2002.)

Rule 21. Transfer for Trial

> **(a) For Prejudice.** Upon the defendant's motion, the court must transfer the proceeding against that defendant to another district if the court is satisfied that so great a prejudice against the defendant exists in the transferring district that the defendant cannot obtain a fair and impartial trial there.
>
> **(b) For Convenience.** Upon the defendant's motion, the court may transfer the proceeding, or one or more counts, against that defendant to another district for the convenience of the parties and witnesses and in the interest of justice.
>
> **(c) Proceedings on Transfer.** When the court orders a transfer, the clerk must send to the transferee district the file, or a certified copy, and any bail taken. The prosecution will then continue in the transferee district.
>
> **(d) Time to File a Motion to Transfer.** A motion to transfer may be made at or before arraignment or at any other time the court or these rules prescribe.

(As amended Feb. 28, 1966, eff. July 1, 1966; Mar. 9, 1987, eff. Aug. 1, 1987; Apr. 29, 2002, eff. Dec. 1, 2002.)

Rule 22. [Transferred]

TITLE VI. TRIAL

Rule 23. Jury or Nonjury Trial

> **(a) Jury Trial.** If the defendant is entitled to a jury trial, the trial must be by jury unless:
>
> (1) the defendant waives a jury trial in writing;
>
> (2) the government consents; and
>
> (3) the court approves.

(b) **Jury Size.**
  (1) *In General.* A jury consists of 12 persons unless this rule provides otherwise.
  (2) *Stipulation for a Smaller Jury.* At any time before the verdict, the parties may, with the court's approval, stipulate in writing that:
    (A) the jury may consist of fewer than 12 persons; or
    (B) a jury of fewer than 12 persons may return a verdict if the court finds it necessary to excuse a juror for good cause after the trial begins.
  (3) *Court Order for a Jury of 11.* After the jury has retired to deliberate, the court may permit a jury of 11 persons to return a verdict, even without a stipulation by the parties, if the court finds good cause to excuse a juror.
(c) **Nonjury Trial.** In a case tried without a jury, the court must find the defendant guilty or not guilty. If a party requests before the finding of guilty or not guilty, the court must state its specific findings of fact in open court or in a written decision or opinion.

(As amended Feb. 28, 1966, eff. July 1, 1966; July 30, 1977, eff. Oct. 1, 1977; Apr. 28, 1983, eff. Aug. 1, 1983; Apr. 29, 2002, eff. Dec. 1, 2002.)

Rule 24. Trial Jurors

(a) **Examination.**
  (1) *In General.* The court may examine prospective jurors or may permit the attorneys for the parties to do so.
  (2) *Court Examination.* If the court examines the jurors, it must permit the attorneys for the parties to:
    (A) ask further questions that the court considers proper; or
    (B) submit further questions that the court may ask if it considers them proper.
(b) **Peremptory Challenges.** Each side is entitled to the number of peremptory challenges to prospective jurors specified below. The court may allow additional peremptory challenges to multiple defendants, and may allow the defendants to exercise those challenges separately or jointly.
  (1) *Capital Case.* Each side has 20 peremptory challenges when the government seeks the death penalty.
  (2) *Other Felony Case.* The government has 6 peremptory challenges and the defendant or defendants jointly have 10 peremptory challenges when the defendant is charged with a crime punishable by imprisonment of more than one year.
  (3) *Misdemeanor Case.* Each side has 3 peremptory challenges when the defendant is charged with a crime punishable by fine, imprisonment of one year or less, or both.
(c) **Alternate Jurors.**
  (1) *In General.* The court may impanel up to 6 alternate jurors to replace any jurors who are unable to perform or who are disqualified from performing their duties.
  (2) *Procedure.*
    (A) Alternate jurors must have the same qualifications and be selected and sworn in the same manner as any other juror.

      (B) Alternate jurors replace jurors in the same sequence in which the alternates were selected. An alternate juror who replaces a juror has the same authority as the other jurors.

  (3) *Retaining Alternate Jurors.* The court may retain alternate jurors after the jury retires to deliberate. The court must ensure that a retained alternate does not discuss the case with anyone until that alternate replaces a juror or is discharged. If an alternate replaces a juror after deliberations have begun, the court must instruct the jury to begin its deliberations anew.

  (4) *Peremptory Challenges.* Each side is entitled to the number of additional peremptory challenges to prospective alternate jurors specified below. These additional challenges may be used only to remove alternate jurors.

      (A) *One or Two Alternates.* One additional peremptory challenge is permitted when one or two alternates are impaneled.

      (B) *Three or Four Alternates.* Two additional peremptory challenges are permitted when three or four alternates are impaneled.

      (C) *Five or Six Alternates.* Three additional peremptory challenges are permitted when five or six alternates are impaneled.

(As amended Feb. 28, 1966, eff. July 1, 1966; Mar. 9, 1987, eff. Aug. 1, 1987; Apr. 26, 1999, eff. Dec. 1, 1999; Apr. 29, 2002, eff. Dec. 1, 2002.)

Rule 25. Judge's Disability

  (a) **During Trial.** Any judge regularly sitting in or assigned to the court may complete a jury trial if:

    (1) the judge before whom the trial began cannot proceed because of death, sickness, or other disability; and

    (2) the judge completing the trial certifies familiarity with the trial record.

  (b) **After a Verdict or Finding of Guilty.**

    (1) *In General.* After a verdict or finding of guilty, any judge regularly sitting in or assigned to a court may complete the court's duties if the judge who presided at trial cannot perform those duties because of absence, death, sickness, or other disability.

    (2) *Granting a New Trial.* The successor judge may grant a new trial if satisfied that:

      (A) a judge other than the one who presided at the trial cannot perform the posttrial duties; or

      (B) a new trial is necessary for some other reason.

(As amended Feb. 28, 1966, eff. July 1, 1966; Mar. 9, 1987, eff. Aug. 1, 1987; Apr. 29, 2002, eff. Dec. 1, 2002.)

Rule 26. Taking Testimony

In every trial the testimony of witnesses must be taken in open court, unless otherwise provided by a statute or by rules adopted under 28 U.S.C. §§2072–2077.

(As amended Nov. 20, 1972, eff. July 1, 1975; Apr. 29, 2002, eff. Dec. 1, 2002.)

Rule 26.1. Foreign Law Determination

A party intending to raise an issue of foreign law must provide the court and all parties with reasonable written notice. Issues of foreign law are questions of law, but in deciding such issues a court may consider any relevant material or source—including testimony—without regard to the Federal Rules of Evidence.

(As added Feb. 28, 1966, eff. July 1, 1966; amended Nov. 20, 1972, eff. July 1, 1975; Apr. 29, 2002, eff. Dec. 1, 2002.)

Rule 26.2. Producing a Witness's Statement

(a) **Motion to Produce.** After a witness other than the defendant has testified on direct examination, the court, on motion of a party who did not call the witness, must order an attorney for the government or the defendant and the defendant's attorney to produce, for the examination and use of the moving party, any statement of the witness that is in their possession and that relates to the subject matter of the witness's testimony.

(b) **Producing the Entire Statement.** If the entire statement relates to the subject matter of the witness's testimony, the court must order that the statement be delivered to the moving party.

(c) **Producing a Redacted Statement.** If the party who called the witness claims that the statement contains information that is privileged or does not relate to the subject matter of the witness's testimony, the court must inspect the statement in camera. After excising any privileged or unrelated portions, the court must order delivery of the redacted statement to the moving party. If the defendant objects to an excision, the court must preserve the entire statement with the excised portion indicated, under seal, as part of the record.

(d) **Recess to Examine a Statement.** The court may recess the proceedings to allow time for a party to examine the statement and prepare for its use.

(e) **Sanction for Failure to Produce or Deliver a Statement.** If the party who called the witness disobeys an order to produce or deliver a statement, the court must strike the witness's testimony from the record. If an attorney for the government disobeys the order, the court must declare a mistrial if justice so requires.

(f) **"Statement" Defined.** As used in this rule, a witness's "statement" means:
   (1) a written statement that the witness makes and signs, or otherwise adopts or approves;
   (2) a substantially verbatim, contemporaneously recorded recital of the witness's oral statement that is contained in any recording or any transcription of a recording; or
   (3) the witness's statement to a grand jury, however taken or recorded, or a transcription of such a statement.

(g) **Scope.** This rule applies at trial, at a suppression hearing under Rule 12, and to the extent specified in the following rules:
   (1) Rule 5.1(h) (preliminary hearing);
   (2) Rule 32(i)(2) (sentencing);
   (3) Rule 32.1(e) (hearing to revoke or modify probation or supervised release);

    (4)   Rule 46(j) (detention hearing); and

    (5)   Rule 8 of the Rules Governing Proceedings under 28 U.S.C. §2255.

(As added Apr. 30, 1979, eff. Dec. 1, 1980; amended Mar. 9, 1987, eff. Aug. 1, 1987; Apr. 22, 1993, eff. Dec. 1, 1993; Apr. 24, 1998, eff. Dec. 1, 1998; Apr. 29, 2002, eff. Dec. 1, 2002.)

Rule 26.3. Mistrial

Before ordering a mistrial, the court must give each defendant and the government an opportunity to comment on the propriety of the order, to state whether that party consents or objects, and to suggest alternatives.

(As added Apr. 22, 1993, eff. Dec. 1, 1993; amended Apr. 29, 2002, eff. Dec. 1, 2002.)

Rule 27. Proving an Official Record

A party may prove an official record, an entry in such a record, or the lack of a record or entry in the same manner as in a civil action.

(As amended Apr. 29, 2002, eff. Dec, 1, 2002.)

Rule 28. Interpreters

The court may select, appoint, and set the reasonable compensation for an interpreter. The compensation must be paid from funds provided by law or by the government, as the court may direct.

(As amended Feb. 28, 1966, eff. July 1, 1966; Nov. 20, 1972, eff. July 1, 1975; Apr. 29, 2002, eff. Dec. 1, 2002.)

Rule 29. Motion for a Judgment of Acquittal

    (a) **Before Submission to the Jury.** After the government closes its evidence or after the close of all the evidence, the court on the defendant's motion must enter a judgment of acquittal of any offense for which the evidence is insufficient to sustain a conviction. The court may on its own consider whether the evidence is insufficient to sustain a conviction. If the court denies a motion for a judgment of acquittal at the close of the government's evidence, the defendant may offer evidence without having reserved the right to do so.

    (b) **Reserving Decision.** The court may reserve decision on the motion, proceed with the trial (where the motion is made before the close of all the evidence), submit the case to the jury, and decide the motion either before the jury returns a verdict or after it returns a verdict of guilty or is discharged without having returned a verdict. If the court reserves decision, it must decide the motion on the basis of the evidence at the time the ruling was reserved.

    (c) **After Jury Verdict or Discharge.**

        (1) *Time for a Motion.* A defendant may move for a judgment of acquittal, or renew such a motion, within seven days after a guilty verdict or after the court discharges the jury, whichever is later.

(2) **Ruling on the Motion.** If the jury has returned a guilty verdict, the court may set aside the verdict and enter an acquittal. If the jury has failed to return a verdict, the court may enter a judgment of acquittal.

(3) **No Prior Motion Required.** A defendant is not required to move for a judgment of acquittal before the court submits the case to the jury as a prerequisite for making such a motion after jury discharge.

(d) **Conditional Ruling on a Motion for a New Trial.**

(1) **Motion for a New Trial.** If the court enters a judgment of acquittal after a guilty verdict, the court must also conditionally determine whether any motion for a new trial should be granted if the judgment of acquittal is later vacated or reversed. The court must specify the reasons for that determination.

(2) **Finality.** The court's order conditionally granting a motion for a new trial does not affect the finality of the judgment of acquittal.

(3) **Appeal.**

(A) *Grant of a Motion for a New Trial.* If the court conditionally grants a motion for a new trial and an appellate court later reverses the judgment of acquittal, the trial court must proceed with the new trial unless the appellate court orders otherwise.

(B) *Denial of a Motion for a New Trial.* If the court conditionally denies a motion for a new trial, an appellee may assert that the denial was erroneous. If the appellate court later reverses the judgment of acquittal, the trial court must proceed as the appellate court directs.

(As amended Feb. 28, 1966, eff. July 1, 1966; Nov. 10, 1986, eff. Dec. 10, 1986; Apr. 29, 1994, eff. Dec. 1, 1994; Apr. 29, 2002, eff. Dec. 1, 2002; Apr. 25, 2005, eff. Dec. 1, 2005.)

Rule 29.1. Closing Argument

Closing arguments proceed in the following order:
(a) the government argues;
(b) the defense argues; and
(c) the government rebuts.

(As added Apr. 22, 1974, eff. Dec. 1, 1975; amended Apr. 29, 2002, eff. Dec. 1, 2002.)

Rule 30. Jury Instructions

(a) **In General.** Any party may request in writing that the court instruct the jury on the law as specified in the request. The request must be made at the close of the evidence or at any earlier time that the court reasonably sets. When the request is made, the requesting party must furnish a copy to every other party.

(b) **Ruling on a Request.** The court must inform the parties before closing arguments how it intends to rule on the requested instructions.

(c) **Time for Giving Instructions.** The court may instruct the jury before or after the arguments are completed, or at both times.

(d) **Objections to Instructions.** A party who objects to any portion of the instructions or to a failure to give a requested instruction must inform the court of the specific objection and the grounds for the objection before the jury retires to deliberate. An opportunity must be given to object out of the jury's hearing and, on request, out of the jury's presence. Failure to object in accordance with this rule precludes appellate review, except as permitted under Rule 52(b).

(As amended Feb. 28, 1966, eff. July 1, 1966; Mar. 9, 1987, eff. Aug. 1, 1987; Apr. 25, 1988, eff. Aug. 1, 1988; Apr. 29, 2002, eff. Dec. 1, 2002.)

Rule 31. Jury Verdict

(a) **Return.** The jury must return its verdict to a judge in open court. The verdict must be unanimous.

(b) **Partial Verdicts, Mistrial, and Retrial.**

    (1) *Multiple Defendants.* If there are multiple defendants, the jury may return a verdict at any time during its deliberations as to any defendant about whom it has agreed.

    (2) *Multiple Counts.* If the jury cannot agree on all counts as to any defendant, the jury may return a verdict on those counts on which it has agreed.

    (3) *Mistrial and Retrial.* If the jury cannot agree on a verdict on one or more counts, the court may declare a mistrial on those counts. The government may retry any defendant on any count on which the jury could not agree.

(c) **Lesser Offense or Attempt.** A defendant may be found guilty of any of the following:

    (1) an offense necessarily included in the offense charged;

    (2) an attempt to commit the offense charged; or

    (3) an attempt to commit an offense necessarily included in the offense charged, if the attempt is an offense in its own right.

(d) **Jury Poll.** After a verdict is returned but before the jury is discharged, the court must on a party's request, or may on its own, poll the jurors individually. If the poll reveals a lack of unanimity, the court may direct the jury to deliberate further or may declare a mistrial and discharge the jury.

(As amended Apr. 24, 1972, eff. Oct. 1, 1972; Apr. 24, 1998, eff. Dec. 1, 1998; Apr. 17, 2000, eff. Dec. 1, 2000; Apr. 29, 2002, eff. Dec. 1, 2002.)

TITLE VII. POSTCONVICTION PROCEDURES

Rule 32. Sentencing and Judgment

(a) **Definitions.** The following definitions apply under this rule:

    (1) "Crime of violence or sexual abuse" means:

        (A) a crime that involves the use, attempted use, or threatened use of physical force against another's person or property; or

        (B) a crime under 18 U.S.C. §§2241–2248 or §§2251–2257.

    (2) "Victim" means an individual against whom the defendant committed an offense for which the court will impose sentence.

(b) **Time of Sentencing.**

    (1) *In General.* The court must impose sentence without unnecessary delay.

    (2) *Changing Time Limits.* The court may, for good cause, change any time limits prescribed in this rule.

(c) Presentence Investigation.

    (1) *Required Investigation.*

        (A) *In General.* The probation officer must conduct a presentence investigation and submit a report to the court before it imposes sentence unless:

            (i)   18 U.S.C. §3593(c) or another statute requires otherwise; or

            (ii) the court finds that the information in the record enables it to meaningfully exercise its sentencing authority under 18 U.S.C. §3553, and the court explains its finding on the record.

        (B) *Restitution.* If the law requires restitution, the probation officer must conduct an investigation and submit a report that contains sufficient information for the court to order restitution.

    (2) *Interviewing the Defendant.* The probation officer who interviews a defendant as part of a presentence investigation must, on request, give the defendant's attorney notice and a reasonable opportunity to attend the interview.

(d) Presentence Report.

    (1) *Applying the Sentencing Guidelines.* The presentence report must:

        (A) identify all applicable guidelines and policy statements of the Sentencing Commission;

        (B) calculate the defendant's offense level and criminal history category;

        (C) state the resulting sentencing range and kinds of sentences available;

        (D) identify any factor relevant to:

            (i)   the appropriate kind of sentence, or

            (ii) the appropriate sentence within the applicable sentencing range; and

        (E) identify any basis for departing from the applicable sentencing range.

    (2) *Additional Information.* The presentence report must also contain the following information:

        (A) the defendant's history and characteristics, including:

            (i)   any prior criminal record;

            (ii) the defendant's financial condition; and

            (iii) any circumstances affecting the defendant's behavior that may be helpful in imposing sentence or in correctional treatment;

        (B) verified information, stated in a nonargumentative style, that assesses the financial, social, psychological, and medical impact on any individual against whom the offense has been committed;

        (C) when appropriate, the nature and extent of nonprison programs and resources available to the defendant;

        (D) when the law provides for restitution, information sufficient for a restitution order;

        (E) if the court orders a study under 18 U.S.C. §3552(b), any resulting report and recommendation; and

        (F) any other information that the court requires.

    (3) *Exclusions.* The presentence report must exclude the following:

        (A) any diagnoses that, if disclosed, might seriously disrupt a rehabilitation program;

        (B) any sources of information obtained upon a promise of confidentiality; and

(C) any other information that, if disclosed, might result in physical or other harm to the defendant or others.

(e) Disclosing the Report and Recommendation.

(1) *Time to Disclose.* Unless the defendant has consented in writing, the probation officer must not submit a presentence report to the court or disclose its contents to anyone until the defendant has pleaded guilty or nolo contendere, or has been found guilty.

(2) *Minimum Required Notice.* The probation officer must give the presentence report to the defendant, the defendant's attorney, and an attorney for the government at least 35 days before sentencing unless the defendant waives this minimum period.

(3) *Sentence Recommendation.* By local rule or by order in a case, the court may direct the probation officer not to disclose to anyone other than the court the officer's recommendation on the sentence.

(f) Objecting to the Report.

(1) *Time to Object.* Within 14 days after receiving the presentence report, the parties must state in writing any objections, including objections to material information, sentencing guideline ranges, and policy statements contained in or omitted from the report.

(2) *Serving Objections.* An objecting party must provide a copy of its objections to the opposing party and to the probation officer.

(3) *Action on Objections.* After receiving objections, the probation officer may meet with the parties to discuss the objections. The probation officer may then investigate further and revise the presentence report as appropriate.

(g) Submitting the Report. At least seven days before sentencing, the probation officer must submit to the court and to the parties the presentence report and an addendum containing any unresolved objections, the grounds for those objections, and the probation officer's comments on them.

(h) Notice of Possible Departure from Sentencing Guidelines. Before the court may depart from the applicable sentencing range on a ground not identified for departure either in the presentence report or in a party's prehearing submission, the court must give the parties reasonable notice that it is contemplating such a departure. The notice must specify any ground on which the court is contemplating a departure.

(i) Sentencing.

(1) *In General.* At sentencing, the court:

(A) must verify that the defendant and the defendant's attorney have read and discussed the presentence report and any addendum to the report;

(B) must give to the defendant and an attorney for the government a written summary of—or summarize in camera—any information excluded from the presentence report under Rule 32(d)(3) on which the court will rely in sentencing, and give them a reasonable opportunity to comment on that information;

(C) must allow the parties' attorneys to comment on the probation officer's determinations and other matters relating to an appropriate sentence; and

(D) may, for good cause, allow a party to make a new objection at any time before sentence is imposed.

(2) *Introducing Evidence; Producing a Statement.* The court may permit the parties to introduce evidence on the objections. If a witness testifies at sentencing, Rule 26.2(a)–(d) and (f) applies. If a party fails to comply with a Rule 26.2 order to produce a witness's statement, the court must not consider that witness's testimony.

(3) *Court Determinations.* At sentencing, the court:

    (A) may accept any undisputed portion of the presentence report as a finding of fact;

    (B) must—for any disputed portion of the presentence report or other controverted matter—rule on the dispute or determine that a ruling is unnecessary either because the matter will not affect sentencing, or because the court will not consider the matter in sentencing; and

    (C) must append a copy of the court's determinations under this rule to any copy of the presentence report made available to the Bureau of Prisons.

(4) *Opportunity to Speak.*

    (A) *By a Party.* Before imposing sentence, the court must:

        (i) provide the defendant's attorney an opportunity to speak on the defendant's behalf;

        (ii) address the defendant personally in order to permit the defendant to speak or present any information to mitigate the sentence; and

        (iii) provide an attorney for the government an opportunity to speak equivalent to that of the defendant's attorney.

    (B) *By a Victim.* Before imposing sentence, the court must address any victim of a crime of violence or sexual abuse who is present at sentencing and must permit the victim to speak or submit any information about the sentence. Whether or not the victim is present, a victim's right to address the court may be exercised by the following persons if present:

        (i) a parent or legal guardian, if the victim is younger than 18 years or is incompetent; or

        (ii) one or more family members or relatives the court designates, if the victim is deceased or incapacitated.

    (C) *In Camera Proceedings.* Upon a party's motion and for good cause, the court may hear in camera any statement made under Rule 32(i)(4).

(j) Defendant's Right to Appeal.

    (1) *Advice of a Right to Appeal.*

        (A) *Appealing a Conviction.* If the defendant pleaded not guilty and was convicted, after sentencing the court must advise the defendant of the right to appeal the conviction.

        (B) *Appealing a Sentence.* After sentencing—regardless of the defendant's plea—the court must advise the defendant of any right to appeal the sentence.

        (C) *Appeal Costs.* The court must advise a defendant who is unable to pay appeal costs of the right to ask for permission to appeal in forma pauperis.

    (2) *Clerk's Filing of Notice.* If the defendant so requests, the clerk must immediately prepare and file a notice of appeal on the defendant's behalf.

(k) Judgment.

    (1) *In General.* In the judgment of conviction, the court must set forth the plea, the jury verdict or the court's findings, the adjudication, and the sentence. If the defendant is found not guilty or is otherwise entitled to be discharged, the court must so order. The judge must sign the judgment, and the clerk must enter it.

    (2) *Criminal Forfeiture.* Forfeiture procedures are governed by Rule 32.2.

(As amended Feb. 28, 1966, eff. July 1, 1966; Apr. 24, 1972, eff. Oct. 1, 1972; Apr. 22, 1974, eff. Dec. 1, 1975; July 31, 1975, eff. Dec. 1, 1975; Apr. 30, 1979, eff. Aug. 1, 1979, and Dec. 1, 1980; Oct. 12, 1982; Apr. 28, 1983, eff. Aug. 1, 1983; Oct. 12, 1984, eff. Nov. 1, 1987; Mar. 9, 1987, eff. Aug. 1, 1987; Apr. 25, 1989, eff. Dec. 1, 1989; Apr. 30, 1991, eff. Dec. 1, 1991; Apr. 22, 1993, eff. Dec. 1, 1993; Apr. 29, 1994, eff. Dec. 1, 1994; Sept. 13, 1994, eff. Dec. 1, 1994; Apr. 23, 1996, eff. Dec. 1, 1996; Apr. 24, 1996; Apr. 17, 2000, eff. Dec. 1, 2000; Apr. 29, 2002, eff. Dec. 1, 2002.)

Rule 32.1. Revoking or Modifying Probation or Supervised Release

(a) Initial Appearance.

    (1) *Person In Custody.* A person held in custody for violating probation or supervised release must be taken without unnecessary delay before a magistrate judge.

        (A) If the person is held in custody in the district where an alleged violation occurred, the initial appearance must be in that district.

        (B) If the person is held in custody in a district other than where an alleged violation occurred, the initial appearance must be in that district, or in an adjacent district if the appearance can occur more promptly there.

    (2) *Upon a Summons.* When a person appears in response to a summons for violating probation or supervised release, a magistrate judge must proceed under this rule.

    (3) *Advice.* The judge must inform the person of the following:

        (A) the alleged violation of probation or supervised release;

        (B) the person's right to retain counsel or to request that counsel be appointed if the person cannot obtain counsel; and

        (C) the person's right, if held in custody, to a preliminary hearing under Rule 32.1(b)(1).

    (4) *Appearance in the District with Jurisdiction.* If the person is arrested or appears in the district that has jurisdiction to conduct a revocation hearing—either originally or by transfer of jurisdiction—the court must proceed under Rule 32.1(b)–(e).

    (5) *Appearance in a District Lacking Jurisdiction.* If the person is arrested or appears in a district that does not have jurisdiction to conduct a revocation hearing, the magistrate judge must:

        (A) if the alleged violation occurred in the district of arrest, conduct a preliminary hearing under Rule 32.1(b) and either:

            (i) transfer the person to the district that has jurisdiction, if the judge finds probable cause to believe that a violation occurred; or

            (ii) dismiss the proceedings and so notify the court that has jurisdiction, if the judge finds no probable cause to believe that a violation occurred; or

(B) if the alleged violation did not occur in the district of arrest, transfer the person to the district that has jurisdiction if:

    (i) the government produces certified copies of the judgment, warrant, and warrant application, or produces copies of those certified documents by reliable electronic means; and

    (ii) the judge finds that the person is the same person named in the warrant.

(6) *Release or Detention.* The magistrate judge may release or detain the person under 18 U.S.C. §3143(a) pending further proceedings. The burden of establishing that the person will not flee or pose a danger to any other person or to the community rests with the person.

(b) Revocation.

  (1) *Preliminary Hearing.*

    (A) *In General.* If a person is in custody for violating a condition of probation or supervised release, a magistrate judge must promptly conduct a hearing to determine whether there is probable cause to believe that a violation occurred. The person may waive the hearing.

    (B) *Requirements.* The hearing must be recorded by a court reporter or by a suitable recording device. The judge must give the person:

      (i) notice of the hearing and its purpose, the alleged violation, and the person's right to retain counsel or to request that counsel be appointed if the person cannot obtain counsel;

      (ii) an opportunity to appear at the hearing and present evidence; and

      (iii) upon request, an opportunity to question any adverse witness, unless the judge determines that the interest of justice does not require the witness to appear.

    (C) *Referral.* If the judge finds probable cause, the judge must conduct a revocation hearing. If the judge does not find probable cause, the judge must dismiss the proceeding.

  (2) *Revocation Hearing.* Unless waived by the person, the court must hold the revocation hearing within a reasonable time in the district having jurisdiction. The person is entitled to:

    (A) written notice of the alleged violation;

    (B) disclosure of the evidence against the person;

    (C) an opportunity to appear, present evidence, and question any adverse witness unless the court determines that the interest of justice does not require the witness to appear;

    (D) notice of the person's right to retain counsel or to request that counsel be appointed if the person cannot obtain counsel; and

    (E) an opportunity to make a statement and present any information in mitigation.

(c) Modification.

  (1) *In General.* Before modifying the conditions of probation or supervised release, the court must hold a hearing, at which the person has the right to counsel and an opportunity to make a statement and present any information in mitigation.

(2) *Exceptions.* A hearing is not required if:

(A) the person waives the hearing; or

(B) the relief sought is favorable to the person and does not extend the term of probation or of supervised release; and

(C) an attorney for the government has received notice of the relief sought, has had a reasonable opportunity to object, and has not done so.

(d) **Disposition of the Case.** The court's disposition of the case is governed by 18 U.S.C. §3563 and §3565 (probation) and §3583 (supervised release).

(e) **Producing a Statement.** Rule 26.2(a)–(d) and (f) applies at a hearing under this rule. If a party fails to comply with a Rule 26.2 order to produce a witness's statement, the court must not consider that witness's testimony.

(As added Apr. 30, 1979, eff. Dec. 1, 1980; amended Nov. 10, 1986, eff. Dec. 10, 1986; Mar. 9, 1987, eff. Aug. 1, 1987; Apr. 25, 1989, eff. Dec. 1, 1989; Apr. 30, 1991, eff. Dec. 1, 1991; Apr. 22, 1993, eff. Dec. 1, 1993; Apr. 29, 2002, eff. Dec. 1, 2002; Apr. 25, 2005, eff. Dec. 1, 2005; Apr. 12, 2006, eff. Dec. 1, 2006.)

Rule 32.2. Criminal Forfeiture

(a) **Notice to the Defendant.** A court must not enter a judgment of forfeiture in a criminal proceeding unless the indictment or information contains notice to the defendant that the government will seek the forfeiture of property as part of any sentence in accordance with the applicable statute.

(b) **Entering a Preliminary Order of Forfeiture.**

(1) *In General.* As soon as practicable after a verdict or finding of guilty, or after a plea of guilty or nolo contendere is accepted, on any count in an indictment or information regarding which criminal forfeiture is sought, the court must determine what property is subject to forfeiture under the applicable statute. If the government seeks forfeiture of specific property, the court must determine whether the government has established the requisite nexus between the property and the offense. If the government seeks a personal money judgment, the court must determine the amount of money that the defendant will be ordered to pay. The court's determination may be based on evidence already in the record, including any written plea agreement or, if the forfeiture is contested, on evidence or information presented by the parties at a hearing after the verdict or finding of guilt.

(2) *Preliminary Order.* If the court finds that property is subject to forfeiture, it must promptly enter a preliminary order of forfeiture setting forth the amount of any money judgment or directing the forfeiture of specific property without regard to any third party's interest in all or part of it. Determining whether a third party has such an interest must be deferred until any third party files a claim in an ancillary proceeding under Rule 32.2(c).

(3) *Seizing Property.* The entry of a preliminary order of forfeiture authorizes the Attorney General (or a designee) to seize the specific property subject to forfeiture; to conduct any discovery the court considers proper in identifying, locating, or disposing of the property; and to commence proceedings that comply with any statutes governing third-party rights. At sentencing—or at

any time before sentencing if the defendant consents—the order of forfeiture becomes final as to the defendant and must be made a part of the sentence and be included in the judgment. The court may include in the order of forfeiture conditions reasonably necessary to preserve the property's value pending any appeal.

(4) *Jury Determination.* Upon a party's request in a case in which a jury returns a verdict of guilty, the jury must determine whether the government has established the requisite nexus between the property and the offense committed by the defendant.

(c) Ancillary Proceeding; Entering a Final Order of Forfeiture.

(1) *In General.* If, as prescribed by statute, a third party files a petition asserting an interest in the property to be forfeited, the court must conduct an ancillary proceeding, but no ancillary proceeding is required to the extent that the forfeiture consists of a money judgment.

  (A) In the ancillary proceeding, the court may, on motion, dismiss the petition for lack of standing, for failure to state a claim, or for any other lawful reason. For purposes of the motion, the facts set forth in the petition are assumed to be true.

  (B) After disposing of any motion filed under Rule 32.2(c)(1)(A) and before conducting a hearing on the petition, the court may permit the parties to conduct discovery in accordance with the Federal Rules of Civil Procedure if the court determines that discovery is necessary or desirable to resolve factual issues. When discovery ends, a party may move for summary judgment under Federal Rule of Civil Procedure 56.

(2) *Entering a Final Order.* When the ancillary proceeding ends, the court must enter a final order of forfeiture by amending the preliminary order as necessary to account for any third-party rights. If no third party files a timely petition, the preliminary order becomes the final order of forfeiture if the court finds that the defendant (or any combination of defendants convicted in the case) had an interest in the property that is forfeitable under the applicable statute. The defendant may not object to the entry of the final order on the ground that the property belongs, in whole or in part, to a codefendant or third party; nor may a third party object to the final order on the ground that the third party had an interest in the property.

(3) *Multiple Petitions.* If multiple third-party petitions are filed in the same case, an order dismissing or granting one petition is not appealable until rulings are made on all the petitions, unless the court determines that there is no just reason for delay.

(4) *Ancillary Proceeding Not Part of Sentencing.* An ancillary proceeding is not part of sentencing.

(d) Stay Pending Appeal. If a defendant appeals from a conviction or an order of forfeiture, the court may stay the order of forfeiture on terms appropriate to ensure that the property remains available pending appellate review. A stay does not delay the ancillary proceeding or the determination of a third party's rights or interests. If the court rules in favor of any third party while an appeal is pending, the court may amend the order of forfeiture but must not transfer any property interest to a third party until the decision on appeal becomes final, unless the defendant consents in writing or on the record.

(e) Subsequently Located Property; Substitute Property.

(1) *In General.* On the government's motion, the court may at any time enter an order of forfeiture or amend an existing order of forfeiture to include property that:

(A) is subject to forfeiture under an existing order of forfeiture but was located and identified after that order was entered; or

(B) is substitute property that qualifies for forfeiture under an applicable statute.

(2) *Procedure.* If the government shows that the property is subject to forfeiture under Rule 32.2(e)(1), the court must:

(A) enter an order forfeiting that property, or amend an existing preliminary or final order to include it; and

(B) if a third party files a petition claiming an interest in the property, conduct an ancillary proceeding under Rule 32.2(c).

(3) *Jury Trial Limited.* There is no right to a jury trial under Rule 32.2(e).

(As added Apr. 17, 2000, eff. Dec. 1, 2000; amended Apr. 29, 2002, eff. Dec. 1, 2002.)

Rule 33. New Trial

(a) Defendant's Motion. Upon the defendant's motion, the court may vacate any judgment and grant a new trial if the interest of justice so requires. If the case was tried without a jury, the court may take additional testimony and enter a new judgment.

(b) Time to File.

(1) *Newly Discovered Evidence.* Any motion for a new trial grounded on newly discovered evidence must be filed within three years after the verdict or finding of guilty. If an appeal is pending, the court may not grant a motion for a new trial until the appellate court remands the case.

(2) *Other Grounds.* Any motion for a new trial grounded on any reason other than newly discovered evidence must be filed within seven days after the verdict or finding of guilty.

(As amended Feb. 28, 1966, eff. July 1, 1966; Mar. 9, 1987, eff. Aug. 1, 1987; Apr. 24, 1998, eff. Dec. 1, 1998; Apr. 29, 2002, eff. Dec. 1, 2002; Apr. 25, 2005, eff. Dec. 1, 2005.)

Rule 34. Arresting Judgment

(a) In General. Upon the defendant's motion or on its own, the court must arrest judgment if:

(1) the indictment or information does not charge an offense; or

(2) the court does not have jurisdiction of the charged offense.

(b) Time to File. The defendant must move to arrest judgment within seven days after the court accepts a verdict or finding of guilty, or after a plea of guilty or nolo contendere.

(As amended Feb. 28, 1966, eff. July 1, 1966; Apr. 29, 2002, eff. Dec. 1, 2002; Apr. 25, 2005, eff. Dec. 1, 2005.)

Rule 35. Correcting or Reducing a Sentence

(a) **Correcting Clear Error.** Within seven days after sentencing, the court may correct a sentence that resulted from arithmetical, technical, or other clear error.

(b) **Reducing a Sentence for Substantial Assistance.**

    (1) *In General.* Upon the government's motion made within one year of sentencing, the court may reduce a sentence if:

        (A) the defendant, after sentencing, provided substantial assistance in investigating or prosecuting another person; and

        (B) reducing the sentence accords with the Sentencing Commission's guidelines and policy statements.

    (2) *Later Motion.* Upon the government's motion made more than one year after sentencing, the court may reduce a sentence if the defendant's substantial assistance involved:

        (A) information not known to the defendant until one year or more after sentencing;

        (B) information provided by the defendant to the government within one year of sentencing, but which did not become useful to the government until more than one year after sentencing; or

        (C) information the usefulness of which could not reasonably have been anticipated by the defendant until more than one year after sentencing and which was promptly provided to the government after its usefulness was reasonably apparent to the defendant.

    (3) *Evaluating Substantial Assistance.* In evaluating whether the defendant has provided substantial assistance, the court may consider the defendant's presentence assistance.

    (4) *Below Statutory Minimum.* When acting under Rule 35(b), the court may reduce the sentence to a level below the minimum sentence established by statute.

(c) **'Sentencing" Defined.** As used in this rule, "sentencing" means the oral announcement of the sentence.

(As amended Feb. 28, 1966, eff. July 1, 1966; Apr. 30, 1979, eff. Aug. 1, 1979; Apr. 28, 1983, eff. Aug. 1, 1983; Oct. 12, 1984, eff. Nov. 1, 1987; Apr. 29, 1985, eff. Aug. 1, 1985; Oct. 27, 1986, eff. Nov. 1, 1987; Apr. 30, 1991, eff. Dec. 1, 1991; Apr. 24, 1998, eff. Dec. 1, 1998; Apr. 29, 2002, eff. Dec. 1, 2002; Apr. 26, 2004, eff. Dec. 1, 2004.)

Rule 36. Clerical Error

After giving any notice it considers appropriate, the court may at any time correct a clerical error in a judgment, order, or other part of the record, or correct an error in the record arising from oversight or omission.

(As amended Apr. 29, 2002, eff. Dec. 1, 2002.)

Rule 37. [Reserved]

Rule 38. Staying a Sentence or a Disability

(a) **Death Sentence.** The court must stay a death sentence if the defendant appeals the conviction or sentence.

(b) **Imprisonment.**

    (1) *Stay Granted.* If the defendant is released pending appeal, the court must stay a sentence of imprisonment.

    (2) *Stay Denied; Place of Confinement.* If the defendant is not released pending appeal, the court may recommend to the Attorney General that the defendant be confined near the place of the trial or appeal for a period reasonably necessary to permit the defendant to assist in preparing the appeal.

(c) **Fine.** If the defendant appeals, the district court, or the court of appeals under Federal Rule of Appellate Procedure 8, may stay a sentence to pay a fine or a fine and costs. The court may stay the sentence on any terms considered appropriate and may require the defendant to:

    (1) deposit all or part of the fine and costs into the district court's registry pending appeal;

    (2) post a bond to pay the fine and costs; or

    (3) submit to an examination concerning the defendant's assets and, if appropriate, order the defendant to refrain from dissipating assets.

(d) **Probation.** If the defendant appeals, the court may stay a sentence of probation. The court must set the terms of any stay.

(e) **Restitution and Notice to Victims.**

    (1) *In General.* If the defendant appeals, the district court, or the court of appeals under Federal Rule of Appellate Procedure 8, may stay—on any terms considered appropriate—any sentence providing for restitution under 18 U.S.C. §3556 or notice under 18 U.S.C. §3555.

    (2) *Ensuring Compliance.* The court may issue any order reasonably necessary to ensure compliance with a restitution order or a notice order after disposition of an appeal, including:

        (A) a restraining order;

        (B) an injunction;

        (C) an order requiring the defendant to deposit all or part of any monetary restitution into the district court's registry; or

        (D) an order requiring the defendant to post a bond.

(f) **Forfeiture.** A stay of a forfeiture order is governed by Rule 32.2(d).

(g) **Disability.** If the defendant's conviction or sentence creates a civil or employment disability under federal law, the district court, or the court of appeals under Federal Rule of Appellate Procedure 8, may stay the disability pending appeal on any terms considered appropriate. The court may issue any order reasonably necessary to protect the interest represented by the disability pending appeal, including a restraining order or an injunction.

(As amended Dec. 27, 1948, eff. Jan. 1, 1949; Feb. 28, 1966, eff. July 1, 1966; Dec. 4, 1967, eff. July 1, 1968; Apr. 24, 1972, eff. Oct. 1, 1972; Oct. 12, 1984, eff. Nov. 1, 1987; Mar. 9, 1987, eff. Aug. 1, 1987; Apr. 17, 2000, eff. Dec. 1, 2000; Apr. 29, 2002, eff. Dec. 1, 2002.)

Rule 39. [Reserved]

TITLE VIII. SUPPLEMENTARY AND SPECIAL PROCEEDINGS

Rule 40. Arrest for Failing to Appear in Another District or for Violating Conditions of Release Set in Another District

(a) **In General.** A person must be taken without unnecessary delay before a magistrate judge in the district of arrest if the person has been arrested under a warrant issued in another district for:
  (i) failing to appear as required by the terms of that person's release under 18 U.S.C. §§3141–3156 or by a subpoena; or
  (ii) violating conditions of release set in another district.
(b) **Proceedings.** The judge must proceed under Rule 5(c)(3) as applicable.
(c) **Release or Detention Order.** The judge may modify any previous release or detention order issued in another district, but must state in writing the reasons for doing so.

(As amended Feb. 28, 1966, eff. July 1, 1966; Apr. 24, 1972, eff. Oct. 1, 1972; Apr. 30, 1979, eff. Aug. 1, 1979; Apr. 28, 1982, eff. Aug. 1, 1982; Oct. 12, 1984, eff. Oct. 12, 1984, and Nov. 1, 1987; Mar. 9, 1987, eff. Aug. 1, 1987; Apr. 25, 1989, eff. Dec. 1, 1989; Apr. 22, 1993, eff. Dec. 1, 1993; Apr. 29, 1994, eff. Dec. 1, 1994; Apr. 27, 1995, eff. Dec. 1, 1995; Apr. 29, 2002, eff. Dec. 1, 2002; Apr. 12, 2006, eff. Dec. 1, 2006.)

Rule 41. Search and Seizure

(a) **Scope and Definitions.**
  (1) *Scope.* This rule does not modify any statute regulating search or seizure, or the issuance and execution of a search warrant in special circumstances.
  (2) *Definitions.* The following definitions apply under this rule:
    (A) "Property" includes documents, books, papers, any other tangible objects, and information.
    (B) "Daytime" means the hours between 6:00 A.M. and 10:00 P.M. according to local time.
    (C) "Federal law enforcement officer" means a government agent (other than an attorney for the government) who is engaged in enforcing the criminal laws and is within any category of officers authorized by the Attorney General to request a search warrant.
    (D) "Domestic terrorism" and "international terrorism" have the meanings set out in 18 U.S.C. §2331.
    (E) "Tracking device" has the meaning set out in 18 U.S.C. §3117(b).
(b) **Authority to Issue a Warrant.** At the request of a federal law enforcement officer or an attorney for the government:
  (1) a magistrate judge with authority in the district—or if none is reasonably available, a judge of a state court of record in the district—has authority to

issue a warrant to search for and seize a person or property located within the district;

(2) a magistrate judge with authority in the district has authority to issue a warrant for a person or property outside the district if the person or property is located within the district when the warrant is issued but might move or be moved outside the district before the warrant is executed;

(3) a magistrate judge—in an investigation of domestic terrorism or international terrorism—with authority in any district in which activities related to the terrorism may have occurred has authority to issue a warrant for a person or property within or outside that district; and

(4) a magistrate judge with authority in the district has authority to issue a warrant to install within the district a tracking device; the warrant may authorize use of the device to track the movement of a person or property located within the district, outside the district, or both.

(c) **Persons or Property Subject to Search or Seizure.** A warrant may be issued for any of the following:

(1) evidence of a crime;

(2) contraband, fruits of crime, or other items illegally possessed;

(3) property designed for use, intended for use, or used in committing a crime; or

(4) a person to be arrested or a person who is unlawfully restrained.

(d) **Obtaining a Warrant.**

(1) *In General.* After receiving an affidavit or other information, a magistrate judge—or if authorized by Rule 41(b), a judge of a state court of record—must issue the warrant if there is probable cause to search for and seize a person or property or to install and use a tracking device.

(2) *Requesting a Warrant in the Presence of a Judge.*

(A) *Warrant on an Affidavit.* When a federal law enforcement officer or an attorney for the government presents an affidavit in support of a warrant, the judge may require the affiant to appear personally and may examine under oath the affiant and any witness the affiant produces.

(B) *Warrant on Sworn Testimony.* The judge may wholly or partially dispense with a written affidavit and base a warrant on sworn testimony if doing so is reasonable under the circumstances.

(C) *Recording Testimony.* Testimony taken in support of a warrant must be recorded by a court reporter or by a suitable recording device, and the judge must file the transcript or recording with the clerk, along with any affidavit.

(3) *Requesting a Warrant by Telephonic or Other Means.*

(A) *In General.* A magistrate judge may issue a warrant based on information communicated by telephone or other reliable electronic means.

(B) *Recording Testimony.* Upon learning that an applicant is requesting a warrant under Rule 41(d)(3)(A), a magistrate judge must:

(i) place under oath the applicant and any person on whose testimony the application is based; and

(ii) make a verbatim record of the conversation with a suitable recording device, if available, or by a court reporter, or in writing.

(C) *Certifying Testimony.* The magistrate judge must have any recording or court reporter's notes transcribed, certify the transcription's accuracy, and file a copy of the record and the transcription with the clerk. Any written verbatim record must be signed by the magistrate judge and filed with the clerk.

(D) *Suppression Limited.* Absent a finding of bad faith, evidence obtained from a warrant issued under Rule 41(d)(3)(A) is not subject to suppression on the ground that issuing the warrant in that manner was unreasonable under the circumstances.

(e) Issuing the Warrant.

    (1) ***In General.*** The magistrate judge or a judge of a state court of record must issue the warrant to an officer authorized to execute it.

    (2) ***Contents of the Warrant.***

        (A) *Warrant to Search for and Seize a Person or Property.* Except for a tracking-device warrant, the warrant must identify the person or property to be searched, identify any person or property to be seized, and designate the magistrate judge to whom it must be returned. The warrant must command the officer to:

            (i) execute the warrant within a specified time no longer than ten days;

            (ii) execute the warrant during the daytime, unless the judge for good cause expressly authorizes execution at another time; and

            (iii) return the warrant to the magistrate judge designated in the warrant.

        (B) *Warrant for a Tracking Device.* A tracking-device warrant must identify the person or property to be tracked, designate the magistrate judge to whom it must be returned, and specify a reasonable length of time that the device may be used. The time must not exceed 45 days from the date the warrant was issued. The court may, for good cause, grant one or more extensions for a reasonable period not to exceed 45 days each. The warrant must command the officer to:

            (i) complete any installation authorized by the warrant within a specified time no longer than ten calendar days;

            (ii) perform any installation authorized by the warrant during the daytime, unless the judge for good cause expressly authorizes installation at another time; and

            (iii) return the warrant to the judge designated in the warrant.

    (3) ***Warrant by Telephonic or Other Means.*** If a magistrate judge decides to proceed under Rule 41(d)(3)(A), the following additional procedures apply:

        (A) *Preparing a Proposed Duplicate Original Warrant.* The applicant must prepare a "proposed duplicate original warrant" and must read or otherwise transmit the contents of that document verbatim to the magistrate judge.

        (B) *Preparing an Original Warrant.* If the applicant reads the contents of the proposed duplicate original warrant, the magistrate judge must enter those contents into an original warrant. If the applicant transmits the contents by reliable electronic means, that transmission may serve as the original warrant.

(C) *Modification.* The magistrate judge may modify the original warrant. The judge must transmit any modified warrant to the applicant by reliable electronic means under Rule 41(e)(3)(D) or direct the applicant to modify the proposed duplicate original warrant accordingly.

(D) *Signing the Warrant.* Upon determining to issue the warrant, the magistrate judge must immediately sign the original warrant, enter on its face the exact date and time it is issued, and transmit it by reliable electronic means to the applicant or direct the applicant to sign the judge's name on the duplicate original warrant.

(f) **Executing and Returning the Warrant.**

(1) *Warrant to Search for and Seize a Person or Property.*

(A) *Noting the Time.* The officer executing the warrant must enter on it the exact date and time it was executed.

(B) *Inventory.* An officer present during the execution of the warrant must prepare and verify an inventory of any property seized. The officer must do so in the presence of another officer and the person from whom, or from whose premises, the property was taken. If either one is not present, the officer must prepare and verify the inventory in the presence of at least one other credible person.

(C) *Receipt.* The officer executing the warrant must give a copy of the warrant and a receipt for the property taken to the person from whom, or from whose premises, the property was taken or leave a copy of the warrant and receipt at the place where the officer took the property.

(D) *Return.* The officer executing the warrant must promptly return it—together with a copy of the inventory—to the magistrate judge designated on the warrant. The judge must, on request, give a copy of the inventory to the person from whom, or from whose premises, the property was taken and to the applicant for the warrant.

(2) *Warrant for a Tracking Device.*

(A) *Noting the Time.* The officer executing a tracking-device warrant must enter on it the exact date and time the device was installed and the period during which it was used.

(B) *Return.* Within ten calendar days after the use of the tracking device has ended, the officer executing the warrant must return it to the judge designated in the warrant.

(C) *Service.* Withing ten calendar days after the use of the tracking device has ended, the officer executing a tracking-device warrant must serve a copy of the warrant on the person who was tracked or whose property was tracked. Service may be accomplished by delivering a copy to the person who, or whose property, was tracked; or by leaving a copy at the person's residence or usual place of abode with an individual of suitable age and discretion who resides at that location and by mailing a copy to the person's last known address. Upon request of the government, the judge may delay notice as provided in Rule 41(f)(3).

(3) *Delayed Notice.* Upon the government's request, a magistrate judge—or if authorized by Rule 41(b), a judge of a state court of record—may delay any notice required by this rule if the delay is authorized by statute.

(g) **Motion to Return Property.** A person aggrieved by an unlawful search and seizure of property or by the deprivation of property may move for the property's return. The motion must be filed in the district where the property was seized. The court must receive evidence on any factual issue necessary to decide the motion. If it grants the motion, the court must return the property to the movant, but may impose reasonable conditions to protect access to the property and its use in later proceedings.

(h) **Motion to Suppress.** A defendant may move to suppress evidence in the court where the trial will occur, as Rule 12 provides.

(i) **Forwarding Papers to the Clerk.** The magistrate judge to whom the warrant is returned must attach to the warrant a copy of the return, of the inventory, and of all other related papers and must deliver them to the clerk in the district where the property was seized.

(As amended Dec. 27, 1948, eff. Oct. 20, 1949; Apr. 9, 1956, eff. July 8, 1956; Apr. 24, 1972, eff. Oct. 1, 1972; Mar. 18, 1974, eff. July 1, 1974; Apr. 26 and July 8, 1976, eff. Aug. 1, 1976; July 30, 1977, eff. Oct. 1, 1977; Apr. 30, 1979, eff. Aug. 1, 1979; Mar. 9, 1987, eff. Aug. 1, 1987; Apr. 25, 1989, eff. Dec. 1, 1989; May 1, 1990, eff. Dec. 1, 1990; Apr. 22, 1993, eff. Dec. 1, 1993; Oct. 26, 2001; Apr. 29, 2002, eff. Dec. 1, 2002; Apr. 12, 2006, eff. Dec. 1, 2006.)

Rule 42. Criminal Contempt

(a) **Disposition After Notice.** Any person who commits criminal contempt may be punished for that contempt after prosecution on notice.

    (1) *Notice.* The court must give the person notice in open court, in an order to show cause, or in an arrest order. The notice must:

        (A) state the time and place of the trial;

        (B) allow the defendant a reasonable time to prepare a defense; and

        (C) state the essential facts constituting the charged criminal contempt and describe it as such.

    (2) *Appointing a Prosecutor.* The court must request that the contempt be prosecuted by an attorney for the government, unless the interest of justice requires the appointment of another attorney. If the government declines the request, the court must appoint another attorney to prosecute the contempt.

    (3) *Trial and Disposition.* A person being prosecuted for criminal contempt is entitled to a jury trial in any case in which federal law so provides and must be released or detained as Rule 46 provides. If the criminal contempt involves disrespect toward or criticism of a judge, that judge is disqualified from presiding at the contempt trial or hearing unless the defendant consents. Upon a finding or verdict of guilty, the court must impose the punishment.

(b) **Summary Disposition.** Notwithstanding any other provision of these rules, the court (other than a magistrate judge) may summarily punish a person who commits criminal contempt in its presence if the judge saw or heard the contemptuous conduct and so certifies; a magistrate judge may summarily punish a person as provided in 28 U.S.C. §636(e). The contempt order must recite the facts, be signed by the judge, and be filed with the clerk.

(As amended Mar. 9, 1987, eff. Aug. 1, 1987; Apr. 29, 2002, eff. Dec. 1, 2002.)

TITLE IX. GENERAL PROVISIONS

Rule 43. Defendant's Presence

(a) **When Required.** Unless this rule, Rule 5, or Rule 10 provides otherwise, the defendant must be present at:
  (1) the initial appearance, the initial arraignment, and the plea;
  (2) every trial stage, including jury impanelment and the return of the verdict; and
  (3) sentencing.

(b) **When Not Required.** A defendant need not be present under any of the following circumstances:
  (1) *Organizational Defendant.* The defendant is an organization represented by counsel who is present.
  (2) *Misdemeanor Offense.* The offense is punishable by fine or by imprisonment for not more than one year, or both, and with the defendant's written consent, the court permits arraignment, plea, trial, and sentencing to occur in the defendant's absence.
  (3) *Conference or Hearing on a Legal Question.* The proceeding involves only a conference or hearing on a question of law.
  (4) *Sentence Correction.* The proceeding involves the correction or reduction of sentence under Rule 35 or 18 U.S.C. §3582(c).

(c) **Waiving Continued Presence.**
  (1) *In General.* A defendant who was initially present at trial, or who had pleaded guilty or nolo contendere, waives the right to be present under the following circumstances:
    (A) when the defendant is voluntarily absent after the trial has begun, regardless of whether the court informed the defendant of an obligation to remain during trial;
    (B) in a noncapital case, when the defendant is voluntarily absent during sentencing; or
    (C) when the court warns the defendant that it will remove the defendant from the courtroom for disruptive behavior, but the defendant persists in conduct that justifies removal from the courtroom.
  (2) *Waiver's Effect.* If the defendant waives the right to be present, the trial may proceed to completion, including the verdict's return and sentencing, during the defendant's absence.

(As amended Apr. 22, 1974, eff. Dec. 1, 1975; July 31, 1975, eff. Dec. 1, 1975; Mar. 9, 1987, eff. Aug. 1, 1987; Apr. 27, 1995, eff. Dec. 1, 1995; Apr. 24, 1998, eff. Dec. 1, 1998; Apr. 29, 2002, eff. Dec. 1, 2002.)

Rule 44. Right to and Appointment of Counsel

(a) **Right to Appointed Counsel.** A defendant who is unable to obtain counsel is entitled to have counsel appointed to represent the defendant at every stage of the proceeding from initial appearance through appeal, unless the defendant waives this right.

(b) **Appointment Procedure.** Federal law and local court rules govern the procedure for implementing the right to counsel.

(c) Inquiry into Joint Representation.

    (1) *Joint Representation.* Joint representation occurs when:

        (A) two or more defendants have been charged jointly under Rule 8(b) or have been joined for trial under Rule 13; and

        (B) the defendants are represented by the same counsel, or counsel who are associated in law practice.

    (2) *Court's Responsibilities in Cases of Joint Representation.* The court must promptly inquire about the propriety of joint representation and must personally advise each defendant of the right to the effective assistance of counsel, including separate representation. Unless there is good cause to believe that no conflict of interest is likely to arise, the court must take appropriate measures to protect each defendant's right to counsel.

(As amended Feb. 28, 1966, eff. July 1, 1966; Apr. 24, 1972, eff. Oct. 1, 1972; Apr. 30, 1979, eff. Dec. 1, 1980; Mar. 9, 1987, eff. Aug. 1, 1987; Apr. 22, 1993, eff. Dec. 1, 1993; Apr. 29, 2002, eff. Dec. 1, 2002.)

Rule 45. Computing and Extending Time

(a) Computing Time. The following rules apply in computing any period of time specified in these rules, any local rule, or any court order:

    (1) *Day of the Event Excluded.* Exclude the day of the act, event, or default that begins the period.

    (2) *Exclusion from Brief Periods.* Exclude intermediate Saturdays, Sundays, and legal holidays when the period is less than 11 days.

    (3) *Last Day.* Include the last day of the period unless it is a Saturday, Sunday, legal holiday, or day on which weather or other conditions make the clerk's office inaccessible. When the last day is excluded, the period runs until the end of the next day that is not a Saturday, Sunday, legal holiday, or day when the clerk's office is inaccessible.

    (4) *"Legal Holiday" Defined.* As used in this rule, "legal holiday" means:

        (A) the day set aside by statute for observing:

            (i)   New Year's Day;

            (ii)   Martin Luther King, Jr.'s Birthday;

            (iii) Washington's Birthday;

            (iv) Memorial Day;

            (v)   Independence Day;

            (vi) Labor Day;

            (vii) Columbus Day;

            (viii)Veterans' Day;

            (ix) Thanksgiving Day;

            (x)   Christmas Day; and

        (B) any other day declared a holiday by the president, the Congress, or the state where the district court is held.

(b) Extending Time.

    (1) *In General.* When an act must or may be done within a specified period, the court on its own may extend the time, or for good cause may do so on a party's motion made:

      (A) before the originally prescribed or previously extended time expires; or

      (B) after the time expires if the party failed to act because of excusable neglect.

    (2) *Exception.* The court may not extend the time to take any action under Rule 35, except as stated in that rule.

  (c) **Additional Time After Service.** When these rules permit or require a party to act within a specified period after a notice or a paper has been served on that party, three days are added to the period if service occurs in the manner provided under Federal Rule of Civil Procedure 5(b)(2)(B), (C), or (D).

(As amended Feb. 28, 1966, eff. July 1, 1966; Dec. 4, 1967, eff. July 1, 1968; Mar. 1, 1971, eff. July 1, 1971; Apr. 28, 1982, eff. Aug. 1, 1982; Apr. 29, 1985, eff. Aug. 1, 1985; Mar. 9, 1987, eff. Aug. 1, 1987; Apr. 29, 2002, eff. Dec. 1, 2002; Apr. 25, 2005, eff. Dec. 1, 2005.)

Rule 46. Release from Custody; Supervising Detention

  (a) **Before Trial.** The provisions of 18 U.S.C. §§3142 and 3144 govern pretrial release.

  (b) **During Trial.** A person released before trial continues on release during trial under the same terms and conditions. But the court may order different terms and conditions or terminate the release if necessary to ensure that the person will be present during trial or that the person's conduct will not obstruct the orderly and expeditious progress of the trial.

  (c) **Pending Sentencing or Appeal.** The provisions of 18 U.S.C. §3143 govern release pending sentencing or appeal. The burden of establishing that the defendant will not flee or pose a danger to any other person or to the community rests with the defendant.

  (d) **Pending Hearing on a Violation of Probation or Supervised Release.** Rule 32.1(a)(6) governs release pending a hearing on a violation of probation or supervised release.

  (e) **Surety.** The court must not approve a bond unless any surety appears to be qualified. Every surety, except a legally approved corporate surety, must demonstrate by affidavit that its assets are adequate. The court may require the affidavit to describe the following:

    (1) the property that the surety proposes to use as security;

    (2) any encumbrance on that property;

    (3) the number and amount of any other undischarged bonds and bail undertakings the surety has issued; and

    (4) any other liability of the surety.

  (f) **Bail Forfeiture.**

    (1) *Declaration.* The court must declare the bail forfeited if a condition of the bond is breached.

    (2) *Setting Aside.* The court may set aside in whole or in part a bail forfeiture upon any condition the court may impose if:

      (A) the surety later surrenders into custody the person released on the surety's appearance bond; or

      (B) it appears that justice does not require bail forfeiture.

(3) *Enforcement.*

    (A) *Default Judgment and Execution.* If it does not set aside a bail forfeiture, the court must, upon the government's motion, enter a default judgment.

    (B) *Jurisdiction and Service.* By entering into a bond, each surety submits to the district court's jurisdiction and irrevocably appoints the district clerk as its agent to receive service of any filings affecting its liability.

    (C) *Motion to Enforce.* The court may, upon the government's motion, enforce the surety's liability without an independent action. The government must serve any motion, and notice as the court prescribes, on the district clerk. If so served, the clerk must promptly mail a copy to the surety at its last known address.

(4) *Remission.* After entering a judgment under Rule 46(f)(3), the court may remit in whole or in part the judgment under the same conditions specified in Rule 46(f)(2).

(g) Exoneration. The court must exonerate the surety and release any bail when a bond condition has been satisfied or when the court has set aside or remitted the forfeiture. The court must exonerate a surety who deposits cash in the amount of the bond or timely surrenders the defendant into custody.

(h) Supervising Detention Pending Trial.

    (1) *In General.* To eliminate unnecessary detention, the court must supervise the detention within the district of any defendants awaiting trial and of any persons held as material witnesses.

    (2) *Reports.* An attorney for the government must report biweekly to the court, listing each material witness held in custody for more than ten days pending indictment, arraignment, or trial. For each material witness listed in the report, an attorney for the government must state why the witness should not be released with or without a deposition being taken under Rule 15(a).

(i) Forfeiture of Property. The court may dispose of a charged offense by ordering the forfeiture of 18 U.S.C. §3142(c)(1)(B)(xi) property under 18 U.S.C. §3146(d), if a fine in the amount of the property's value would be an appropriate sentence for the charged offense.

(j) Producing a Statement.

    (1) *In General.* Rule 26.2(a)–(d) and (f) applies at a detention hearing under 18 U.S.C. §3142, unless the court for good cause rules otherwise.

    (2) *Sanctions for Not Producing a Statement.* If a party disobeys a Rule 26.2 order to produce a witness's statement, the court must not consider that witness's testimony at the detention hearing.

(As amended Apr. 9, 1956, eff. July 8, 1956; Feb. 28, 1966, eff. July 1, 1966; Apr. 24, 1972, eff. Oct. 1, 1972; Oct. 12, 1984; Mar. 9, 1987, eff. Aug. 1, 1987; Apr. 30, 1991, eff. Dec. 1, 1991; Apr. 22, 1993, eff. Dec. 1, 1993; Sept. 13, 1994; Apr. 29, 2002, eff. Dec. 1, 2002.)

Rule 47. Motions and Supporting Affidavits

(a) In General. A party applying to the court for an order must do so by motion.

(b) Form and Content of a Motion. A motion—except when made during a trial or hearing—must be in writing, unless the court permits the party to make the motion by other means. A motion must state the grounds on which it is based and the relief or order sought. A motion may be supported by affidavit.

(c) **Timing of a Motion.** A party must serve a written motion— other than one that the court may hear ex parte—and any hearing notice at least five days before the hearing date, unless a rule or court order sets a different period. For good cause, the court may set a different period upon ex parte application.

(d) **Affidavit Supporting a Motion.** The moving party must serve any supporting affidavit with the motion. A responding party must serve any opposing affidavit at least one day before the hearing, unless the court permits later service.

(As amended Apr. 29, 2002, eff. Dec. 1, 2002.)

Rule 48. Dismissal

(a) **By the Government.** The government may, with leave of court, dismiss an indictment, information, or complaint. The government may not dismiss the prosecution during trial without the defendant's consent.

(b) **By the Court.** The court may dismiss an indictment, information, or complaint if unnecessary delay occurs in:
   (1) presenting a charge to a grand jury;
   (2) filing an information against a defendant; or
   (3) bringing a defendant to trial. (As amended Apr. 29, 2002, eff. Dec. 1, 2002.)

Rule 49. Serving and Filing Papers

(a) **When Required.** A party must serve on every other party any written motion (other than one to be heard ex parte), written notice, designation of the record on appeal, or similar paper.

(b) **How Made.** Service must be made in the manner provided for a civil action. When these rules or a court order requires or permits service on a party represented by an attorney, service must be made on the attorney instead of the party, unless the court orders otherwise.

(c) **Notice of a Court Order.** When the court issues an order on any post-arraignment motion, the clerk must provide notice in a manner provided for in a civil action. Except as Federal Rule of Appellate Procedure 4(b) provides otherwise, the clerk's failure to give notice does not affect the time to appeal, or relieve—or authorize the court to relieve—a party's failure to appeal within the allowed time.

(d) **Filing.** A party must file with the court a copy of any paper the party is required to serve. A paper must be filed in a manner provided for in a civil action.

(As amended Feb. 28, 1966, eff. July 1, 1966; Dec. 4, 1967, eff. July 1, 1968; Apr. 29, 1985, eff. Aug. 1, 1985; Mar. 9, 1987, eff. Aug. 1, 1987; Apr. 22, 1993, eff. Dec. 1, 1993; Apr. 27, 1995, eff. Dec. 1, 1995; Apr. 29, 2002, eff. Dec. 1, 2002.)

Rule 50. Prompt Disposition

Scheduling preference must be given to criminal proceedings as far as practicable.

(As amended Apr. 24, 1972, eff. Oct. 1, 1972; Mar. 18, 1974, eff. July 1, 1974; Apr. 26 and July 8, 1976, eff. Aug. 1, 1976; Apr. 22, 1993, eff. Dec. 1, 1993; Apr. 29, 2002, eff. Dec. 1, 2002.)

Rule 51. Preserving Claimed Error

(a) **Exceptions Unnecessary.** Exceptions to rulings or orders of the court are unnecessary.

(b) **Preserving a Claim of Error.** A party may preserve a claim of error by informing the court—when the court ruling or order is made or sought—of the action the party wishes the court to take, or the party's objection to the court's action and the grounds for that objection. If a party does not have an opportunity to object to a ruling or order, the absence of an objection does not later prejudice that party. A ruling or order that admits or excludes evidence is governed by Federal Rule of Evidence 103.

(As amended Mar. 9, 1987, eff. Aug. 1, 1987; Apr. 29, 2002, eff. Dec. 1, 2002.)

Rule 52. Harmless and Plain Error

(a) **Harmless Error.** Any error, defect, irregularity, or variance that does not affect substantial rights must be disregarded.

(b) **Plain Error.** A plain error that affects substantial rights may be considered even though it was not brought to the court's attention.

(As amended Apr. 29, 2002, eff. Dec. 1, 2002.)

Rule 53. Courtroom Photographing and Broadcasting Prohibited

Except as otherwise provided by a statute or these rules, the court must not permit the taking of photographs in the courtroom during judicial proceedings or the broadcasting of judicial proceedings from the courtroom.

(As amended Apr. 29, 2002, eff. Dec. 1, 2002.)

Rule 54. [Transferred][1]

Rule 55. Records

The clerk of the district court must keep records of criminal proceedings in the form prescribed by the Director of the Administrative Office of the United States Courts. The clerk must enter in the records every court order or judgment and the date of entry.

(As amended Dec. 27, 1948, eff. Oct. 20, 1949; Feb. 28, 1966, eff. July 1, 1966; Apr. 24, 1972, eff. Oct. 1, 1972; Apr. 28, 1983, eff. Aug. 1, 1983; Apr. 22, 1993, eff. Dec. 1, 1993; Apr. 29, 2002, eff. Dec. 1, 2002.)

Rule 56. When Court Is Open

(a) **In General.** A district court is considered always open for any filing, and for issuing and returning process, making a motion, or entering an order.

(b) **Office Hours.** The clerk's office—with the clerk or a deputy in attendance—must be open during business hours on all days except Saturdays, Sundays, and legal holidays.

(c) **Special Hours.** A court may provide by local rule or order that its clerk's office will be open for specified hours on Saturdays or legal holidays other than than those set aside by statute for observing New Year's Day, Martin Luther King, Jr.'s Birthday,

Washington's Birthday, Memorial Day, Independence Day, Labor Day, Columbus Day, Veterans' Day, Thanksgiving Day, and Christmas Day.

(As amended Dec. 27, 1948, eff. Oct. 20, 1949; Feb. 28, 1966, eff. July 1, 1966; Dec. 4, 1967, eff. July 1, 1968; Mar. 1, 1971, eff. July 1, 1971; Apr. 25, 1988, eff. Aug. 1, 1988; Apr. 29, 2002, eff. Dec. 1, 2002.)

Rule 57. District Court Rules

(a) **In General.**

   (1) *Adopting Local Rules.* Each district court acting by a majority of its district judges may, after giving appropriate public notice and an opportunity to comment, make and amend rules governing its practice. A local rule must be consistent with—but not duplicative of—federal statutes and rules adopted under 28 U.S.C. §2072 and must conform to any uniform numbering system prescribed by the Judicial Conference of the United States.

   (2) *Limiting Enforcement.* A local rule imposing a requirement of form must not be enforced in a manner that causes a party to lose rights because of an unintentional failure to comply with the requirement.

(b) **Procedure When There Is No Controlling Law.** A judge may regulate practice in any manner consistent with federal law, these rules, and the local rules of the district. No sanction or other disadvantage may be imposed for noncompliance with any requirement not in federal law, federal rules, or the local district rules unless the alleged violator was furnished with actual notice of the requirement before the noncompliance.

(c) **Effective Date and Notice.** A local rule adopted under this rule takes effect on the date specified by the district court and remains in effect unless amended by the district court or abrogated by the judicial council of the circuit in which the district is located. Copies of local rules and their amendments, when promulgated, must be furnished to the judicial council and the Administrative Office of the United States Courts and must be made available to the public.

(As amended Dec. 27, 1948, eff. Oct. 20, 1949; Dec. 4, 1967, eff. July 1, 1968; Apr. 29, 1985, eff. Aug. 1, 1985; Apr. 22, 1993, eff. Dec. 1, 1993; Apr. 27, 1995, eff. Dec. 1, 1995; Apr. 29, 2002, eff. Dec. 1, 2002.)

Rule 58. Petty Offenses and Other Misdemeanors

(a) Scope.

   (1) *In General.* These rules apply in petty offense and other misdemeanor cases and on appeal to a district judge in a case tried by a magistrate judge, unless this rule provides otherwise.

   (2) *Petty Offense Case Without Imprisonment.* In a case involving a petty offense for which no sentence of imprisonment will be imposed, the court may follow any provision of these rules that is not inconsistent with this rule and that the court considers appropriate.

   (3) *Definition.* As used in this rule, the term "petty offense for which no sentence of imprisonment will be imposed" means a petty offense for which the court determines that, in the event of conviction, no sentence of imprisonment will be imposed.

(b) Pretrial Procedure.

    (1) *Charging Document.* The trial of a misdemeanor may proceed on an indictment, information, or complaint. The trial of a petty offense may also proceed on a citation or violation notice.

    (2) *Initial Appearance.* At the defendant's initial appearance on a petty offense or other misdemeanor charge, the magistrate judge must inform the defendant of the following:

        (A) the charge, and the minimum and maximum penalties, including imprisonment, fines, any special assessment under 18 U.S.C. §3013, and restitution under 18 U.S.C. §3556;

        (B) the right to retain counsel;

        (C) the right to request the appointment of counsel if the defendant is unable to retain counsel—unless the charge is a petty offense for which the appointment of counsel is not required;

        (D) the defendant's right not to make a statement, and that any statement made may be used against the defendant;

        (E) the right to trial, judgment, and sentencing before a district judge—unless:

            (i) the charge is a petty offense; or

            (ii) the defendant consents to trial, judgment, and sentencing before a magistrate judge;

        (F) the right to a jury trial before either a magistrate judge or a district judge—unless the charge is a petty offense; and

        (G) any right to a preliminary hearing under Rule 5.1, and the general circumstances, if any, under which the defendant may secure pretrial release.

    (3) *Arraignment.*

        (A) *Plea Before a Magistrate Judge.* A magistrate judge may take the defendant's plea in a petty offense case. In every other misdemeanor case, a magistrate judge may take the plea only if the defendant consents either in writing or on the record to be tried before a magistrate judge and specifically waives trial before a district judge. The defendant may plead not guilty, guilty, or (with the consent of the magistrate judge) nolo contendere.

        (B) *Failure to Consent.* Except in a petty offense case, the magistrate judge must order a defendant who does not consent to trial before a magistrate judge to appear before a district judge for further proceedings.

(c) Additional Procedures in Certain Petty Offense Cases. The following procedures also apply in a case involving a petty offense for which no sentence of imprisonment will be imposed:

    (1) *Guilty or Nolo Contendere Plea.* The court must not accept a guilty or nolo contendere plea unless satisfied that the defendant understands the nature of the charge and the maximum possible penalty.

    (2) *Waiving Venue.*

        (A) *Conditions of Waiving Venue.* If a defendant is arrested, held, or present in a district different from the one where the indictment, information, complaint, citation, or violation notice is pending, the defendant may state in writing a desire to plead guilty or nolo contendere; to waive venue and trial in the district where the proceeding is pending; and to consent to the court's disposing of the case in the district where the defendant was arrested, is held, or is present.

(B) *Effect of Waiving Venue.* Unless the defendant later pleads not guilty, the prosecution will proceed in the district where the defendant was arrested, is held, or is present. The district clerk must notify the clerk in the original district of the defendant's waiver of venue. The defendant's statement of a desire to plead guilty or nolo contendere is not admissible against the defendant.

(3) *Sentencing.* The court must give the defendant an opportunity to be heard in mitigation and then proceed immediately to sentencing. The court may, however, postpone sentencing to allow the probation service to investigate or to permit either party to submit additional information.

(4) *Notice of a Right to Appeal.* After imposing sentence in a case tried on a not-guilty plea, the court must advise the defendant of a right to appeal the conviction and of any right to appeal the sentence. If the defendant was convicted on a plea of guilty or nolo contendere, the court must advise the defendant of any right to appeal the sentence.

(d) **Paying a Fixed Sum in Lieu of Appearance.**

(1) *In General.* If the court has a local rule governing forfeiture of collateral, the court may accept a fixed-sum payment in lieu of the defendant's appearance and end the case, but the fixed sum may not exceed the maximum fine allowed by law.

(2) *Notice to Appear.* If the defendant fails to pay a fixed sum, request a hearing, or appear in response to a citation or violation notice, the district clerk or a magistrate judge may issue a notice for the defendant to appear before the court on a date certain. The notice may give the defendant an additional opportunity to pay a fixed sum in lieu of appearance. The district clerk must serve the notice on the defendant by mailing a copy to the defendant's last known address.

(3) *Summons or Warrant.* Upon an indictment, or upon a showing by one of the other charging documents specified in Rule 58(b)(1) of probable cause to believe that an offense has been committed and that the defendant has committed it, the court may issue an arrest warrant or, if no warrant is requested by an attorney for the government, a summons. The showing of probable cause must be made under oath or under penalty of perjury, but the affiant need not appear before the court. If the defendant fails to appear before the court in response to a summons, the court may summarily issue a warrant for the defendant's arrest.

(e) **Recording the Proceedings.** The court must record any proceedings under this rule by using a court reporter or a suitable recording device.

(f) **New Trial.** Rule 33 applies to a motion for a new trial.

(g) **Appeal.**

(1) *From a District Judge's Order or Judgment.* The Federal Rules of Appellate Procedure govern an appeal from a district judge's order or a judgment of conviction or sentence.

(2) *From a Magistrate Judge's Order or Judgment.*

(A) *Interlocutory Appeal.* Either party may appeal an order of a magistrate judge to a district judge within ten days of its entry if a district judge's order could similarly be appealed. The party appealing must file a notice with the clerk specifying the order being appealed and must serve a copy on the adverse party.

(B) *Appeal from a Conviction or Sentence.* A defendant may appeal a magistrate judge's judgment of conviction or sentence to a district judge within ten days of its entry. To appeal, the defendant must file a notice with the clerk specifying the judgment being appealed and must serve a copy on an attorney for the government.

(C) *Record.* The record consists of the original papers and exhibits in the case; any transcript, tape, or other recording of the proceedings; and a certified copy of the docket entries. For purposes of the appeal, a copy of the record of the proceedings must be made available to a defendant who establishes by affidavit an inability to pay or give security for the record. The Director of the Administrative Office of the United States Courts must pay for those copies.

(D) *Scope of Appeal.* The defendant is not entitled to a trial de novo by a district judge. The scope of the appeal is the same as in an appeal to the court of appeals from a judgment entered by a district judge.

(3) *Stay of Execution and Release Pending Appeal.* Rule 38 applies to a stay of a judgment of conviction or sentence. The court may release the defendant pending appeal under the law relating to release pending appeal from a district court to a court of appeals.

(As added May 1, 1990, eff. Dec. 1, 1990; amended Apr. 30, 1991, eff. Dec. 1, 1991; Apr. 22, 1993, eff. Dec. 1, 1993; Apr. 11, 1997, eff. Dec. 1, 1997; Apr. 29, 2002, eff. Dec. 1, 2002; Apr. 12, 2006, eff. Dec. 1, 2006.)

Rule 59. Matters Before a Magistrate Judge

(a) **Nondispositive Matters.** A district judge may refer to a magistrate judge for determination any matter that does not dispose of a charge or defense. The magistrate judge must promptly conduct the required proceedings and, when appropriate, enter on the record an oral or written order stating the determination. A party may serve and file objections to the order within ten days after being served with a copy of a written order or after the oral order is stated on the record, or at some other time the court sets. The district judge must consider timely objections and modify or set aside any part of the order that is contrary to law or clearly erroneous. Failure to object in accordance with this rule waives a party's right to review.

(b) **Dispositive Matters.**

(1) *Referral to Magistrate Judge.* A district judge may refer to a magistrate judge for recommendation a defendant's motion to dismiss or quash an indictment or information, a motion to suppress evidence, or any matter that may dispose of a charge or defense. The magistrate judge must promptly conduct the required

proceedings. A record must be made of any evidentiary proceeding and of any other proceeding if the magistrate judge considers it necessary. The magistrate judge must enter on the record a recommendation for disposing of the matter, including any proposed findings of fact. The clerk must immediately serve copies on all parties.

(2) ***Objections to Findings and Recommendations.*** Within ten days after being served with a copy of the recommended disposition, or at some other time the court sets, a party may serve and file specific written objections to the proposed findings and recommendations. Unless the district judge directs otherwise, the objecting party must promptly arrange for transcribing the record, or whatever portions of it the parties agree to or the magistrate judge considers sufficient. Failure to object in accordance with this rule waives a party's right to review.

(3) ***De Novo Review of Recommendations.*** The district judge must consider de novo any objection to the magistrate judge's recommendation. The district judge may accept, reject, or modify the recommendation, receive further evidence, or resubmit the matter to the magistrate judge with instructions.

(As added Apr. 25, 2005, eff. Dec. 1, 2005.)

Rule 60. Title

These rules may be known and cited as the Federal Rules of Criminal Procedure.

(As amended Apr. 29, 2002, eff. Dec. 1, 2002.)

NOTES

KAPLAN) *pmbr*